THE BOOK OF GENERAL IGNORANCE

This 'quite interesting' catalogue of frequent misconceptions in 'common knowledge' will make you wonder why anyone bothers to go to school. If you still think that Henry VIII had six wives, that water has no colour, that Mount Everest is the world's highest mountain, and that Earth has only one moon, then you need this book. Urgently. *The Book of General Ignorance* throws fresh light on a question which has obsessed philosophers, scientists and men in pubs for most of history: what is truth and what is total hogwash? With a foreword by Stephen Fry.

THE BOOK OF GENERAL IGNORANCE

A Quite Interesting Book

John Lloyd and John Michinson

WINDSOR
PARAGON

First published 2006
by Faber and Faber Limited
This Large Print edition published 2008
by BBC Audiobooks Ltd
by arrangement with
Faber and Faber

Hardcover ISBN: 978 1 405 68716 4
Softcover   ISBN: 978 1 405 68717 1

British Library Cataloguing in Publication Data available

Printed and bound in Great Britain by
Antony Rowe Ltd., Chippenham, Wiltshire

CONTENTS

FOREWORD | Stephen Fry   xiv
FOUR WORDS | Alan Davies   xvi
INTRODUCTION | John Lloyd   xvii

How many wives did Henry VIII have?   1
How many nostrils have you got?   2
Where is the driest place on earth?   3
Where is the highest mountain?   4
What's the name of the tallest mountain in the world?   5
What's the largest living thing?   7
What's the biggest thing a blue whale can swallow?   8
Which bird lays the smallest egg for its size?   9
How long can a chicken live without its head?   10
What has a three-second memory?   11
What's the most dangerous animal that has ever lived?   12
Do marmots kill people?   14
How do lemmings die?   15
What do chameleons do?   16
How do polar bears disguise themselves?   18
How many galaxies are visible to the naked eye?   20
What man-made artefacts can be seen from the Moon?   21
What did the Chinese invent?   22
Where did Marco Polo come from?   23
Who introduced tobacco and potatoes to England?   25
Who invented the steam engine?   26
Who invented the telephone?   28

What's quite interesting about Scotland? 29
Where does Chicken Tikka Masala come from? 31
Is French toast from France? 33
Who invented champagne? 34
Where was the guillotine invented? 36
Who was freed by the storming of the Bastille? 38
Who said, 'Let them eat cake'? 39
How well do you know the Swiss? 41
What does a St Bernard carry round its neck? 42
What goes hunk-hunk? 43
What noise does the largest frog in the world
    make? 44
Which owl says 'Tu-whit tu-whoo'? 46
What did Darwin do to dead owls? 47
When does 'ring-a-ring o' roses' date from? 48
What were Nelson's last words? 50
Which eye did Nelson wear his eye-patch on? 51
How many senses does a human being have? 53
How many states of matter are there? 54
What's the normal state of glass? 56
Which metal is liquid at room temperature? 57
Which metal is the best conductor? 58
What's the densest element? 59
Where do diamonds come from? 61
How do we measure earthquakes? 63
What's the commonest material in the world? 64
What does the Moon smell like? 66
Does the Earth go round the Moon? 67
How many moons does the Earth have? 67
How many planets are there in the solar system? 68
How would you fly through an asteroid belt? 70
What's in an atom? 71
What's the main ingredient of air? 73
Where would you go for a lungful of ozone? 74
What speed does light at travel at ? 75

How do moths feel about flames? 76

How many legs does a centipede have? 77

How many toes has a two-toed sloth? 78

How many eyes does a no-eyed, big-eyed wolf spider have? 79

How many penises does a European earwig have? 80

Which animals are the best-endowed of all? 81

What's a rhino's horn made from? 83

Which African mammal kills more humans than any other? 85

Where do most tigers live? 86

What would you use to overpower a crocodile? 88

What's three times as dangerous as war? 89

What killed you in an eighteenth-century sea battle? 91

Which war killed most British soldiers? 92

What's the word for Napoleon's most humiliating defeat? 93

Who blew the nose off the Sphinx? 94

What's the name of the statue in Piccadilly Circus? 95

What did Nero do while Rome burned? 97

What's more likely: being killed by lightning or by an asteroid? 98

How many people died in the Great Fire of London? 100

How did Roman emperors order the death of a gladiator? 101

What happened to most English witches? 103

What's the Number of the Beast? 104

Which crime did Burke and Hare commit? 106

What are chastity belts for? 107

What was Tutankhamun's curse? 109

What did feminists do with their bras? 110

What colour is the universe?	111
What colour is Mars?	113
What colour is water?	114
What colour was the sky in ancient Greece?	115
How much of the Earth is water?	117
Which way does the bathwater go down the plughole?	118
What do camels store in their humps?	119
Where do camels come from?	121
Who is America named after?	122
How many states are there in the USA?	123
Who was the first American President?	124
What were George Washington's false teeth made from?	125
What did Buffalo Bill do to buffaloes?	127
Where was baseball invented?	128
What was Billy the Kid's real name?	130
What do we have Thomas Crapper to thank for?	131
What was Mozart's middle name?	133
How did Nome in Alaska get its name?	134
What's the name of the capital city of Thailand?	134
What's the world's largest city?	136
What's the single largest man-made structure on Earth?	137
Where's the coolest place in the universe?	139
When did the most recent Ice Age end?	140
Who lives in igloos?	142
Would you call someone an Eskimo?	143
How many words do Eskimos have for snow?	144
What did human beings evolve from?	146
Who coined the phrase 'the survival of the fittest'?	148
Who invented the ball-point pen?	149
What do we use to write on a blackboard?	151
What's made of celluloid?	152

Who invented rubber boots?   154

What Edison invention do English speakers use
every day?   155

Was the first computer bug a real insect?   157

What's the most likely survivor of a nuclear
war?   158

What's the best use for Marmite?   159

Which is the hottest part of a chilli?   160

Where do tulips come from?   161

How many crocuses does it take to make a kilo
of saffron?   163

What was the first invention to break the sound
barrier?   164

What kind of music charms snakes most?   165

What are violin strings made from?   166

What's the best floor of a building to throw a
cat from?   167

Why did the dodo die out?   169

What buries its head in the sand?   170

Where do gorillas sleep?   171

What's the commonest bird in the world?   172

What's the 'sport of kings'?   174

What's Britain's smallest bird?   175

What animal are the Canary Islands named
after?   177

What's the smallest dog in the world?   178

How do dogs mate?   180

How did Catherine the Great die?   181

What surprised John Ruskin on his wedding
night?   183

How long do your fingernails and hair grow
after death?   184

What did Atlas carry on his shoulders?   186

How high is Cloud Nine?   187

What makes champagne fizz?   189

What shape is a raindrop?	189
What produces most of the Earth's oxygen?	190
What were First World War German uniforms made from?	191
Who discovered penicillin?	192
What causes stomach ulcers?	194
What are guinea pigs used for?	195
What was the first animal in space?	197
Which has the most neck bones, a mouse or a giraffe?	198
How long have the Celts lived in Britain?	199
Who was the first man to circumnavigate the globe?	201
Who was the first to claim that the Earth goes round the Sun?	202
Who invented the Theory of Relativity?	203
What shape did Columbus think the Earth was?	205
What shape did medieval people think the Earth was?	207
Who first discovered that the world was round?	208
Why do bees buzz?	210
What has the largest brain in comparison to its size?	211
How much of our brains do we use?	213
What colour is your brain?	214
What effect does alcohol have on brain cells?	216
What do dolphins drink?	217
What was James Bond's favourite drink?	218
What shouldn't you drink if you're dehydrated?	220
What contains the most caffeine: tea or coffee?	221
What kind of fruit are Jaffa Cakes made from?	222
What do digestive biscuits do?	223
How was Teflon discovered?	225
Which organisation invented Quaker Oats?	226

What shouldn't you do twenty minutes after
    eating? 227
How does television damage your health? 229
How much sleep should you have every night? 230
What will be the biggest killer in the world by
    2030? 232
What illness do British doctors treat most often? 233
Is the answer to depression just to 'walk it off'? 234
Which country has the world's highest suicide
    rate? 236
Was Hitler a vegetarian? 237
Which nation invented the concentration camp? 239
Which aeroplane won the Battle of Britain? 240
When did the last survivor of the Crimean War
    die? 242
How many dog years equal one human year? 243
How long is a day? 244
What's the longest animal? 245
What's the loudest thing in the ocean? 247
Why are flamingos pink? 248
What colour is a panther? 250
What makes an animal see red? 251
What colour were the original Oompa-Loompas? 252
What colour were Robin Hood's tights? 253
What colour are carrots? 255
Do carrots help us see in the dark? 256
What do bananas grow on? 258
Which of the following are berries? 259
Which of the following are nuts? 260
Who goes gathering nuts in May? 262
What's inside a coconut? 263
What did Captain Cook give his men to cure
    scurvy? 264
Who discovered Australia? 266
What does 'kangaroo' mean in Aboriginal? 268

xi

What's 'pom' short for? 268

What's the biggest rock in the world? 270

What were boomerangs used for? 271

What's wrong with this picture? 272

Which religion curses people by sticking pins
  into dolls? 274

How many Wise Men visited Jesus? 275

Where does Santa Claus come from? 276

What are Bugs Bunny, Brer Rabbit and the
  Easter Bunny? 278

What were Cinderella's slippers made from? 279

Where do loofahs come from? 281

What's the strongest wood? 282

What do you get if you suck your pencil? 282

Where was the log cabin invented? 284

Where did Stone Age people live? 285

What was the first animal to be domesticated? 286

What was odd about Rudolph the Red-nosed
  Reindeer? 288

Where do turkeys come from? 288

Who was born by Immaculate Conception? 290

Was Jesus born in a stable? 291

How many sheep were there on Noah's Ark? 292

Where were the first modern Olympics held? 294

Why is a marathon 26 miles and 385 yards
  long? 295

What does the Queen say to someone she's
  knighted? 297

Who was the first King of England? 298

Who fought at the battle of Culloden? 299

Which was the last country invaded by
  Scotland? 301

Where do Panama hats come from? 303

Can you name an Irish saint? 304

What nationality was the Duke of Wellington? 306

Who was Britain's first Prime Minister?   307
Who invented the Penny Post?   309
What do you get when you're 100 years old?   310

WHAT IS QUITE INTERESTING?   312

FOREWORD | Stephen Fry

People sometimes accuse me of knowing a lot. 'Stephen,' they say, accusingly, 'you know a lot.' This is a bit like telling a person who has a few grains of sand clinging to him that he owns much sand. When you consider the vast amount of sand there is in the world such a person is, to all intents and purposes, sandless. We are all sandless. We are all ignorant. There are beaches and deserts and dunes of knowledge whose existence we have never even guessed at, let alone visited.

It's the ones who think they know what there is to be known that we have to look out for. 'All is explained in this text—there is nothing else you need to know,' they tell us. For thousands of years we put up with this kind of thing. Those who said, 'Hang on, I think we might be ignorant, let's see...' were made to drink poison, or had their eyes put out and their bowels drawn out through their botties.

We are perhaps now more in danger of thinking we know everything than we were even in those dark times of religious superstition (if indeed they have gone away). Today we have the whole store of human knowledge a mouse-click away, which is all very fine and dandy, but it's in danger of becoming just another sacred text. What we need is a treasure house, not of knowledge, but of ignorance. Something that gives not answers but questions. Something that shines light, not on already garish facts, but into the dark, damp corners of ignorance. And the volume you have in your hands is just such a blazing torch which can help us embark upon the journey of dumbing up.

Read it wisely, Little One, for the power of ignorance is great.

FOUR WORDS | Alan Davies

Will this do, Stephen?

INTRODUCTION | John Lloyd

There's an idea going about that the human race basically understands how the universe works. Not you and me, obviously, but 'scientists' perhaps, or 'experts'. Regrettably, this is not the case. In the words of Thomas Edison, the man who didn't invent the light bulb, 'We don't know a millionth of one per cent about anything.'

This book is for the people who know they don't know very much. It contains hundreds of things that the average person doesn't know. But it doesn't begin to scratch the surface of human ignorance, because it's the kind of stuff that has answers. The really interesting questions aren't like that. What is life? Nobody knows. What is light? Or love? Or laughter?

It's a very well-kept secret, which they don't teach you at school, that nobody has the faintest notion what gravity is. Or consciousness, or electricity or viruses. We don't know why there is something and not nothing and we do not know either how, or why, the universe began. Worse, 96 per cent of the universe appears to be missing. The world is not solid; it is made of empty space and energy. But nobody knows what energy is and they're beginning to suspect there is no such thing as emptiness.

One of the many things we don't understand is: what is interestingness? The Romans, interestingly, had no word for 'interesting'. Nobody has ever successfully defined what interestingness actually is—or worked out why what you don't know is much more interesting than what you do know.

Biologists say our primal drives are food, sex and shelter, no different from the animals. We say there is a fourth drive which makes us uniquely human— curiosity. Porcupines do not worry about the meaning of existence. Moths and aardvarks do not look up at the night sky and wonder what the twinkly bits are. People do. In the words of W. H. Auden, 'Those who run to the apes to explain our behaviour are chuckle-heads too dumb to know their arse from a hole-in-the-ground.'

The human brain is the most complex single object in the cosmos. It can make more connections than there are positively charged particles in the visible universe. Nobody knows why it is so massively complicated, or what we are supposed to do with all that astonishing computing power.

At QI, we think we know the answer. Ask more questions.

Here are 230 of them.

THE BOOK
OF
GENERAL IGNORANCE

By ignorance the truth is known.
Henry Suso (1300–65), The Little Book of Truth

HOW MANY WIVES DID HENRY VIII HAVE?

We make it two.

Or four if you're a Catholic.

Henry's fourth marriage to Anne of Cleves was annulled. This is very different from divorce. Legally, it means the marriage never took place.

There were two grounds for the annulment. Anne and Henry never consummated the marriage; that is, they never had intercourse. Refusal or inability to consummate a marriage is still grounds for annulment today.

In addition, Anne was already betrothed to Francis, Duke of Lorraine when she married Henry. At that time, the formal act of betrothal was a legal bar to marrying someone else.

All parties agreed no legal marriage had taken place. So that leaves five.

The Pope declared Henry's second marriage to Anne Boleyn illegal, because the King was still married to his first wife, Catherine of Aragon.

Henry, as head of the new Church of England, declared in turn that his *first* marriage was invalid on the legal ground that a man could not sleep with his brother's widow. The King cited the Old Testament, which he claimed as 'God's Law', whether the Pope liked it or not.

Depending on whether you believe the Pope or the King, this brings it down to either four or three marriages.

Henry annulled his marriage to Anne Boleyn just

before he had her executed for adultery. This was somewhat illogical: if the marriage had never existed, Anne could hardly be accused of betraying it.

He did the same with his fifth wife, Catherine Howard. All the evidence suggests she was unfaithful to him before and during their marriage. This time, Henry passed a special act making it treasonable for a queen to commit adultery. Once again, he also had the marriage annulled.

So that makes four annulments, and only two incontestably legal marriages.

Apart from Henry's last wife, Catherine Parr (who outlived him), the lady who got off lightest was Anne of Cleves. After their annulment, the King showered her with gifts and the official title of 'beloved sister'. She visited court often, swapping cooks, recipes, and household gadgets with the man who had never been her husband.

HOW MANY NOSTRILS HAVE YOU GOT?

Four. Two you can see; two you can't.

This discovery came from observing how fish breathe. Fish get their oxygen from water. Most of them have two pairs of nostrils, a forward-facing set for letting water in and a pair of 'exhaust pipes' for letting it out again.

The question is, if humans evolved from fishes, where did the other pair of nostrils go?

The answer is that they migrated back inside the head to become internal nostrils called *choannae*— Greek for 'funnels'. These connect to the throat and are what allow us to breathe through our noses.

To do this they somehow had to work their way back through the teeth. This sounds unlikely but scientists in China and Sweden have recently found a fish called *To see what is in front of one's nose requires constant struggle.* **GEORGE ORWELL**

Kenichthys campbelli—a 395-million-year-old fossil —that shows this process at its half-way stage. The fish has two nostril-like holes between its front teeth.

Kenichthys campbelli is a direct ancestor of land animals, able to breathe in both air and water. One set of nostrils allowed it to lie in the shallows and eat while the other poked out of the water a bit like a crocodile's.

Similar gaps between the teeth can also be seen at an early stage of the human embryo. When they fail to join up, the result is a cleft palate. So one ancient fish explains two ancient human mysteries.

The most recent research on noses, incidentally, shows that we use each of our two external nostrils to detect different smells, breathing different amounts of air into each to create a kind of nasal stereo.

WHERE IS THE DRIEST PLACE ON EARTH?

Antarctica. Parts of the continent have seen no rain for two million years.

A desert is technically defined as a place that receives less than 254 mm (10 inches) of rain a year.

The Sahara gets just 25 mm (1 inch) of rain a year.

Antarctica's average annual rainfall is about the

3

same, but 2 per cent of it, known as the Dry Valleys, is free of ice and snow and it never rains there at all.

The next-driest place in the world is the Atacama Desert in Chile. In some areas, no rain has fallen there for 400 years and its average annual rainfall is a tiny 0.1 mm (0.004 inches). Taken as a whole, this makes it the world's driest desert, 250 times as dry as the Sahara.

As well as the driest place on earth, Antarctica can also claim to be the wettest and the windiest. Seventy per cent of the world's water is found there in the form of ice, and its wind speeds are the fastest ever recorded.

The unique conditions in the Dry Valleys of Antarctica are caused by so-called katabatic winds (from the Greek word for 'going down'). These occur when cold, dense air is pulled downhill simply by the force of gravity. The winds can reach speeds of 320 kph (200 mph) evaporating all moisture—water, ice and snow—in the process.

Though Antarctica is a desert, these completely dry parts of it are called, somewhat ironically, oases. They are so similar to conditions on Mars that NASA used them to test the Viking mission.

WHERE IS THE HIGHEST MOUNTAIN?

It's on Mars.

The giant volcano Mount Olympus—or *Olympus Mons* in Latin—is the highest mountain in the solar system and in the known universe.

At 22 km high (14 miles) and 624 km (388 miles) across, it is almost three times the height of Mount

4

Everest and so wide that its base would cover Arizona, or the whole of the area of the British Isles. The crater on the top is around 72 km (45 miles) wide and over 3 km (nearly 2 miles) deep, easily big enough to swallow London.

Mons Olympus doesn't conform to most people's idea of a mountain. It is flat-topped—like a vast plateau in a sea drained of water—and its sides aren't even steep. Their slight incline of between one and three degrees means you wouldn't even break sweat if you climbed it.

We traditionally measure mountains by their height. If we measured them by their size, it would be meaningless to isolate one mountain in a range from the rest. That being so, Mount Everest would dwarf Olympus Mons. It is part of the gigantic Himalaya–Karakoram–Hindu-Kush–Pamir range which is nearly 2,400 km (1,500 miles) long.

WHAT'S THE NAME OF THE TALLEST MOUNTAIN IN THE WORLD?

Mauna Kea, the highest point on the island of Hawaii.

The inactive volcano is a modest 4,206 m (13,799 feet) above sea level, but when measured from the seabed to its summit, it is 10,200 m (33,465 feet) high—about three-quarters of a mile taller than Mount Everest.

As far as mountains are concerned, the current convention is that 'highest' means measured from sea level to summit; 'tallest' means measured from the bottom of the mountain to the top.

So, while Mount Everest, at 8,848 m (29,029 feet) is the highest mountain in the world, it is not the tallest.

Measuring mountains is trickier than it looks. It's easy enough to see where the top is, but where exactly is the 'bottom' of a mountain?

For example, some argue that Mount Kilimanjaro in Tanzania—at 5,895 m (19,340 feet)—is taller than Everest because it rises straight out of the African plain, whereas Everest is merely one of many peaks topping the enormous base of the Himalayas, shared by the world's next thirteen highest mountains.

Others claim that the most logical measure ought to be the distance of a mountain's peak from the centre of the Earth.

Because the Earth is a flattened rather than a perfect sphere, the equator is about 21 km (13 miles) further from the centre of the Earth than the poles.

This is good news for the reputation of those mountains that are very close to the equator—like Mount Chimborazo in the Andes—but it also means accepting that even the beaches in Ecuador are 'higher' than the Himalayas.

Though massive, the Himalayas are surprisingly young. When they were formed, the dinosaurs had been dead for 25 million years.

In Nepal, Everest is known as *Chomolungma*—'Mother of the Universe'. In Tibet, it is called *Sagamartha*—'Forehead of the Sky'. Like any healthy youngster, it is still growing—at the not very exciting rate of 4 mm (less than a quarter of an inch) a year.

WHAT'S THE LARGEST LIVING THING?

It's a mushroom.

And it's not even a particularly rare one. You've probably got the honey fungus (*Armillaria ostoyae*) in your garden, growing on a dead tree-stump.

For your sake, let's hope it doesn't reach the size of the largest recorded specimen, in Malheur National Forest in Oregon. It covers 890 hectares (2,200 acres) and is between 2,000 and 8,000 years old. Most of it is underground in the form of a massive mat of tentacle-like white *mycelia* (the mushroom's equivalent of roots). These spread along tree roots, killing the trees and peeping up through the soil occasionally as innocent-looking clumps of honey mushrooms.

I confess that nothing frightens me more than the appearance of mushrooms on the table, especially in a small provincial town.
ALEXANDRE DUMAS

The giant honey fungus of Oregon was initially thought to grow in separate clusters throughout the forest, but researchers have now confirmed it is the world's single biggest organism, connected under the soil.

WHAT'S THE BIGGEST THING A BLUE WHALE CAN SWALLOW?

a) A very large mushroom
b) A small family car
c) A grapefruit
d) A sailor

A grapefruit.

Quite interestingly, a blue whale's throat is almost exactly the same diameter as its belly button (which is about the size of a side plate), but a little smaller than its eardrum (which is more the size of a dinner plate).

For eight months of the year, blue whales eat virtually nothing, but during the summer they feed almost continuously, scooping up three tons of food a day. As you may remember from biology lessons, their diet consists of tiny, pink, shrimp-like crustaceans called *krill*, which slip down a treat. Krill come conveniently served in huge swarms that can weigh over 100,000 tons.

The word krill is Norwegian. It comes from the Dutch word *kriel*, meaning 'small fry' but now also used to mean both pygmies and 'small potatoes'. Krill sticks have been marketed with reasonable success in Chile but krill mince was a bit of a disaster in Russia, Poland and South Africa owing to dangerously high levels of fluoride. It came from the krill's shells which were too small to pick off individually before mincing.

The narrow gauge of a blue whale's throat means it couldn't have swallowed Jonah. The only whale with

8

a throat wide enough to swallow a person whole is the sperm whale and, once inside, the intense acidity of the sperm whale's stomach juices would make survival impossible. The celebrated case of the 'Modern Jonah' in 1891, in which James Bartley claimed to have been swallowed by a sperm whale and rescued by his crew mates fifteen hours later, has been nailed as a fraud.

Aside from its throat, everything else about the blue whale is *big*. At 32 m (105 feet) in length, it is the largest creature that has ever lived—three times the size of the biggest dinosaur and equivalent in weight to 2,700 people. Its tongue weighs more than an elephant; its heart is the size of a family car; its stomach can hold more than a ton of food. It also makes the loudest noise of any individual animal: a low frequency 'hum' that can be detected by other whales over 16,000 km (10,000 miles) away.

WHICH BIRD LAYS THE SMALLEST EGG FOR ITS SIZE?

The ostrich.

Although it is the largest single cell in nature, an ostrich egg is less than 1½ per cent of the weight of the mother. A wren's egg, by comparison, is 13 per cent of its weight.

The largest egg in comparison with the size of the bird is that of the Little Spotted kiwi. Its egg accounts for 26 per cent of its own weight: the equivalent of a woman giving birth to a six-year-old child.

An ostrich egg weighs as much as twenty-four hen's eggs; to soft-boil one takes forty-five minutes.

Queen Victoria tucked into one for breakfast and declared it among the best meals she had ever eaten.

The largest egg laid by any animal—including the dinosaurs—belonged to the elephant bird of Madagascar, which became extinct in 1700. It was ten times the size of an ostrich egg, nine litres in volume and the equivalent of 180 chicken's eggs.

The elephant bird (*Aepyornis maximus*) is thought to be the basis for the legend of the fierce *roc* that Sinbad battles in the *Arabian Nights*.

HOW LONG CAN A CHICKEN LIVE WITHOUT ITS HEAD?

About two years.

On 10 September 1945, a plump young cockerel in Fruita, Colorado, had his head chopped off and lived. Incredibly, the axe had missed the jugular vein and left enough of the brain stem attached to the neck for him to survive, even thrive.

Mike, as he was known, became a national celebrity, touring the country and featuring in *Time* and *Life* magazines. His owner, Lloyd Olsen, charged twenty-five cents for a chance to meet 'Mike the Headless Wonder Chicken' in sideshows across the USA. Mike would appear complete with a dried chicken's head purporting to be his own—in fact, the Olsens' cat had made off with the original. At the height of his fame, Mike was making $4,500 a month, and was valued at $10,000. His success resulted in a wave of copycat chicken beheadings, though none of the unfortunate victims lived for more than a day or two.

Mike was fed and watered using an eyedropper. In the two years after he lost his head, he put on nearly six pounds and spent his time happily preening and 'pecking' for food with his neck. One person who knew Mike well commented: 'He was a big fat chicken who didn't know he didn't have a head.'

Tragedy struck one night in a motel room in Phoenix, Arizona. Mike started to choke and Lloyd Olsen, to his horror, realised he'd left the eyedropper at the previous day's show. Unable to clear his airways, Mike choked to death.

Mike remains a cult figure in Colorado and, every May since 1999, Fruita has marked his passing with a 'Mike the Headless Chicken' Day.

WHAT HAS A THREE-SECOND MEMORY?

Not a goldfish, for starters.

Despite its status as a proverbial fact, a goldfish's memory isn't a few seconds long.

Research by the School of Psychology at the University of Plymouth in 2003 demonstrated beyond reasonable doubt that goldfish have a memory-span of at least three months and can distinguish between different shapes, colours and sounds. They were trained to push a lever to earn a food reward; when the lever was fixed to work only for an hour a day, the fish soon learned to activate it at the correct time. A number of similar studies have shown that farmed fish can easily be trained to feed at particular times and places in response to an audible signal.

Goldfish don't swim into the side of the bowl, not because they can see it, but because they are using a pressure-sensing system called the lateral line. Certain species of blind cave fish are able to navigate perfectly well in their lightless environment by using their lateral line system alone.

While we're dealing with goldfish myths, a pregnant goldfish isn't, hasn't and can't be called a 'twit'. Goldfish don't get pregnant: they lay eggs that the males fertilise in the water.

In principle, there *could* be a word for a female fish with egg development—such as 'twit', 'twat' or 'twerp'—but none is listed in any proper dictionary.

WHAT'S THE MOST DANGEROUS ANIMAL THAT HAS EVER LIVED?

Half the human beings who have ever died, perhaps as many as 45 billion people, have been killed by female mosquitoes (the males only bite plants).

Mosquitoes carry more than a hundred potentially fatal diseases including malaria, yellow fever, dengue fever, encephalitis, filariasis and elephantiasis. Even today, they kill one person every twelve seconds.

If you think you are too small to make a difference, try sleeping in a closed room with a mosquito.
AFRICAN PROVERB

Amazingly, nobody had any idea that mosquitoes were dangerous until the end of the nineteenth century. In 1877, the British doctor Sir Patrick Manson—known as 'Mosquito' Manson— proved that elephantiasis was caused by mosquito bites.

12

Seventeen years later, in 1894, it occurred to him that malaria might also be caused by mosquitoes. He encouraged his pupil Ronald Ross, then a young doctor based in India, to test the hypothesis.

Ross was the first person to show how female mosquitoes transmit the *Plasmodium* parasite through their saliva. He tested his theory using birds. Manson went one better. To show that the theory worked for humans, he infected his own son—using mosquitoes carried in the diplomatic bag from Rome. (Fortunately, after an immediate dose of quinine, the boy recovered.)

Ross won the Nobel Prize for Medicine in 1902. Manson was elected a Fellow of the Royal Society, knighted and founded the London School of Tropical Medicine.

There are 2,500 known species of mosquito, 400 of them are members of the *Anopheles* family, and, of these, 40 species are able to transmit malaria.

The females use the blood they suck to mature their eggs, which are laid on water. The eggs hatch into aquatic larvae or 'wrigglers'. Unlike most insects, the pupae of mosquitoes, known as 'tumblers', are active and swim about.

Male mosquitoes hum at a higher pitch than females: they can be sexually enticed by the note of a B-natural tuning fork.

Female mosquitoes are attracted to their hosts by moisture, milk, carbon dioxide, body heat and movement. Sweaty people and pregnant women have a higher chance of being bitten.

Mosquito means 'small fly' in Spanish and Portuguese.

DO MARMOTS KILL PEOPLE?

Yes, they cough them to death.

Marmots are benign, pot-bellied members of the squirrel family. They are about the size of a cat and squeak loudly when alarmed. Less appealingly, the bobac variety, found on the Mongolian steppe, is particularly susceptible to a lung infection caused by the bacterium *Yersinia pestis*, commonly known as bubonic plague.

They spread it around by coughing on their neighbours, infecting fleas, rats and, ultimately, humans. All the great plagues that swept through Eastern Asia to Europe came from marmots in Mongolia. The estimated death-toll is over a billion, making the marmot second only to the malarial mosquito as a killer of humans.

When marmots and humans succumb to plague, the lymph glands under the armpits and in the groin become black and swollen (these sores are called 'buboes', from Greek *boubon*, 'groin', hence 'bubonic'). Mongolians will never eat a marmot's armpits because 'they contain the soul of a dead hunter'.

The other parts of the marmot are a delicacy in Mongolia. Hunters have complicated rituals to stalk their prey that include wearing false rabbit-ears, dancing and waving the tail of a yak. The captured marmots are barbecued whole over hot stones. In Europe, the fat of the alpine marmot is valued as a salve for rheumatism.

Other species of marmot include the American prairie dog and the woodchuck, or groundhog.

14

Groundhog Day is on 2 February. Each year, a marmot known as Punxsutawney Phil is pulled out of his electrically heated burrow at Gobbler's Knob, Pennsylvania by his tuxedo-clad 'keepers' who ask him if he can see his shadow. If he whispers 'yes', it means winter has six weeks to go. Since 1887, Phil has never been wrong.

Bubonic plague is still with us today—the last serious outbreak occurred in India in 1994—and it is one of the three diseases listed in the US as requiring quarantine (the other two being yellow fever and cholera).

HOW DO LEMMINGS DIE?

Not by mass suicide, if that's what you're thinking.

The suicide idea seems to have originated in the work of nineteenth-century naturalists who had witnessed (but not understood) the four-year boom-and-bust population cycle of the Norwegian lemming (*Lemmus lemmus*).

Lemmings have a phenomenal reproductive capacity. A single female can produce up to eighty offspring a year. Sudden surges in their numbers once led Scandinavians to think they were spontaneously generated by the weather.

What actually happens is that mild winters lead to overpopulation that in turn leads to over-grazing. The lemmings set off into unfamiliar territory in search of food until they pile up against natural obstacles like cliffs, lakes and seas. The lemmings keep coming. Panic and violence ensue. Accidents happen. But it isn't suicide.

A secondary myth has evolved which is that the whole idea of mass suicide was invented by the 1958 Walt Disney film *White Wilderness*. It's true that the film was a complete fake. It was filmed in land-locked, lemming-free Alberta, Canada: the lemmings had to be bussed in from several hundred miles away in Manitoba. The shots of the 'migration' were made using a few lemmings on a snow-covered turntable. The notorious final scene—where lemmings plunge into the sea to the doom-laden voice-over of Winston Hibbler: 'This is the last chance to turn back, yet over they go, casting themselves out bodily into space'— was created by the film-makers simply throwing the lemmings into a river.

But Disney was only guilty of trying to recreate an already entrenched story. Here it is described in the most influential children's reference book of the early twentieth century, Arthur Mee's *Children's Encyclopaedia*, published in 1908:

'They march straight forward, over hill and dell, through gardens, farms, villages, into wells and ponds to poison water and cause typhoid ... on and on to the sea, then into the water to destruction ... It is sad and terrible, but if the dismal exodus did not occur lemmings would long ago have eaten Europe bare.'

WHAT DO CHAMELEONS DO?

They don't change colour to match the background.

Never have; never will. Complete myth. Utter fabrication. Total lie.

They change colour as a result of different

16

emotional states. If they happen to match the background it's entirely coincidental.

Chameleons change colour when frightened or picked up or when they beat another chameleon in a fight. They change colour when a member of the opposite sex steps into view and they sometimes change colour due to fluctuations in either light or temperature.

A chameleon's skin contains several layers of specialised cells called *chromataphores* (from Greek *chroma,* colour, and *pherein,* to carry), each with different coloured pigments. Altering the balance between these layers causes the skin to reflect different kinds of light, making chameleons a kind of walking colour-wheel.

It's odd how persistent the belief that they change colour to match the background is. The myth first appears in the work of a minor Greek writer of entertaining stories and potted biographies called Antigonus of Carystus in about 240 BC. Aristotle, far more influential and writing a century earlier, had already, quite correctly, linked the colour-change to fear and, by the Renaissance, the 'background' theory had, once again, been almost entirely abandoned. But it's come back with a vengeance since and to this day is perhaps the only thing most people think they 'know' about chameleons.

Chameleons can remain completely motionless for several hours at a time. Because of this, and the fact that they eat very little, they were, for many centuries, believed to live on air. This, of course, isn't true either.

The word chameleon is Greek for 'ground-lion'. The smallest species is the *Brookesia minima*, which is 25 mm (1 inch) long; the largest is the *Chaemaeleo parsonnii*, which is more than 610 mm (2 feet) long. The Common Chameleon glories in the Latin name *Chamaeleo chamaeleon*, which sounds like the opening to a song.

Chameleons can rotate and focus either eye independently to look in two completely different directions at once, but they are stone deaf.

The Bible forbids the eating of chameleons.

HOW DO POLAR BEARS DISGUISE THEMSELVES?

They cover their black nose with their white paw, don't they?

Adorable but unfounded, unfortunately. And they're not left-handed either. Naturalists have observed polar bears for many hundreds of hours and have never seen any evidence of discreet nose-covering or of left-handedness.

They like toothpaste, though. There are regular reports of polar bears wreaking havoc in Arctic tourist camps, knocking over tents and trampling equipment, all in order to suck on a tube of Pepsodent.

This may be one of the reasons the town of Churchill in Manitoba has a large concrete 'polar-bear jail'. Any bear moseying into town is apprehended and incarcerated there. Some serve sentences of several months before being released back into the community, embittered, institutionalised and jobless. Formerly the morgue for a military base, it is officially designated Building D-20. It can hold twenty-three bears at a time. Polar bears don't eat during the summer, so some of the inmates aren't fed for months at a time. They're held until spring or the autumn—their hunting seasons—so that when they're released they go off fishing and don't just wander back to Churchill.

The earliest-known captive polar bear belonged to Ptolemy II of Egypt (308–246 BC), and was kept in his private zoo in Alexandria. In AD 57, the Roman writer Calpurnius Siculus wrote of polar bears pitted against seals in a flooded amphitheatre. Viking hunters captured polar bear cubs by killing and skinning the mother, spreading her pelt on the snow, and nabbing the cubs when they came to lie on it.

The scientific names can be a bit misleading. *Ursus arctos* isn't the polar bear, it's the Brown Bear. *Ursus* means 'bear' in Latin and *arctos* means 'bear' in Greek. The Arctic is named after the bear, not the other way around; it was 'the region of the bear', where bears lived and where the great bear in the sky, the constellation Ursa Major, pointed. The polar bear is *Ursus maritimus*—the sea bear.

The constellation Ursa Major has been identified as a bear by a number of cultures including the Ainu of Japan in the east, the American Indians in the west and ourselves in the middle. Even though all polar bears are born, literally, under the constellation of the Great Bear, astrologically they are all Capricorns, born in late December or early January.

The Brown Bear is the same species as the Grizzly, which is the term applied to Brown Bears living in inland North America. Male and female bears are known as boars and sows, despite being about as closely related to pigs as koalas are to seals. Bears' closest relatives are actually dogs.

HOW MANY GALAXIES ARE VISIBLE TO THE NAKED EYE?

Five thousand? Two million? Ten billion?

The answer is four—although from where you are sitting, you can only see two; and one of those is the Milky Way (the one we're in).

Given that there are estimated to be more than 100 billion galaxies in the universe, each containing between 10 and 100 billion stars, it's a bit disappointing. In total, only four galaxies are visible from Earth with the naked eye, only half of which can be seen at once (two from each hemisphere). In the Northern Hemisphere, you can see the Milky Way and Andromeda (M31), while in the Southern Hemisphere you can see the Large and Small Magellanic Clouds.

Some people with exceptional eyesight claim to be able to see three more: M33 in Triangulum, M81 in Ursa Major and M83 in Hydra, but it's very hard to prove.

The number of stars supposedly visible to the naked eye varies wildly, but everyone agrees that the total is substantially less than 10,000. Most amateur-astronomy computer software uses the same database: it lists 9,600 stars as 'naked-eye visible'. But no one really believes this figure. Other estimates vary from around 8,000 down to fewer than 3,000.

It used to be said that there were more cinemas (around 5,200) in the former Soviet Union than there are stars visible in the night sky.

At the Canadian website www.starregistry.ca you can have a star named after yourself or a friend for

$98 CDN (or $175 CDN with a framed certificate). They list 2,873 stars as being visible to the naked eye. None of these are available as they already have historical or scientific names.

WHAT MAN-MADE ARTEFACTS CAN BE SEEN FROM THE MOON?

Deduct ten points if you said the Great Wall of China.

No human artefacts at all can be seen from the Moon with the naked eye.

The idea that the Great Wall is the 'only man-made object that can be seen from the Moon' is all-pervasive, but it confuses 'the Moon' with space.

'Space' is quite close. It starts about 100 km (60 miles) from the Earth's surface. From there, many artificial objects are visible: motorways, ships on the sea, railways, cities, fields of crops, and even some individual buildings.

However, at an altitude of only a few thousand miles after leaving the Earth's orbit, no man-made objects are visible at all. From the Moon—over 400,000 km (some 250,000 miles) away—even the continents are barely visible.

And, despite *Trivial Pursuit* telling you otherwise, there is no point in between the two where 'only' the Great Wall of China is visible.

WHICH OF THESE ARE CHINESE INVENTIONS?

  a) Glass
  b) Rickshaws
  c) Chop suey
  d) Fortune cookies

Chop suey. There are many fanciful stories about its American origin but it is a Chinese dish.

In E. N. Anderson's definitive *The Food of China* (1988), chop suey is named as a dish local to Toisan in southern Canton. They called it *tsap seui*, which means 'miscellaneous scraps' in Cantonese. Most of the early immigrants to California came from this region, hence its early appearance in America.

Glass isn't Chinese: the earliest-known glass artefacts are from ancient Egypt in 1350 BC. The earliest Chinese porcelain dates from the Han dynasty (206 BC–AD 220). Ancient China built a whole culture on porcelain, but they never got to grips with transparent glass. This is sometimes used to explain the fact that they never had a scientific revolution comparable with the one in the West, which was made possible by the development of lenses and transparent glassware.

The rickshaw was invented by an American missionary, Jonathan Scobie, who first used it to wheel his invalid wife through the streets of Yokohama in Japan in 1869.

Fortune cookies are also American, though they were probably invented by a Japanese immigrant, Makato Hagiwara, a landscape designer who created the Golden Gate tearoom in San Francisco. He served small, sweet Japanese buns with thank-you notes inside from about 1907 onwards.

Seek knowledge, even if it be in China.
MUHAMMAD

Restaurant owners in the city's Chinatown copied them and the notes soon started to tell fortunes.

But who's complaining? Chinese resourcefulness has given us: the abacus, bells, brandy, the calendar, the compass, the crossbow, the decimal system, drilling for oil, fireworks, the fishing reel, the flamethrower, the flush toilet, gunpowder, the helicopter, the horse collar, the iron plough, the kite, lacquer, magic mirrors, matches, the mechanical clock, miniature hot-air balloons, negative numbers, paper, parachutes, porcelain, printmaking, relief maps, rudders, seismographs, silk, stirrups, the suspension bridge, the umbrella, the water pump and the wheelbarrow.

WHERE DID MARCO POLO COME FROM?

Croatia.

Marco Polo (or 'Mark Chicken' in English) was born Marko Pilić in Korcula, Dalmatia, in 1254, then a protectorate of Venice.

We shall probably never know whether he really went to the Far East as a seventeen-year-old with his merchant uncles or if he simply recorded the tales of Silk Road traders who stopped off at their Black Sea trading post.

What is certain is that his famous book of travels was largely the work of a romance writer called

Rustichello da Pisa with whom he shared a cell after being captured by the Genoans in 1296. Polo dictated it; Rustichello wrote it in French, a language Polo didn't speak.

The result, which appeared in 1306, was designed to entertain, and it became a best-seller in the era before printing. As an accurate history its status is less secure.

Its original title was *Il Milione*—'the Million'—for reasons that are now obscure, although it quickly became nicknamed 'the million lies', and Polo—now a rich and successful merchant—was known as 'Mr Million'. It was probably just a catchy thirteenth-century version of a title like 'Wonder Book of Wonders'. No original manuscripts survive.

Marco Polo is also supposed to have brought pasta and ice cream to Italy.

In fact, pasta was known in Arab countries in the ninth century and dried macaroni is mentioned in Genoa in 1279, twenty-five years before Polo claimed to have returned. According to the food historian Alan Davidson, the myth itself only dates back as far as 1929 when it was mentioned in an American pasta-trade journal.

Ice cream may well be a Chinese invention but it seems unlikely to have been introduced to the West by Polo, as it doesn't get mentioned again until the middle of the seventeenth century.

WHO INTRODUCED TOBACCO AND POTATOES TO ENGLAND?

It's not who you think it is.

Walter Raleigh, poet, courtier, explorer and Renaissance man, is a perfect example of how popular myths attach themselves to attractive characters. His fame now rests almost entirely on things he didn't do.

The first report of a smoking Englishman is of a sailor in Bristol, seen 'emitting smoke from his nostrils'. This was in 1556, four years before Raleigh was born.

Raleigh never personally visited Virginia or any other part of North America. It was a Frenchman named Jean Nicot, from whose name the word 'nicotine' is derived, who introduced tobacco to France in 1560, and it was from France, not the New World, that tobacco reached England.

Raleigh was a keen smoker and probably helped popularise the tobacco habit after he was introduced to it by Sir Francis Drake.

The term 'smoking' is a late seventeenth-century coinage; until then it was referred to as 'drinking smoke'.

Potatoes were known in Spain by the mid-sixteenth century, and probably reached the British Isles from Europe, rather than directly from America. As a member of the nightshade family the plant was assumed to be poisonous (as, indeed, the upper portions are). When Raleigh planted one in his garden in Ireland, his neighbours threatened to burn his house down.

25

Potatoes gradually caught on. By the middle of the seventeenth century the surgeon Dr William Salmon was claiming they could cure tuberculosis, rabies and 'increase seed and provoke lust, causing fruitfulness in both sexes'.

As for the cloak spread across the puddle for the Queen, the story originated after Raleigh's death with the historian Thomas Fuller. It only became famous as a result of Walter Scott's 1821 Elizabethan romance, *Kenilworth*.

Raleigh's name was spelt many different ways but it seems to have been pronounced 'Raw Lie'. His first name was probably pronounced 'water'.

He spent fifteen years on death row writing his projected five-volume *History of the World* but never got further than 1300 BC.

After his execution, his head was embalmed and presented to his wife. She carried it with her at all times in a velvet bag until she died twenty-nine years later and it was returned to Raleigh's tomb at St Margaret's, Westminster.

WHO INVENTED THE STEAM ENGINE?

a) James Watt
b) George Stephenson
c) Richard Trevithick
d) Thomas Newcomen
e) A Heron from Egypt

Heron (sometimes called Hero) takes the prize, some 1,600 years before Newcomen's engine of 1711.

Heron lived in Alexandria around AD 62, and is

best known as a mathematician and geometer. He was also a visionary inventor and his *aeolopile* or 'wind-ball' was the first working steam engine. Using the same principle as jet propulsion, a steam-driven metal sphere spun round at 1,500 rpm. Unfortunately for Heron, no one was able to see its practical function, so it was considered nothing more than an amusing novelty.

Amazingly, had Heron but known it, the railway had already been invented 700 years earlier by Periander, tyrant of Corinth. Called the Diolkos, or Slipway, it ran for 6 km (4 miles) across the isthmus of Corinth in Greece, and consisted of a roadway paved with limestone blocks in which were cut parallel grooves 1.5 m (5 feet) apart. Trolleys ran along these tracks, on to which ships were loaded. These were pushed by gangs of slaves forming a sort of 'land-canal' offering a short cut between the Aegean and the Ionian seas.

The Diolkos was in use for some 1,500 years until it fell into disrepair around AD 900. The principle of railways was then completely forgotten about for almost another 500 years, until people had the idea of using them in mines in the fourteenth century.

The historian Arnold Toynbee wrote a brilliant essay speculating what would have happened if the two inventions had been combined to create a global Greek empire, based on a fast rail network, Athenian democracy and a Buddhist-style religion founded on the teachings of Pythagoras. He refers in passing to a failed prophet who lived at 4, Railway Cuttings, Nazareth.

Heron also invented the vending machine—for four drachmas you got a shot of holy water—and a

27

portable device to ensure that no one else could drink the wine you brought along to a bottle party.

WHO INVENTED THE TELEPHONE?

Antonio Meucci.

An erratic, sometimes brilliant, Florentine inventor, Meucci arrived in the USA in 1850. In 1860, he first demonstrated a working model of an electric device he called the *teletrofono*. He filed a caveat (a kind of stopgap patent) in 1871, five years before Alexander Graham Bell's telephone patent.

In the same year, Meucci fell ill after he was badly scalded when the Staten Island ferry's boiler exploded. Unable to speak much English, and living on the dole, he failed to send the $10 required to renew his caveat in 1874.

When Bell's patent was registered in 1876, Meucci sued. He'd sent his original sketches and working models to the lab at Western Union. By an extraordinary coincidence, Bell worked in the very same lab and the models had mysteriously disappeared.

Meucci died in 1889, while his case against Bell was still under way. As a result, it was Bell, not Meucci who got the credit for the invention. In 2004, the balance was partly redressed by the US House of Representatives who passed a resolution that 'the life and achievements of Antonio Meucci should be recognized, and his work in the invention of the telephone should be acknowledged.'

One day there will be a telephone in every major city in the USA.
ALEXANDER GRAHAM BELL

Not that Bell was a complete fraud. As a young man he did teach his dog to say 'How are you, grandmamma?' as a way of communicating with her when she was in a different room. And he made the telephone a practical tool.

Like his friend Thomas Edison, Bell was relentless in his search for novelty. And, like Edison, he wasn't always successful. His metal detector failed to locate the bullet in the body of the stricken President James Garfield. It seems Bell's machine was confused by the President's metal bed-springs.

Bell's foray into animal genetics was driven by his desire to increase the numbers of twin and triplet births in sheep. He noticed that sheep with more than two nipples produced more twins. All he managed to produce was sheep with more nipples.

On the plus side, he did help to invent a hydrofoil, the HP4, which set the world water-speed record of 114 kph (70.84 mph) in 1919 and stood for ten years. Bell was eighty-two at the time and wisely refused to travel in it.

Bell always referred to himself first and foremost as a 'teacher of the deaf'. His mother and wife were deaf and he taught the young Helen Keller. She dedicated her autobiography to him.

WHAT'S QUITE INTERESTING ABOUT SCOTLAND, KILTS, BAGPIPES, HAGGIS, PORRIDGE, WHISKY AND TARTAN?

None of them is Scottish.

Scotland is named after the Scoti, a Celtic tribe from Ireland, who arrived in what the Romans called

29

Caledonia in the fifth or sixth century AD. By the eleventh century they dominated the whole of mainland Scotland. 'Scots Gaelic' is actually a dialect of Irish.

Kilts were invented by the Irish but the word 'kilt' is Danish (*kilte op*, 'tuck up').

The bagpipes are ancient and were probably invented in Central Asia. They are mentioned in the Old Testament (Daniel 3: 5, 10, 15) and in Greek poetry of the fourth century BC. The Romans probably brought them to Britain but the earliest Pictish carvings date from the eighth century AD.

Haggis was an ancient Greek sausage (Aristophanes mentions one exploding in *The Clouds* in 423 BC).

Oat porridge has been found in the stomachs of 5,000-year-old Neolithic bog bodies in central Europe and Scandinavia.

Whisky was invented in ancient China. It arrived in Ireland before Scotland, first distilled by monks. The word derives from the Irish *uisge beatha*, from the Latin *aqua vitae* or 'water of life'.

The elaborate system of clan tartans is a complete myth stemming from the early nineteenth century. All Highland dress, including what tartan or plaid there was, was banned after the 1745 rebellion. The English garrison regiments started designing their own tartans as an affectation, and to mark the state visit of King George IV to Edinburgh in 1822. Queen Victoria encouraged the trend, and it soon became a Victorian craze.

Hae'ing said a' that, they've nae been idle, ye ken. Scots inventions and discoveries include adhesive stamps, the Bank of England, bicycle pedals, Bovril, the breech-loading rifle, the cell nucleus, chloroform, the cloud chamber, colour photography, cornflour, the cure for malaria, the decimal point, electro-magnetism, the *Encyclopaedia Britannica*, finger-printing, the fountain pen, hypnosis, hypodermic syringes, insulin, the kaleidoscope, the Kelvin scale, the lawnmower, lime cordial, logarithms, lorries, marmalade, motor insurance, the MRI scanner, the paddle steamer, paraffin, piano pedals, pneumatic tyres, the postmark, radar, the raincoat, the reflecting telescope, savings banks, the screw propeller, the speedometer, the steam hammer, tarmac, the teleprinter, tubular steel, the typhoid vaccine, the ultrasound scanner, the United States Navy, Universal Standard Time, vacuum flasks, wave-powered electricity generators and wire rope.

WHERE DOES CHICKEN TIKKA MASALA COME FROM?

Glasgow.

Britain exports chicken tikka masala to India.

Invented in Glasgow in the late 1960s, chicken tikka masala, or CTM, is Britain's most popular dish. There is no standard recipe. In a recent survey, the *Real Curry Guide* tested forty-eight different versions and found the only common ingredient was chicken.

Chicken tikka is a traditional Bangladeshi dish in which pieces of marinated chicken are cooked in a clay oven called a *tandoor*. This ancient style of cooking originated in the Middle East, the word deriving from the Babylonian *tinuru*, meaning 'fire'.

The first chicken tandoori on a British restaurant

31

menu was at the Gaylord in Mortimer Street, London, in 1966—the same restaurant where *Not the Nine O'Clock News* was invented in 1979. The recipe reached Glasgow shortly afterwards and when, as the legend goes, a customer asked for some gravy to go with it, the chef improvised with tomato soup, spices and cream.

Masala means a mixture of spices, and the usual CTM contains ginger and garlic, tomatoes, butter and cream, spiced with cardamom, cloves, cumin, nutmeg, mild red chilli powder and paprika, fenugreek and turmeric.

It is the turmeric that gives it the bright yellow colour, although the synthetic dye tartrazine is often substituted. (It is tartrazine, among other unpleasant things, that makes curry stains impossible to remove from clothing.) CTM doesn't have a standard style or colour: it can be yellow, brown, red, or green and chilli hot; creamy and mild; or very smooth and sweet.

In 2001, the Foreign Secretary, Robin Cook, declared that: 'Chicken tikka masala is now a true British national dish, not only because it is the most popular, but because it is a perfect illustration of the way Britain absorbs and adapts external influences.'

One in seven curries sold in the UK are CTMs—23 million portions each year. Many of the schools and charities in the city of Sylhet in Bangladesh are funded by profits from the British chicken tikka masala boom.

There are now 8,000 Indian restaurants in Britain, turning over in excess of £2 billion and employing 70,000 workers.

IS FRENCH TOAST FROM FRANCE?

Yes and no. Dipping bread in eggs and frying it is a pretty universal solution to making stale bread go further.

The French certainly had a medieval version called *tostees dorees*, 'golden toast', and this later became *pain perdu*, 'lost bread', a name that has been enthusiastically adopted for the de luxe versions served in Cajun cooking.

The earliest recorded recipe for the dish occurs in the work of the Roman cook Apicius in the first century AD. In his book *The Art of Cooking*, he writes, rather casually, that it's just 'another sweet dish': 'Break fine white bread, crust removed, into rather large pieces. Soak them in milk, fry in oil, cover in honey and serve.'

There are references in early French documents to this recipe as *pain à la Romaine*, 'Roman bread'. So, that makes it Italian Toast. As ever, it depends where you are at the time, as there are records of German Toast, Spanish Toast, American Toast and even Nun's Toast being used.

'French toast' is first recorded in English in 1660 when it appears in *The Accomplisht Cook* by Robert May. In the same year, Gervase Markham's influential *The English Huswife* has a rich and spicy version of 'pamperdy' (*pain perdu*), so, as far as the English were concerned, French toast was French, in those days at least.

However, the dish was also sometimes referred to as 'Poor Knights of Windsor'. This finds its counterpart in the German (*arme Ritter*), Danish (*arme riddere*), Swedish (*fattiga riddare*) and Finnish (*köyhät ritarit*) versions—all of which mean 'poor knights'.

One theory offered in explanation is that the most expensive part of a medieval banquet was dessert—spices and nuts were costly imports. Although titled, not all knights were rich, so a dish of fried eggy-bread served with jam or honey would have fulfilled the requirements of etiquette without breaking the bank.

WHO INVENTED CHAMPAGNE?

Not the French.

It may come as a surprise—even an outrage—to them but champagne is an English invention.

As anyone who has made their own ginger beer knows, fermentation naturally produces bubbles. The problem has always been controlling it.

The English developed a taste for fizzy wine in the sixteenth century, importing barrels of green, flat wine from Champagne and adding sugar and molasses to start it fermenting. They also developed the strong coal-fired glass bottles and corks to contain it.

As the records of the Royal Society show, what is now called *méthode champenoise* was first written down in England in 1662. The French added finesse and marketing flair but it wasn't until 1876 that they perfected the modern dry or *brut* style (and even then it was for export to England).

The UK is France's largest customer for champagne. In 2004, 34 million bottles were consumed in Britain. This is almost a third of the entire export market—twice as much as the USA, three times as much as the Germans and twenty times as much as the Spanish.

The Benedictine monk Dom Pérignon (1638–1715) did not invent champagne: in fact he spent most of his time trying to remove the bubbles.

His famous exclamation: 'Come quickly, I am drinking the stars', was devised for an advertisement in the late nineteenth century. Pérignon's real legacy to champagne was in the skilful blending of grape varieties from different vineyards and the use of a wire or hempen cage for the cork.

A legal loophole uniquely allows Americans to call their sparkling wines champagne. The Treaty of Madrid (1891) decreed that only the Champagne region may use that name. This was reaffirmed by the Treaty of Versailles (1919) but the US signed a separate peace agreement with Germany.

When prohibition was lifted, American wine-merchants took advantage of this loophole, freely selling their own 'Champagne', much to the annoyance of the French.

The saucer-like *coupe* from which champagne is sometimes drunk is *not* based on a mould of Marie Antoinette's breast. It was first manufactured in 1663 (in England), well before her reign. No alternative English topless model has yet been suggested.

WHERE WAS THE GUILLOTINE INVENTED?

Halifax in Yorkshire.

The Halifax Gibbet consisted of two fifteen-foot wooden uprights between which hung an iron axe mounted on a lead-filled cross-beam controlled by a rope and pulley. Official records show at least fifty-three people were executed using it between 1286 and 1650.

Medieval Halifax made its fortune from the cloth trade. Large quantities of expensive cloth were left outside the mills to dry on frames. Theft was a serious problem and the town's merchants needed an efficient deterrent.

This, and a similar, later, Scottish device called the Maiden, may well have inspired the French to borrow the idea and come up with their own name.

Dr Joseph Ignace Guillotin was a humane, mild-mannered doctor who disliked public executions. In 1789, he put to the National Assembly an ambitious plan to reform the French penal system and make it more humane. He proposed a standardised mechanical method of execution which didn't discriminate against the poor (who were messily hanged), as opposed to the rich (who were relatively cleanly beheaded).

Most of the proposals were rejected out of hand, but the notion of an efficient killing engine stuck. Guillotin's recommendation was picked up and refined by Dr Antoine Louis, the Secretary of the Academy of Surgeons. It was he, not Guillotin, who produced the first working device with its characteristic diagonal blade in 1792. It was even called, briefly, a *Louison* or *Louisette*, after its sponsor.

But somehow, Guillotin's name became attached to it and, despite the best efforts of his family, there it has stubbornly remained. Contrary to popular folklore, Guillotin was not killed by his eponymous machine; he died in 1814 from an infected carbuncle on his shoulder.

The guillotine became the first 'democratic' method of execution and was adopted throughout France. In its first ten years, historians estimate 15,000 people were decapitated. Only Nazi Germany has used it to execute more, with an estimated 40,000 criminals being guillotined between 1938 and 1945.

The last French person to be guillotined was a Tunisian immigrant called Hamida Djandoubi, for the rape and murder of a young girl in 1977. The death penalty was finally abolished in France in 1981.

It is impossible to test accurately how long a severed head remains conscious, if at all. The best estimate is between five and thirteen seconds.

The more I see of the moneyed classes, the more I understand the guillotine.
GEORGE BERNARD SHAW

HOW MANY PRISONERS WERE FREED BY THE STORMING OF THE BASTILLE?

Seven.

In France, 14 July, Bastille Day, is a national holiday and a glorious national symbol, equivalent to 4 July in the USA.

From the rousing paintings of the scene, you might think hundreds of proud revolutionaries flooded into the streets waving tricolours. In fact, only just over half a dozen people were being held at the time of the siege.

The Bastille was stormed on 14 July 1789. Shortly afterwards ghoulish engravings of prisoners languishing in chains next to skeletons went on sale in the streets of Paris, forming the popular impression of the conditions there ever since.

The thirteenth-century fortress had been a jail for centuries; by the time of Louis XVI it mainly housed people arrested on the orders of the king or his ministers for offences like conspiracy and subversion. Distinguished former inmates included Voltaire, who wrote *Oedipus* there in 1718.

The seven prisoners in residence that day were: four forgers, the Comte de Solanges (inside for 'a sexual misdemeanour') and two lunatics (one of whom was an English or Irish man named Major Whyte who sported a waist-length beard and thought he was Julius Caesar).

One hundred lives were lost in the attack, including that of the governor, whose head was carried through Paris on a pike.

The prison guard were a contingent of *invalides*—soldiers invalided out of regular service—and conditions were fairly comfortable for most inmates, with relaxed visiting hours and furnished lodgings.

The painter Jean Fragonard's sketch of visiting day in 1785 shows fashionable ladies promenading around the courtyard with the prisoners, who were given a generous spending allowance, plenty of tobacco and alcohol, and were allowed to keep pets.

Jean François Marmontel, an inmate from 1759 to 1760, wrote: 'The wine was not excellent, but was passable. No dessert: it was necessary to be deprived of something. On the whole I found that one dined very well in prison.'

Louis XVI's diary for the day of the storming of the Bastille reads *'Rien'*.

He was referring to the bag in that day's hunt.

WHO SAID, 'LET THEM EAT CAKE'?

Wrong again. It wasn't her.

You probably remember the history lesson as if it were yesterday. It's 1789 and the French Revolution is under way. The poor of Paris are rioting because they have no bread and the Queen, Marie Antoinette—callously indifferent, trying to be funny or just plain stupid—comes up with the fatuous suggestion that they eat cake instead.

The first problem is that it wasn't cake, it was brioche (the original French is *Qu'ils mangent de la brioche*). According to Alan Davidson's *Oxford*

Companion to Food, 'Eighteenth-century brioche was only lightly enriched (by modest quantities of butter and eggs) and not very far removed from a good white loaf of bread.' So, the remark might have been an attempt at kindness: 'If they want bread, give them some of the good stuff.'

Except Marie Antoinette didn't say it. The line had been in use in print as an illustration of aristocratic decadence since at least 1760. Jean-Jacques Rousseau claimed he'd first heard it as early as 1740.

Lady Antonia Fraser, Marie Antoinette's most recent biographer, attributes the remark to the Queen Marie-Thérèse, wife of Louis XIV, 'The Sun King', but there is a host of other grand eighteenth-century ladies who might have said it. It's also entirely possible it was made up for propaganda purposes.

There is another story that suggests Marie Antoinette introduced croissants to France from her native Vienna. This seems highly unlikely, as the earliest French reference to a croissant isn't until 1853.

Interestingly, wandering Austrian pastry chefs did introduce the flaky pastry to Denmark at about this time, the eponymous 'Danish' pastries being known there as *wienerbrød* ('Vienna bread').

In Vienna, they are called *Kopenhagener*.

HOW WELL DO YOU KNOW THE SWISS?

a) They eat swiss rolls
b) They eat dogs
c) They invented the cuckoo clock
d) They have no army

Swiss rolls are not Swiss: nobody knows why they are called 'Swiss' in Britain and nowhere else. The Swiss equivalents are called either *Biscuitrolle* or *gâteau roulé*; the Spanish call them *brazo de gitano*, or 'gypsies' arms' and the Americans call them jelly rolls (jelly being American for 'jam').

Despite Orson Welles's famous soliloquy in Carol Reed's film *The Third Man* (1949), the cuckoo clock was invented in Germany in 1738.

The Swiss are responsible for several more modern and useful contributions to modern life including rayon, cellophane, Velcro, milk chocolate and the Swiss Army knife.

The Swiss are neutral but they are not pacifists. Every Swiss man aged between twenty and forty is in the Swiss national militia and keeps a rifle at home. If the Swiss had to fight a war, their 'Army' would be 500,000 strong. During the Second World War, the Swiss air force nonchalantly shot down both German and Allied aircraft.

That leaves us with dog-eating. The sensible, law-abiding Swiss are the only Europeans who eat dog meat.

No one knows how many dogs end up salted, smoked or made into sausages in remote Alpine villages, but it certainly happens. Cats, too. Their defence: it's a reasonable way to recycle a much-loved pet and it's good for you. After eating the tastiest parts of the dog, the rest is made into lard and used to cure coughs.

WHAT DOES A ST BERNARD CARRY ROUND ITS NECK?

St Bernards have never, ever carried brandy barrels.

The dog's mission is entirely teetotal—apart from anything else giving brandy to someone with hypothermia is a disastrous mistake—but tourists have always loved the idea, so they still pose wearing them.

Before they were trained as mountain rescue dogs, they were used by the monks at the hospice in the Great St Bernard Pass—the Alpine route that links Switzerland to Italy—to carry food, as their large size and docile temperament made them good pack animals.

The brandy barrel was the idea of a young English artist named Sir Edwin Landseer (1802–73), who was much favoured by Queen Victoria. He was a renowned painter of landscapes and animals, best known for his painting *The Monarch of the Glen* and for sculpting the lions around the base of Nelson's Column.

In 1831, he painted a scene called *Alpine Mastiffs Reanimating a Distressed Traveller* featuring two St Bernards, one of them carrying a miniature brandy barrel around its neck, which he added 'for interest'. St Bernards have been saddled with the association ever since. Landseer is also credited with popularising the name St Bernard (rather than Alpine Mastiff) for the breed.

Originally, St Bernards were known as Barry hounds, a corruption of the German *Bären*, meaning 'bears'. One of the first lifesavers was known as 'Barry the Great', who rescued forty people between 1800 and 1814 but was unfortunately killed by the forty-first, who mistook him for a wolf.

Barry was stuffed and now has pride of place in the Natural History Museum in Berne. In his honour, the best male pup from each litter at the St Bernard's Hospice is named Barry.

Sometimes, the Hospice's duty to provide food and shelter for all who ask can prove troublesome. One night in 1708, Canon Vincent Camos had to provide food for over 400 travellers. To save manpower, he had a device built like a large hamster-wheel attached to a spit. Inside, a St Bernard trotted along turning the meat skewer.

It's estimated the dogs have made over 2,500 rescues since 1800, though none at all in the last fifty years. As a result, the monastery has decided to sell them off and replace them with helicopters.

WHAT GOES HUNK-HUNK?

An Albanian pig.
Albanian dogs go *ham ham*.
In Catalan, dogs go *bup bup*. The Chinese dogs say *wang wang*, the Greek dogs go *gav gav*, the Slovenians *hov hov* and the Ukrainians *haf haf*. In Iceland, it's a *voff*, in Indonesia, it's a *gong gong,* and in Italian, it's a *bau bau.*

Interestingly, when there is less variety in an

43

animal's noise, languages seem to agree more commonly on its interpretation. For example, nearly every language has a cow going *moo*, a cat going *meow* and a cuckoo going *cuckoo*.

Dogs even develop regional accents, according to researchers at the Canine Behaviour Centre in Cumbria. Scouse and Scots dogs have the most distinctive accents. The Liverpudlians have higher-pitched voices, whereas the Scots have a 'lighter tone'.

To gather their data the Centre asked for owners and their dogs to leave messages on their answering machine; experts then compared the pitch, tone, volume and length of the sounds made by humans and dogs.

They concluded that dogs imitate their owners in order to bond with them; the closer the bond, the closer the similarity in sound.

Dogs also mimic their owners' behaviour. A terrier owned by a young family will tend to be lively and difficult to control. The same dog living with an old lady will end up quiet, inactive and prone to long periods of sleep.

WHAT NOISE DOES THE LARGEST FROG IN THE WORLD MAKE?

None at all. Particularly not *RIBBIT*.

The three-foot-long Goliath frog from central Africa is mute.

There are 4,360 known species of frog, but only one of them goes 'ribbit'. Each species has its own unique call. The reason everyone thinks all frogs go 'ribbit' is that 'ribbit' is the distinctive call of the Pacific tree frog (*Hyla regilla*). This is the frog that lives in Hollywood.

Recorded locally, it has been plastered all over the movies for decades to enhance the atmosphere of anywhere from the Everglades to Vietnamese jungles.

Frogs make a huge variety of noises. They croak, snore, grunt, trill, cluck, chirp, ring, whoop, whistle and growl. They make noises like cattle, squirrels and crickets. The barking tree frog yaps like a dog, the carpenter frog sounds like two carpenters hammering nails out of sync, and Fowler's toad makes a noise like a bleating sheep with a heavy cold. The South American paradoxical frog (*Pseudis paradoxa*) grunts like a pig (it's paradoxical because the tadpoles are three times larger than the frog).

Female frogs are mostly silent. The noise is made by male frogs advertising themselves to potential mates. The loudest frog is the tiny *coquí* of Puerto Rico, whose Latin name, *Eleutherodactylus coqui*, measures more than its body. Male coquís congregate in dense forest—one to every ten square metres—and compete to see who can call loudest. From three feet away, this has been recorded at ninety-five decibels, about the same as a pneumatic drill, and close to the human pain threshold.

Recent research has solved the riddle of how frogs avoid bursting their own eardrums. They use their lungs to hear. By absorbing up the vibrations of their own calls, the lungs equalise the internal and external pressure on the surface of the eardrums, protecting the delicate inner ear.

Frog calls operate rather like radio stations: each species selects its own frequency. So what we hear—

a forest or pond full of competing froggy racket—is much less distracting to the lady frogs, who only tune in to the calls of their own species.

Internationally, frogs are generally regarded as making a similar sound to ducks. But not everywhere. In Thailand, for example they go *ob ob*, in Poland *kum kum*, in Argentina *berp*; Algerian frogs make a *gar gar* noise, similar to the Chinese *guo guo*; Bengali frogs go *gangor-gangor*; in Hindi frogs go *me:ko:me:k-me:ko:me:k* (the colon indicates that the preceding vowel is long and nasalised); Japanese frogs produce a *kerokero* sound and Korean frogs go *gae-gool-gae-gool*.

WHICH OWL SAYS 'TU-WHIT, TU-WHOO'?

William Shakespeare first used the phrase 'tu-whit, tu-whoo' in his poem 'Winter' from *Love's Labour's Lost*:

Then nightly sings the staring owl,
Tu-who;
Tu-whit, tu-who: a merry note,
While greasy Joan doth keel the pot.

No single owl has ever gone 'tu-whit, tu-whoo'.

Barn owls screech. Short-eared owls are largely silent. A long-eared owl makes an extended low pitched 'oo-oo-oo' noise.

The owl noise that most resembles 'tu-whit, tu-whoo' is made by Tawny owls. Two of them.

The male Tawny—also known as a Brown Owl—

calls with a hooting 'hooo-hoo-hooo', and the female replies with a hoarser 'kew-wick'.

WHAT DID DARWIN DO TO DEAD OWLS?

He ate them, although only once.

Charles Darwin was driven by gastronomic, as well as scientific, curiosity. While half-heartedly reading Divinity at Cambridge University, he became a member of the 'Glutton' or 'Gourmet Club' which met once a week and actively sought to eat animals not normally found on menus.

Darwin's son, Francis, commenting on his father's letters, noted that the Gourmet Club enjoyed, among other things, hawk and bittern, but that 'their zeal broke down over an old brown owl,' which they found 'indescribable'.

Over the years, Darwin sharpened up considerably in the academic arena and lost his faith in God, but he never lost his taste for the allure of an interesting menu.

During the voyage of the *Beagle*, he ate armadillos which, he said, 'taste & look like duck' and a chocolate-coloured rodent that was 'the best meat I ever tasted'—probably an agouti, whose family name is *Dasyproctidae*, Greek for 'hairy bum'. In Patagonia, he tucked into a plate of puma (the mountain lion *Felis concolor*) and thought it tasted rather like veal. In fact, he originally thought it *was* veal.

Later, after exhaustively searching Patagonia for the Lesser Rhea, Darwin realised he had already eaten one for his Christmas dinner, while moored off

Port Desire in 1833. The bird had been shot by Conrad Martens, the ship's artist.

Darwin assumed it was one of the common Greater Rheas, or 'ostriches', as he called them, and only realised his mistake when the plates were being cleared: 'It was cooked and eaten before my memory returned. Fortunately the head, neck, legs, wings, many of the larger feathers, and a large part of the skin, had been preserved.' He sent the bits back to the Zoological Society in London and the *Rhea Darwinii* was named after him.

In the Galapagos, Darwin lived on iguana (*Conolophus subcristatus*) and, on James Island, wolfed down a few helpings of giant tortoise. Not realising the importance of giant tortoises to his later evolutionary theory, forty-eight specimens were loaded aboard the *Beagle.* Darwin and his shipmates proceeded to eat them, throwing the shells overboard as they finished.

A Phylum Feast is a shared meal using as many different species as possible, eaten by biologists on 12 February to celebrate Darwin's birthday.

WHEN DOES 'RING-A-RING O' ROSES' DATE FROM?

The seventeenth century, surely? It's about the plague: the rings of roses are skin lesions, the first signs of infection; the posies are the doomed attempts to keep the disease at bay; the sneezing is a symptom of the advancing sickness; 'all fall down' is death.

Like most attempts to attribute precise historical meaning to nursery rhymes this doesn't hold water. It was first advanced in 1961 by the popular novelist James Leasor in his racy account of life in seventeenth-century London, *The Plague and the Fire*. Until then, there was no obvious connection (and absolutely no evidence) that the rhyme had been sung in this form for almost 400 years as a way of preserving the trauma of the plague.

That's because it hadn't. The very earliest recorded version comes from Massachusetts in 1790:

> Ring a ring a rosie
> A bottle full of posie,
> All the girls in our town
> Ring for little Josie.

There are French, German and even Gaelic versions. Several have a second verse where everyone gets up again; others mention wedding bells, pails of water, birds, steeples, Jacks, Jills and other favourite nursery images.

A more credible theory is that the rhyme grew out of a ring game, a staple element of the 'play-parties' which had grown up in Protestant communities in eighteenth-century America and Britain where dancing was forbidden.

'Ring-a-ring o' roses' remains our most popular ring game today.

Henry Bett in his 1924 collection of *Nursery Rhymes and Tales* took the view that the rhyme is of an age 'to be measured in thousands of years, or rather it is so great it cannot be measured at all.'

WHAT WERE NELSON'S LAST WORDS?

'Drink, drink. Fan, fan. Rub, rub.'

These were the absolutely last things the dying admiral said. He was hot and thirsty. His steward stood by to fan him and feed him lemonade and watered wine, while the ship's chaplain, Dr Scott, massaged his chest to ease the pain.

Historians are certain that Nelson did indeed say 'Kiss me, Hardy' rather than, as some have suggested, the more noble 'Kismet' (meaning fate). Eyewitnesses testified that Hardy kissed the admiral twice: once on the cheek and once on the forehead, as Nelson struggled to remain conscious.

Nelson asked his flag-captain not to throw him overboard and to look after 'poor Lady Hamilton'. He then uttered the immortal words. After Hardy's first kiss he said, 'Now I am satisfied.' After the second, 'Who is that?' When he saw it was Hardy he croaked, 'God bless you, Hardy.'

Shortly afterwards he muttered, 'Thank God I have done my duty' and then 'Drink, drink. Fan, fan. Rub, rub.' He lost consciousness, the surgeon was called and Nelson was declared dead at 4.30 p.m.

It seems that Nelson had deliberately decided to die at the moment of his greatest victory at Trafalgar. For a guinea each he bought four large silver stars and had them sewn into his uniform along with the glitzy Neapolitan Order of St Ferdinand. He then stood brazenly in the middle of the deck of HMS *Victory* till he was shot at a range of fifty feet by a French sniper.

It was a comprehensive victory. Though 1,700

British sailors had been killed or wounded, no ships were lost. The French and Spanish fleets had been decimated: 18 ships captured or destroyed, 6,000 men killed or wounded and 20,000 taken prisoner. The risk of an invasion of Britain had passed. Nelson's immortality was assured.

His body was preserved on its way back from Trafalgar in a cask of brandy. Rumour had it that, on the voyage home to England, sailors drank the contents of the barrel, using tubes of macaroni as straws. This is not the case. The barrel was kept under armed guard and, according to eyewitnesses, when it was opened in Portsmouth, seemed well topped-up.

Whether true or not, the legend stuck and the Navy adopted the phrase 'tapping the Admiral' for the surreptitious swigging of rum.

WHICH EYE DID NELSON WEAR HIS EYE-PATCH ON?

Neither. Nelson never wore an eye-patch.

He didn't wear anything at all over his damaged right eye, though he had an eye-shade built into his hat to protect his good left eye from the sun.

Nelson didn't have a 'blind' eye. His right one was badly damaged (but not blinded) at the siege of Calvi in Corsica in 1794. A French cannon ball threw sand and debris into it, but it still looked normal—so normal, in fact, he had difficulty convincing the Royal Navy he was eligible for a disability pension.

There is no contemporary portrait of Nelson wearing an eye-patch, and despite what most people recall having 'seen', the Trafalgar Square column shows him *without* an eye-patch. It was only after his death that the eye-patch was used to add pathos to portraits.

He used the damaged eye to his advantage. At the battle of Copenhagen in 1801, he ignored the recall signal issued by his superior Admiral Sir Hyde Parker. Nelson, who was in a much better position than Parker to see that the Danes were on the run, said to his flag-captain: 'You know, Foley, I only have one eye—I have the right to be blind sometimes.'

He then held his telescope to his blind eye and said: 'I really do not see the signal!' This is usually misquoted as: 'I see no ships.'

Nelson was a brilliant tactician, a charismatic leader and undeniably brave—had he been alive today he would have been eligible for at least three Victoria Crosses—but he was also vain and ruthless.

As captain of HMS *Boreas* in 1784 he ordered 54 of his 122 seamen and 12 of his 20 marines flogged—47 per cent of the men aboard. In June 1799, he treacherously executed 99 prisoners of war in Naples, after the British commander of the garrison had guaranteed their safety.

While in Naples, Nelson began an affair with Lady Emma Hamilton, wife of the British ambassador. Her father had been a blacksmith and she a teenage prostitute in London before marrying Sir William. She was enormously fat and had a Lancashire accent. Another admirer of Nelson was Patrick Brunty, a Yorkshire

Animal courage was the sole mark of Lord Nelson, his private character disgraceful in every sense of the word.
EARL ST VINCENT

52

parson of Irish descent, who changed his surname to Brontë after the King of Naples created Nelson Duke of Bronte. Had he not done so, his famous daughters would have been Charlotte, Emily and Anne Brunty.

In contrast to the public grief at news of Nelson's death, Earl St Vincent and eighteen other admirals of the Royal Navy refused to attend his funeral.

HOW MANY SENSES DOES A HUMAN BEING HAVE?

At least nine.

The five senses we all know about—sight, hearing, taste, smell and touch—were first listed by Aristotle, who, while brilliant, often got things wrong. (For example, he taught that we thought with our hearts, that bees were created by the rotting carcasses of bulls and that flies had only four legs.)

There are four more commonly agreed senses:

1 *Thermoception*, the sense of heat (or its absence) on our skin.

2 *Equilibrioception*—our sense of balance—which is determined by the fluid-containing cavities in the inner ear.

3 *Nociception*—the perception of pain from the skin, joints and body organs. Oddly, this does not include the brain, which has no pain receptors at all. Headaches, regardless of the way it seems, don't come from inside the brain.

4 *Proprioception*—or 'body awareness'. This is the unconscious knowledge of where our

53

body parts are without being able to see or feel them. For example, close your eyes and waggle your foot in the air. You still know where it is in relation to the rest of you.

Every self-respecting neurologist has their own opinion about whether there are more than these nine. Some argue that there are up to twenty-one. What about hunger? Or thirst? The sense of depth, or the sense of meaning, or language? Or the endlessly intriguing subject of synaesthesia, where senses collide and combine so that music can be perceived in colour?

And what about the sense of electricity, or even impending danger, when your hair stands on end?

There are also senses which some animals have but we don't. Sharks have keen *electroception* which allows them to sense electric fields, *magnetoception* detects magnetic fields and is used in the navigation systems of birds and insects, *echolocation* and the 'lateral line' are used by fish to sense pressure, and infrared vision is used by owls and deer to hunt or feed at night.

HOW MANY STATES OF MATTER ARE THERE?

Three, that's easy. Solid, liquid, gas.

Actually, it's more like fifteen, although the list grows almost daily.

Here's our latest best effort:

solid, amorphous solid, liquid, gas, plasma, superfluid, supersolid, degenerate matter, neutronium, strongly symmetric matter, weakly symmetric matter, quark-gluon plasma, fermionic condensate, Bose-Einstein condensate and strange matter.

Without going into impenetrable (and, for most purposes, needless) detail, one of the most curious is Bose-Einstein condensate.

A Bose-Einstein condensate or 'bec' occurs when you cool an element down to a very low temperature (generally a tiny fraction of a degree above absolute zero ($-273\,°C$, the theoretical temperature at which everything stops moving).

When this happens, seriously peculiar things begin to happen. Behaviour normally only seen at atomic level occurs at scales large enough to observe. For example, if you put a 'bec' in a beaker, making sure to keep it cold enough, it will actually climb the sides and de-beaker itself.

This, apparently, is a futile attempt to reduce its own energy (which is already at its lowest possible level).

Bose-Einstein condensate was predicted to exist by Einstein in 1925, after studying the work of Satyendra Nath Bose, but wasn't actually manufactured until 1995 in America—work that earned its creators the 2001 Nobel Prize. Einstein's manuscript itself was only rediscovered in 2005.

WHAT IS THE NORMAL STATE OF GLASS?

It's a solid.

You may have heard it said that glass is a liquid which has cooled but not crystallised, and which just flows fantastically slowly. This is untrue—glass is a *bona fide* solid.

In support of the assertion that glass is a liquid, people often point to old church windows, where the glass is thicker at the bottom of the pane.

The reason for this is not that the glass has flowed over time, but that medieval glaziers sometimes couldn't cast perfectly uniform sheets of glass. When that happened, they preferred to stand the glass into the window with the thick edge at the bottom, for obvious reasons.

The confusion about whether glass is a liquid or solid stems from a misreading of the work of German physicist Gustav Tammann (1861–1938) who studied glass and described its behaviour as it solidifies.

He observed that the molecular structure of glass is irregular and disordered, unlike the neat arrangement of molecules in, say, metals.

Reaching for an analogy, he compared it to 'a frozen supercooled liquid'. But saying glass is like a liquid doesn't mean it is a liquid.

These days, solids are categorised as either crystalline or amorphous. Glass is an amorphous solid.

WHICH METAL IS LIQUID AT ROOM TEMPERATURE?

As well as mercury, gallium, caesium and francium can all be liquids at room temperature. As these liquids are very dense (being metals), bricks, horseshoes and cannon balls theoretically float in them.

Gallium (Ga) was discovered by French chemist Lecoq de Boisbaudran in 1875. Everyone assumed it was a patriotic name but *gallus* is Latin for 'a Gaul' *and* 'rooster'—as in 'Lecoq'. It was the first new element to confirm Dmitri Medeleeyev's prediction of the periodic table. Gallium is used chiefly in silicon chips because of its strange electronic properties. Compact disc players also make use of it because when mixed with arsenic it transforms an electric current directly into laser light, which is used to 'read' the data from the discs.

Caesium (Cs) is most notably used in atomic clocks—it is used to define the atomic second (see page 244) It also explodes extremely violently when it comes into contact with water. Caesium's name means 'sky blue' because of the bright blue lines it produces as part of its spectrum. It was discovered in 1860 by Robert Bunsen using the spectroscope he had invented with Gustav Kirchoff, the man who had earlier discovered that signals travel down telegraph wires at the speed of light.

Francium (Fr) is one of the rarest elements: it has been calculated there are only ever thirty grams of it present on Earth. This is because it is so radioactive it quickly decays into other, more stable elements. So it is a liquid metal, but not for very long—a few seconds at most. It was isolated in 1939 by Marguerite Perey at the Curie Institute in Paris. It was the last element to be found in nature.

These elements are liquid at unusually low temperatures for metals because the arrangement of electrons in their atoms makes it hard for them to get close enough to each other to form a crystalline lattice.

Each atom floats around freely, without being attracted to its neighbours, which is exactly what happens in other liquids.

WHICH METAL IS THE BEST CONDUCTOR?

Silver.

The best conductor of both heat and electricity is also the most reflective of all the elements. Its drawback is that it is expensive. The reason we use copper wire in our electrical equipment is because copper—the second most conductive element—is much cheaper.

As well as its decorative uses, silver is now mostly used in the photographic industry, for long-life batteries and for solar panels.

Silver has the curious property of sterilising water. Only tiny amounts are needed—just ten parts per billion. This remarkable fact has been known since the fifth century BC when Herodotus reported that the Persian king Cyrus the Great travelled with his own personal water supply taken from a special stream, boiled, and sealed in silver vessels.

Both the Romans and Greeks noticed that food and

drink put in silver containers did not spoil so quickly. Silver's strong antibacterial qualities were made use of for many centuries before bacteria were discovered. This may also explain why silver coins are often found at the bottom of ancient wells.

A word of caution before you start filling your silver tankard.

First, while silver will certainly kill bacteria in the lab, whether or not it will do so in the body is controversial. Many of the supposed advantages are unproven: the US Food and Drug Administration has forbidden companies from advertising health benefits.

Second, there is a disease called argyria which is linked to the intake of silver particles diluted in water, the most obvious symptom of which is a conspicuously blue skin.

On the other hand, silver salts in swimming pools are a safe substitute for chlorine and, in the US, athletes' socks are impregnated with silver to stop their feet smelling.

Water is an exceptionally poor conductor of electricity, especially pure water, which is actually used as an insulator. What conducts the electricity is not the H_2O molecules but the chemicals dissolved in it—salt, for example.

Sea water is a hundred times better at conducting electricity than fresh water, but it's a *million* times worse at conducting electricity than silver.

WHAT'S THE DENSEST ELEMENT?

It's either osmium or iridium, depending on how you measure it.

The two metals are extremely close in density and have changed places several times over the years. The third-densest element is platinum, followed by rhenium, neptunium, plutonium and gold. Lead is way, way down the list—it's only half as dense as either osmium or iridium.

Osmium (Os) is a very rare, very hard, silvery-blue metal discovered (along with iridium) in 1803 by the English chemist Smithson Tennant (1761–1815).

Tennant was a vicar's son from Richmond who was also the first man to show that diamond is a form of pure carbon.

He named osmium from *osme*, Greek for smell. It gives off highly toxic osmium tetroxide, which has a pungent, irritating odour and can damage the lungs, skin and eyes and cause intense headaches. Osmium tetroxide has been used in fingerprinting because its vapour reacts with minute traces of oil left by the fingers to form black deposits.

Its extreme hardness and resistance to corrosion made osmium useful in the manufacture of long-life gramophone styluses, compass needles and the nibs of quality fountain-pens—hence the trade name Osmiroid.

Osmium also has an unusually high melting point of 3,054 °C. In 1897, this inspired Karl Auer to create an osmium electric light-bulb filament to improve on the bamboo one used by Edison. Osmium was eventually replaced by tungsten, which melts at 3,407 °C. The name Osram was registered by Auer in 1906. It derives from OSmium and WolfRAM, the German for tungsten.

Less than 100 kg (220 lb) of osmium are produced worldwide every year.

Iridium (Ir) is a yellowish white metal which, like

osmium, is closely related to platinum. The name comes from *iris*, Greek for rainbow, because of the many beautiful colours its compounds produce.

Iridium also has an extremely high melting point (2,446 °C) and is mainly used to make crucibles for metal foundries and to harden platinum.

Iridium is one of the rarest elements on Earth (eighty-fourth out of ninety-two) but improbably large amounts of it are found in the thin geological layer known as the KT boundary laid down about 65 million years ago.

Geologists believe this can only have come from space, and it adds support to the theory that an asteroid impact caused the extinction of the dinosaurs.

WHERE DO DIAMONDS COME FROM?

Volcanoes. All diamonds are formed under immense heat and pressure beneath the earth and are brought to the surface in volcanic eruptions.

They are formed between 160 km to 480 km (about 100 to 300 miles) underground. Most are found inside a volcanic rock called Kimberlite, and mined in areas where volcanic activity is still common. Any other diamonds are found loose, having been washed out of their original Kimberlite.

Twenty countries in the world produce diamonds. South Africa is now the fifth largest after Australia, the Democratic Republic of the Congo, Botswana and Russia.

There are three things that are extremely hard: steel, a diamond, and to know one's self.
BENJAMIN FRANKLIN

Diamonds are made of pure carbon. So is graphite, the stuff that the 'lead' in pencils is made from, but with the carbon atoms arranged differently. Diamond is one of the hardest naturally occurring substances on Earth with a score of ten on the Mohs Hardness scale, but graphite is one of the softest with a score of one and a half, only just harder than talcum powder.

The largest known diamond is 4,000 km (2,500 miles) across and measures ten billion trillion trillion carats. Found directly above Australia (eight light years away) the diamond sits inside the star 'Lucy' in the constellation Centaurus.

'Lucy' got its nickname from the Beatles classic 'Lucy in the Sky with Diamonds', but its technical name is white dwarf BPM 37093. The Beatles song was named after a picture drawn by John Lennon's son Julian of his four-year-old friend Lucy Richardson.

Diamonds were once the world's hardest known material. However, in August 2005, scientists in Germany managed to create a harder one in a laboratory. Called aggregated carbon nanorods (ACNR), it was made by compressing and heating super-strong carbon molecules to 2,226 °C.

Each of these molecules comprises sixty atoms that interweave in pentagonal or hexagonal shapes; they're said to resemble tiny footballs. ACNR is so tough it scratches diamonds effortlessly.

HOW DO WE MEASURE EARTHQUAKES?

The MMS Scale.

In the last decade, the Richter scale has been superseded in seismological circles by the Moment Magnitude Scale or MMS.

The MMS was devised in 1979 by seismologists Hiroo Kanamori and Tom Hanks (no relation) of the California Institute of Technology, who found the Richter scale unsatisfactory because it only measures the strength of the shock waves, which do not fully describe an earthquake's impact. On the Richter scale, large earthquakes may have the same score but cause wildly different degrees of devastation.

The Richter scale measures the seismic waves or vibration as experienced 600 km (373 miles) away. It was devised in 1935 by Charles Richter, who was also, like Kanamori and Hanks, a Caltech seismologist. He developed it with Beno Gutenberg, the first man to measure accurately the radius of the Earth's core. Gutenberg died of flu in 1960 without living to measure the Great Chilean Earthquake (the largest ever recorded, which took place four months later).

The MMS, by contrast, is an expression of the energy released by an earthquake. It multiplies the distance of the slip between the two parts of the fault by the total area affected. It was designed to give values that make sense when compared to their Richter equivalent.

Both scales are logarithmic: a two-point increase means 1,000 times more power. A hand grenade scores 0.5 on the Richter scale, the Nagasaki atom bomb 5.0. The MMS is only used for large earthquakes, above 3.5 on the Richter scale.

According to the US Geological Survey, on the basis of the area of damage (600,000 square km or 231,660 square miles) and the area it was felt in (5,000,000 square km or 1,930,502 square miles) the largest known earthquakes in North America were the little-known Mississippi River valley earthquakes of 1811–12. They created new lakes and changed the whole course of the Mississippi. The area of strong shaking was ten times larger than that in San Francisco in 1906. Church bells rang spontaneously as far away as Massachusetts.

It is impossible to predict when an earthquake will happen. One expert claims that the best way is to count the number of missing cats and dogs in the local newspaper.

Britain has up to 300 earthquakes a year but they are so small that the public notices only about 10 per cent of them.

WHAT'S THE COMMONEST MATERIAL IN THE WORLD?

a) Oxygen
b) Carbon
c) Nitrogen
d) Water

None of the above. The answer is perovskite, a mineral compound of magnesium, silicon and oxygen.

Perovskite accounts for about half the total mass of

the planet. It's what the Earth's mantle is mostly made from. Or so scientists suppose: nobody has yet taken a sample to prove it.

Perovskites are a family of minerals named after the Russian mineralogist Count Lev Perovski in 1839. They may prove to be the Holy Grail of superconductor research—a material that can conduct electricity without resistance at normal temperatures.

This would make a world of 'floating' trains and unimaginably fast computers a reality. At present, superconductors only function at unhelpfully low temperatures (the best so far recorded is -135 °C).

Apart from perovskite, it is thought that the mantle is made from magnesio-wusstite (a form of magnesium oxide also found in meteorites), and a small amount of shistovite (named after Lev Shistov, a graduate student at Moscow University, who synthesised a new high-pressure form of silicon oxide in his lab in 1959).

The Earth's mantle sits between the crust and the core. It is generally assumed to be solid, but some scientists believe that it is actually a very slow-moving liquid.

How do we know any of this? Even the rocks spewed out of volcanoes have only come from the first 200 km (125 miles) below the surface and it's 660 km (over 400 miles) before the lower mantle starts.

By sending pulses of seismic waves downwards and recording the resistance they encounter, both the density and the temperature of the Earth's interior can be estimated.

This can then be matched to what we already know about the structure of minerals we do have samples

65

of—from the crust and in meteorites—and what happens to these minerals under intense heat and high pressure.

But like much else in science, it's really only a highly educated guess.

WHAT DOES THE MOON SMELL LIKE?

Like gunpowder, apparently.

Only twelve people have walked on the moon, all of them American. Obviously, in their airtight space suits the astronauts could not actually smell the Moon, but moondust is clingy stuff, and plenty of it was traipsed back into the cabin when they returned from the Moon's surface.

They reported that moondust feels like snow, smells like gunpowder, and doesn't taste too bad. The dust is actually mostly made of silicon dioxide glass created by meteors slamming into the Moon's surface. It also contains minerals like iron, calcium and magnesium.

NASA employs a small team to sniff every single piece of equipment which goes onto its space flights. This is to ensure that no items which could change the delicate balance of the climate of the International Space Station make it on to shuttles.

The idea that the Moon was made of cheese seems to date from the sixteenth century. The first citation, from John Heywood's *Proverbs* (1564), says 'the moon is made of greene chees'. It is thought that in this context, the word 'greene' means 'new', rather than having a green colour, as young cheeses would often have a more mottled appearance; much like the cratered Moon.

DOES THE EARTH GO ROUND THE MOON OR THE MOON ROUND THE EARTH?

Both. They go round one another.

The two bodies orbit a common centre of gravity located about 1,600 km (1,000 miles) below the surface of the Earth, so the Earth makes three different rotations: around its own axis, around the Sun and around this point.

Confused? Even Newton claimed that thinking about the motion of the Moon gave him a headache.

HOW MANY MOONS DOES THE EARTH HAVE?

At least seven.

Certainly *the* Moon (or Luna, as astronomers call it) is the only celestial body to observe a strict orbit of the Earth. But there are now six other 'Near-Earth' Asteroids (NEAs) which do follow the Earth around the Sun, despite being invisible to the naked eye.

The first of these 'co-orbitals' to be identified was Cruithne (pronounced *Cru-een-ya*, and named after Britain's earliest recorded Celtic tribe), a three-mile-wide satellite, discovered in 1997. It has an odd horseshoe-shaped orbit.

Since then, six more have been identified: the snappily named 2000 PH_5, 2000 WN_{10}, 2002 AA_{29},

2003 YN_{107} and 2004 GU_9.

Are they really moons? Many astronomers would say no, but they are certainly more than just run-of-the-mill asteroids. Like Earth they take roughly a year to orbit the Sun (think of two cars going round a race track at the same speed but in different lanes) and do, occasionally, come close enough to exert a very slight gravitational influence.

So whether you call them pseudo-moons, quasi-satellites, or companion asteroids, they are worth watching, not least because some or all of them may one day settle down into a more regular orbital pattern.

HOW MANY PLANETS ARE THERE IN THE SOLAR SYSTEM?

Eight. If you still think there's nine you've obviously been living in a parallel solar system.

On 24 August 2006, the General Assembly of the International Astronomical Union finally agreed its long overdue definition of a 'planet'. Planets must fulfil three criteria: they have to orbit the sun, have enough mass to be spherical, and to have 'cleared the neighbourhood' around their orbit. Pluto only managed the first two, so was demoted to the status of 'dwarf planet'.

It's not perfect—some astronomers argue that neither Earth, Jupiter or Neptune have cleared their orbits either—but it does resolve the anomalous position of Pluto.

Even the planet's discoverers in 1930 weren't fully convinced of its status, referring to it as a trans-Neptunian object or TNO—something on the edge of the solar system, beyond Neptune.

Pluto is much smaller than all the other planets, a fifth the mass of the Moon and smaller than seven of the moons of other planets. It isn't much larger than its own main moon, Charon (two more, smaller, Plutonian moons were discovered in 2005). Its orbit is eccentric and on a different plane to the other planets, and its composition is completely different.

The four innermost planets are medium-sized and rocky; the next four are gas giants. Pluto is a tiny ball of ice—one of at least 60,000 small, comet-like objects forming the Kuiper belt right on the edge of the solar system.

All these planetoid objects (including asteroids, TNOs and a host of other sub-classifications) are known collectively as minor planets. There are 371,670 of them already registered, around 5,000 new ones are discovered each month and it is estimated there may be almost two million such bodies with diameters of over a kilometre. Most are much too small to be considered as planets but twelve of them look like giving Pluto a run for its money.

One of them, discovered in 2005 as 2003 UB$_{313}$ and now named Eris, is actually larger than Pluto. Others, such as Sedna, Orcus and Quaoar, aren't far off.

Now Pluto, Eris and Ceres—the largest body in the asteroid belt between Mars and Jupiter—have been officially adopted as the first three dwarf planets.

HOW WOULD YOU FLY THROUGH AN ASTEROID BELT?

Keep an eye open, but it's really unlikely you'll collide with anything.

Despite what you may have seen in bad sci-fi films, asteroid belts are typically quite desolate places. Busy when compared with the rest of space, but desolate nonetheless.

Generally, the gap between large asteroids (ones which could do significant damage to a space ship) is about two million kilometres (nearly 1¼ million miles).

Although there are some clusters called 'families' which have been recently formed from a larger body, it would not be too difficult to manoeuvre around an asteroid belt. In fact, if you picked a random course, you'd be lucky to see a single asteroid.

If you did, you might like to give it a name.

These days the International Astronomical Union has a fifteen-person Committee for Small-Body Nomenclature to control the naming of the ever-expanding roll-call of minor planets. It's not an entirely serious business, as these recent examples show:

(15887) *Daveclark*, (14965) *Bonk*, (18932) *Robinhood*, (69961) *Millosevich*, (2829) *Bobhope*, (7328) *Seanconnery*, (5762) *Wanke*, (453) *Tea*, (3904) *Honda*, (17627) *Humptydumpty*, (9941) *Iguanodon*, (9949) *Brontosaurus*, (9778) *Isabelallende,* (4479) *Charlieparker*, (9007) *James Bond*, (39415)

70

Janeausten, (11548) *Jerrylewis*, (19367) *Pink Floyd*, (5878) *Charlene*, (6042) *Cheshirecat*, (4735) *Gary*, (3742) *Sunshine*, (17458) *Dick*, (1629) *Pecker* and (821) *Fanny.*

Smith, Jones, Brown and Robinson are all official names of asteroids; so are Bikki, Bus, Bok, Lick, Kwee, Hippo, MrSpock, Roddenberry and Swissair.

Eccentricity in planet-naming isn't new. Pluto was named in 1930 by an eleven-year-old Oxford schoolgirl called Venetia Burney, whose grandfather passed on her breakfast-time suggestion to his good friend Herbert Hall Turner, the Oxford Professor of Astronomy.

Perhaps 2003 UB_{313} will after all be named Rupert, Douglas Adams's name for the tenth planet in *The Hitch-hiker's Guide to the Galaxy*. Stranger things have happened. The day before Adams suddenly died in 2001, the asteroid (18610) Arthurdent was first named. And now he has one of his very own: (25924) Douglasadams.

WHAT'S IN AN ATOM?

Mostly nothing. The vast majority of an atom is empty space.

To get it into perspective, imagine an atom the size of an international sports stadium. The electrons are right up at the top of the stands, each smaller than a pin-head. The nucleus of the atom is on the centre spot of the pitch, and is about the size of a pea.

For many centuries, atoms, which were entirely theoretical, were thought to be the smallest possible

71

Nothing exists except atoms and empty space; everything else is opinion.
DEMOCRITOS OF ABDERA

units of matter, hence the word, which means 'not-cut' in Greek.

Then, in 1897, the electron was discovered, followed in 1911 by the nucleus. The atom was split and the neutron discovered in 1932.

This was by no means the end of the matter. The positively charged protons and uncharged neutrons in the nucleus are made of still smaller elements.

These even tinier units called quarks are given names like 'strangeness' and 'charm' and come not in different shapes and sizes but 'flavours'.

The distant satellites of the nucleus, the negatively charged electrons, are so odd they are no longer even called that but 'Probability Density Charges'.

By the 1950s, so many new subatomic particles (over 100) had been found that it was becoming an embarrassment. Whatever matter might be, no one seemed able to get to the bottom of it.

Enrico Fermi, the Italian-born physicist who won the Nobel Physics Prize in 1938 for his work on atomic reactors, was quoted as saying: 'If I could remember the names of all these particles, I'd be a botanist.'

Since Fermi's time, scientists have settled on the number of subatomic particles inside an atom at twenty-four. This best guess is known as the Standard Model, giving the impression that we have a pretty good idea what's what.

The universe in general, as far as we can tell, is as underpopulated as the atom itself. Space, on average, contains just a couple of atoms per cubic metre.

Occasionally, gravity pulls them together into

stars, planets and giraffes, which seems equally extraordinary.

WHAT'S THE MAIN INGREDIENT OF AIR?

a) Oxygen
b) Carbon dioxide
c) Hydrogen
d) Nitrogen

Nitrogen. As every twelve-year-old knows, it accounts for 78 per cent of the air.

Less than 21 per cent of air is oxygen. Only three hundredths of 1 per cent of the air is carbon dioxide.

The high percentage of nitrogen in the air is a result of volcanic eruptions during the formation of the Earth. Vast amounts of it were released into the atmosphere. Being heavier than hydrogen or helium it has stayed closer to the surface of the planet.

A person weighing 76 kg contains almost 1 kg of nitrogen.

Nitre is the old name for saltpetre, or potassium nitrate. A key ingredient in gunpowder, it is also used to cure meat, as a preservative in ice cream, and the anaesthetic in toothpaste for sensitive teeth.

For several hundred years, the richest source of saltpetre was the organic mulch that had seeped into the earth floor of human houses. In 1601, the unscrupulous activities of the 'Saltpeetermen' were raised in Parliament. They would break into houses and even churches, dig up the floors and sell the earth for gunpowder.

The word nitrogen means 'soda-forming' in Greek.

Beer cans with pressure-sensitive 'widgets' contain nitrogen, not carbon dioxide. The smaller nitrogen bubbles make a smoother, creamier head.

The only other significant gas in air is argon (1 per cent).

It was discovered by William John Strutt, Lord Rayleigh, who was also the first man to work out why the sky is blue.

WHERE WOULD YOU GO FOR A LUNGFUL OF OZONE?

Don't bother going to the seaside.

The nineteenth-century cult of healthy sea air was based on a fundamental misunderstanding. The bracing, salty tang has nothing to do with ozone, an unstable and dangerous gas.

Ozone was discovered in 1840 by the German chemist Christian Schönbein. Investigating the peculiar odour that lingers around electrical equipment he traced it to a gas, O_3, which he named after the Greek for 'to smell' (*ozein*).

Ozone or 'heavy air' found favour with medical scientists still in the grip of the 'miasma' theory of disease, where ill health was thought to spring from bad smells. Ozone, they thought, was just the thing to clear the lungs of harmful 'effluvia' and the seaside was just the place to get it.

A whole industry grew up around 'ozone cures' and 'ozone hotels' (there are still some carrying the name in Australasia). As late as 1939, Blackpool was still boasting 'the healthiest ozone in Britain'.

Nowadays, we know that the seaside doesn't smell of ozone—it smells of rotting seaweed. There's no evidence this smell does you good or harm (it's mostly compounds of sulphur). It may simply trigger positive associations in your brain, linking back to happy childhood holidays.

As for ozone, the fumes from your car's exhaust (when combined with sunlight) create far more ozone than anything on the beach. If you really want a lungful, the best thing would be to clamp your mouth round an exhaust pipe. This is emphatically not recommended. Apart from doing irreparable damage to your lungs, you could burn your lips.

Ozone is used to make bleach and to kill bacteria in drinking water as a less noxious alternative to chlorine. It is also generated by high-voltage electrical equipment such as televisions and photocopiers.

Some trees, such as oaks and willows, release ozone which can poison nearby vegetation.

The shrinking ozone layer, which protects the planet from dangerous ultra-violet radiation, would be fatal if inhaled. It is 24 km (15 miles) above the Earth's surface and smells faintly of geraniums.

WHAT SPEED DOES LIGHT TRAVEL AT?

That depends.

It's often said that the speed of light is constant, but it isn't. Only in a vacuum does light reach its maximum speed of nearly 300,000 km per second (186,282 miles per second).

In any other medium, the speed of light varies

considerably, always being slower than the figure everyone knows. Through diamonds, for example, it goes less than half as fast: about 130,000 km per second, or 80,000 miles per second.

Until recently, the slowest recorded speed of light (through sodium at −272 °C) was just over 60 kph (38 mph): slower than a bicycle.

In 2000, the same team (at Harvard University) managed to bring light to a complete standstill by shining it into a bec (Bose-Einstein condensate) of the element rubidium.

Rubidium was discovered by Robert Bunsen (1811–99) who didn't invent the Bunsen burner which is named after him.

Astoundingly, light is invisible.

You can't see the light itself, you can only see what it bumps into. A beam of light in a vacuum, shining at right angles to the observer, cannot be seen.

Although this is very odd, it's quite logical. If light itself was visible, it would form a kind of fog between your eyes and everything in front of you.

Darkness is equally strange. It's not there but you can't see through it.

HOW DO MOTHS FEEL ABOUT FLAMES?

They're not attracted to them. They are disorientated by them.

Apart from the odd forest fire, artificial light sources have been in existence for an extremely short time in comparison with the age of the relationship between moths and the Sun and Moon. Many insects use these light sources to navigate by day and night.

Because the Moon and Sun are a long way away, the insects have evolved to expect the light from them to strike their eyes in the same place at different times of day or night, enabling them to calculate how to fly in a straight line.

When people come along with their portable miniature suns and moons and a moth flies past, the light confuses it. It assumes it must somehow be moving in a curved path, because its position in relation to the stationary 'sun' or 'moon', has unexpectedly changed.

The moth then adjusts its course until it sees the light as stationary again. With a light source so close, the only way this is possible for an object which is so close is to fly round and round it in circles.

Moths do not eat clothes. (It's their caterpillars that do it.)

HOW MANY LEGS DOES A CENTIPEDE HAVE?

Not a hundred.

The word centipede is from the Latin for 'a hundred feet', and though centipedes have been extensively studied for over a hundred years, not one has ever been found that has exactly a hundred legs.

Some have more, some less. The one with the number of legs closest to one hundred was discovered in 1999. It has ninety-six legs, and is unique among centipedes in that it is the only known species with an even number of pairs of legs: forty-eight.

All other centipedes have odd numbered pairs of legs ranging from fifteen to 191 pairs.

HOW MANY TOES HAS A TWO-TOED SLOTH?

It's either six or eight.

For reasons known only to taxonomists the sloths in question are called 'two-toed' rather than 'two-fingered'. Both two-toed and three-toed sloths have three 'toes' on each foot. Two-'toed' sloths are distinguished from three-'toed' sloths by the fact that they have two 'fingers' on each 'hand', whereas three-toed sloths have three.

Despite their obvious similarities, three-toed sloths and two-toed sloths are not related to one another. Two-toed sloths are slightly faster. Three-toed sloths have nine bones in their necks; two-toed have six.

Three-toed sloths make good pets, but two-toed sloths are vicious. Three-toed sloths produce shrill whistles through their nostrils. Two-toed sloths will hiss if disturbed.

Sloths, generally, are the world's slowest mammals. Their top speed is slightly over 1.6 km (1 mile) an hour but they mostly inch along at less than 2 metres (about 6 feet) a minute.

They sleep for fourteen to nineteen hours a day and spend their entire lives hanging upside down in trees. They eat, sleep, mate, give birth and die upside-down. Some move so little that two species of algae take root on them, giving

The Spanish for sloth is **perezoso,** *'the slothful one', not to be confused with* **perezosa** *which means 'deckchair'.*

them a greenish tinge, which also acts as useful camouflage. Several species of moth and beetle also make their home in sloth fur.

Their metabolism is slow, too. It takes them more than a month to digest their food and they pass urine and faeces only once a week. They do this at the base of the trees they live in, these unsavoury piles being romantically known as 'trysting places'.

Like reptiles, they practise thermoregulation—basking in the sun to warm up, creeping into the shade to cool down.

This slows down their complex and lethargic digestive rate. During the rainy season when they stay put under leaves to stay dry, some sloths perform the astonishing feat of starving to death on a full stomach.

HOW MANY EYES DOES A NO-EYED, BIG-EYED WOLF SPIDER HAVE?

a) No eyes
b) No eyes, but big ones
c) One big eye that doesn't work
d) 144 eye-like warts

It has no eyes.

The blind arachnid was first discovered in 1973 and the entire population lives in three pitch-black caves on the volcanic island of Kauai in Hawaii.

Like other cave-dwelling beasts, it evolved without needing to see but, as it's a member of the big-eyed wolf spider family, it gets to call itself big-eyed (i.e. if it did have any eyes left, they'd be big ones).

It's about the size of a fifty-pence piece when fully grown. Its rooming buddy and main source of nourishment is the Kauai cave amphipod, a small crustacean that resembles a blind, semi-transparent shrimp.

HOW MANY PENISES DOES A EUROPEAN EARWIG HAVE?

a) Fourteen
b) None at all
c) Two (one for special occasions)
d) Mind your own business

The answer is *c.* The European or Black earwig carries a spare one in case the first one snaps off, which happens quite frequently.

Both penises are very brittle and relatively long; at just over a centimetre in length, they are often longer than the earwig itself. Two gentlemen at Tokyo Metropolitan University discovered this when one of them playfully pinched a male earwig's rear end during the act of sexual intercourse. Its penis snapped off inside the female, but miraculously it produced a back up.

Earwigs are named for the almost universal belief that they crawl into people's ears and burrow into their brain. The word earwig is Anglo-Saxon for 'ear-creature'. Their French name is *perce-oreille* ('ear-piercer'); in German it's *ohrwurm* ('ear-worm'); in Turkish *kulagakacan* ('ear-fugitive').

Earwigs don't crawl into ears any more than any other insect but Pliny the Elder recommended that if one does do so, you spit in the person's ear until the earwig comes out again. They definitely do not burrow into brains.

An alternative suggestion for the name is that the pincers on the rear of an earwig resemble the tool once used for ear-piercing.

This idea seems to have more appeal to Latins. The Spanish have two words for earwig: *contraplumas* (which also means 'penknife'), and *tijereta* (which also means a 'scissor-kick'). In Italian, an earwig is *forbicina* ('little scissors').

A giant species of earwig (8.5 cm, or 3.3 inches long) lived on St Helena, the South Atlantic island where Napoleon Bonaparte spent his final years in exile. They may still be living there, but the last one was sighted in 1967.

Nicknamed the 'Dodo of the Dermaptera' (the order to which they belong, meaning 'skin wing'), the slim hope that they may still exist was enough for environmentalists to prevent a new airport being built on the island in 2005.

Two species of Malayan earwig feed exclusively on the body oozings and dead skin of naked bats.

WHICH ANIMALS ARE THE BEST-ENDOWED OF ALL?

Barnacles. These unassumingly modest beasts have the longest penis relative to their size of any creature. They can be seven times longer than their body.

Most of the 1,220 species of barnacles are hermaphrodites. When one barnacle decides to be 'mother' it lays eggs inside its own shell and at the same time releases some alluring pheromones. A nearby barnacle will respond by playing 'male' and fertilise the eggs by extending its massive penis, releasing sperm into the cavity of the 'female'.

Barnacles stand on their heads and eat with their feet. Using a very strong glue, they attach themselves head-first to a rock or the hull of a ship. The opening we see as the top of the barnacle is actually the bottom; through it their long, feathery legs catch small plants and animals that float past.

Other well-endowed species are the nine-banded armadillo (its penis extends to two-thirds of its body length) and the blue whale, whose penis, despite a relatively modest proportion in comparison to size, is still the biggest physical organ of all, averaging between 1.8 and 3 metres (6 to 10 feet) in length and around 450 mm (18 inches) in girth.

A blue whale's ejaculate is estimated to contain about 20 litres (35 pints) based on its testes, which weigh about 70 kg (over 150 lb) each.

Whale's penises were useful. In Herman Melville's *Moby-Dick* (1851), there is an account of how the outer skin can be transformed into a floor-length waterproof apron, ideal for protection when gutting the dead whale.

Like most other mammals, whales have a penis bone, the *baculum* or *os penis*. These, along with the *baculi* of walruses and polar bears, are used by Eskimo peoples as runners for their sleds or as clubs.

Other uses for mammalian *baculi* ('little rod' in Latin) are as tie-pins, coffee stirrers, or love-tokens. The bones are incredibly diverse in shape—they are probably the most varied of any bone—and are useful in working out the relationships between mammalian species. Humans and spider monkeys are the only primates without them.

Biblical Hebrew does not have a word for penis. This has led two scholars (Gilbert and Zevit in the *American Journal of Medical Genetics* in 2001) to suggest that Eve was made out of Adam's penis bone rather than his rib (Genesis 2: 21–23). This would explain why males and females have the same number of ribs but the man has no penis bone.

The biblical account also states that afterwards 'the Lord God closed up the flesh', the suggestion being that this is the 'scar' (known as the *raphe)* that runs down the underside of the penis and scrotum.

WHAT IS A RHINO'S HORN MADE FROM?

A rhinoceros horn is not, as some people think, made out of hair.

It's made out of tightly packed strands of keratin fibres. Keratin is the protein found in human hair and fingernails as well as animal claws and hooves, birds' feathers, porcupine quills and the shells of armadillos and tortoises.

Rhinos are the only animal to have a horn that is entirely made from keratin; unlike those of cattle, sheep, antelopes and giraffes they don't have any bone core. A dead rhino's skull shows no evidence that it ever had horns; in life they are anchored on a roughened bump on the skin, above the nasal bone.

A rhino's horn sometimes unravels if cut or damaged, but young rhinos can completely re-grow them if that happens. No one knows what their function is, though females with their horns removed fail to look after their offspring properly.

Rhinoceroses are endangered animals largely due to the demand for their horns. Africa's rhinoceros horns have long been in demand for both medicines and traditional dagger handles in the Middle East, especially Yemen. Since 1970 67,050 kg (nearly 150,000 lb) of rhinoceros horn have been imported into Yemen. Based upon an average horn weight of 3 kg (6.6 lb), this volume represents the horns of 22,350 rhinoceroses.

A persistent misconception is that rhino horn is used as an aphrodisiac. Chinese herbalists say this is untrue; its effect is cooling rather than warming, and is used in treating high blood-pressure and fever.

'Rhinoceros' comes from the Greek words *rhino* (nose) and *keras* (horn). There are five living species of rhino: Black, White, Indian, Javan and Sumatran. Only sixty Javan rhinos survive, making it the world's fourth most endangered species after the Vancouver Island marmot and the Seychelles sheath-tailed bat and the South China Tiger.

White rhinos aren't white. It's a corruption of the Afrikaans *Wyd*, meaning 'wide'. This refers to the animal's mouth, rather than its girth—white rhinos lack the agile lip of the black species which is used in grazing tree branches.

A rhinoceros has an excellent sense of smell and hearing but its eyesight is terrible. They are generally solitary animals, coming together only to mate.

When surprised, rhinos urinate and defecate prodigiously. To attack, Asian rhinos bite; African rhinos charge. A black rhino, despite its short legs, can reach speeds of 55 kph (about 35 mph).

WHICH AFRICAN MAMMAL KILLS MORE HUMANS THAN ANY OTHER?

The hippopotamus.

Unfortunately hippos like to hang out near slow-moving fresh water bordered by grass—the same habitat favoured by humans.

Most accidents occur either because a submerged hippo has been inadvertently whacked on the head with a paddle and decides to overturn the boat or because people are out walking at night, just the time when hippos leave the water to graze. Being trampled by a startled hippo is not a dignified way to die.

Hippopotamuses, once believed to be members of the pig family but now shown to be most closely related to whales, are divided into two species: Common and Pygmy. The common hippo is the third-largest land mammal after the African and Asian elephants.

Not many animals are stupid enough to attack a hippo. They are very irritable beasts, especially when they have young. They dispose of lions by plunging them into deep water and drowning them, crocodiles by biting them in half, and sharks by dragging them out of the water and trampling them to death. However, they are strict vegetarians, so their aggression is mostly to do with self-defence. Hippos mainly eat grass.

The skin of a hippopotamus weighs a ton. It is 4 cm (1.5 inches) thick—bullet-proof as far as most guns are concerned—and accounts for 25 per cent of the animal's weight. It exudes an oily red fluid which keeps it from drying out, which used to make people think that hippos sweat blood. Don't be fooled by their bulk. A fully grown hippo can easily outrun a man.

Hippos are the only mammal other than whales and dolphins to mate and give birth under water. They can close their nostrils, flatten their ears and stay completely submerged for up to five minutes at a time.

Hippos have appalling breath. When they appear to be yawning, they are in fact blasting everything around them with halitosis as a warning to stay clear. This is good advice: a hippo's tusks are sharp and a snap of the jaws can easily sever a limb.

Hippos have only four teeth, which are made of ivory. Part of George Washington's set of false teeth was made from hippopotamus ivory.

According to the *Oxford Companion to Food*, the best part of a hippopotamus to eat is their breasts, pot roasted with herbs and spices. Failing that, the back muscles, cooked in the same manner, are acceptable.

WHERE DO MOST TIGERS LIVE?

The USA.

A century ago, there were about 40,000 tigers in India. Now there are between 3,000 and 4,700. Some scientists estimate that there are only between 5,100 and 7,500 wild tigers left on the planet.

On the other hand, there are thought to be 4,000 tigers living in captivity in Texas alone. The American Zoo and Aquarium Association estimate that up to 12,000 tigers are being kept as private pets in the USA. Mike Tyson personally owns four of them.

Part of the reason for America's enormous tiger population relates to legislation. Only nineteen states have banned private ownership of tigers, fifteen require only a licence, and sixteen states have no regulations at all.

They're not particularly expensive either. A tiger cub will set you back a mere $1,000 while $3,500 will buy you a pair of Bengal tigers; $15,000 is enough for a fashionable blue-eyed white tiger.

Ironically, it is the success of breeding programmes at American zoos and circuses that has driven this. An overabundance of cubs in the 1980s and 90s brought the prices right down. The Society for the Prevention of Cruelty to Animals estimate that there are now 500 lions, tigers and other big cats in private ownership just in the Houston area.

Wild tiger populations were crippled during the twentieth century. Tigers were extinct around the Caspian Sea by the 1950s, and the tigers on the islands of Bali and Java disappeared between 1937 and 1972. The South China tiger is nearly extinct in the wild, with only thirty animals remaining.

Despite the efforts of conservationists, all species of tiger are expected to be extinct in the wild by the end of the current century.

A domestic cat is about 1 per cent the size of a tiger.

Tigers cannot abide the smell of alcohol. They will savage anyone who has been drinking.

Tigers fade as they get older, and who can blame them.

WHAT WOULD YOU USE TO OVERPOWER A CROCODILE?

a) Paper clip
b) Crocodile clip
c) Paper bag
d) Handbag
e) Rubber band

For crocodiles up to 2 m (6.5 feet) long, an ordinary rubber band should be sufficient for you to make your escape.

The muscles that close the jaws of a crocodile or alligator are so strong that they have the same downward force of a truck falling off a cliff. But the muscles that open their jaws are weak enough for you to hold their mouths shut with one hand.

The technical difference between alligators and crocodiles is that crocs have a longer, narrower snout, eyes further forward, and their fourth tooth sticks out from the lower jaw rather than fitting neatly into the upper jaw. Also, some crocodiles live in salty water; alligators generally live in fresh water.

'Crocodile' means lizard, from the Greek *krokodeilos*. This name was first recorded by Herodotus who remarked on them basking on the pebbly banks of the Nile. 'Alligator' is a corruption of the Spanish *el lagarto das Indias*, 'the lizard of the Indies'.

Neither animal cries as it savages you to death. Crocodile tears are a myth from medieval travellers' tales. Sir John Mandeville, writing in 1356, observed,

'In many places of Inde are many cokadrilles—that is, a manner of long serpent. These serpents slay men and eat them weeping.'

No call alligator long mouth till you cross the river.
JAMAICAN
PROVERB

Crocodiles do have tear ducts, but they discharge straight into the mouth, so no tears are visible externally. The origin of the legend may be in the proximity of the throat to the glands which lubricate the eye. These can cause the eye to water a little from the effort of swallowing something large or reluctant. They can't smile either: crocodiles and alligators have no lips.

The digestive juices of crocodiles contain enough hydrochloric acid to dissolve iron and steel. On the other hand, there is no need to worry about alligators living in city sewers. They can't survive without the ultraviolet radiation from the sun that enables them to process calcium. This urban legend can be traced back to a *New York Times* article in 1935, which reported that some boys had dragged an alligator out of a sewer in Harlem and beat it to death with shovels. It probably swam up a storm conduit after falling from a boat.

WHAT'S THREE TIMES AS DANGEROUS AS WAR?

Work is a bigger killer than drink, drugs or war.

Around two million people die every year from work-related accidents and diseases, as opposed to a mere 650,000 who are killed in wars.

Worldwide, the most dangerous jobs are in

agriculture, mining and construction. According to the United States Bureau of Labor Statistics, in the year 2000, 5,915 people died at work—including those who had a heart attack at their desks.

Lumberjacks had the most dangerous job, with 122 deaths per 100,000 employed. The second most dangerous job was fishing and the third was airplane pilots—with a death rate of 101 per 100,000. Nearly all of the pilots, you'll be reassured to hear, died in small-plane crashes, not passenger jets.

Structural-metalworkers and people in mining and drilling came fourth and fifth, though the death rate for both was less than half that of timber cutters.

The third most common cause of death on the job in all occupations was murder, which claimed 677 workers. Fifty policemen were murdered. But so were 205 salespeople.

Falls were the second most common cause of death, accounting for 12 per cent of the total. Roofers and structural-metalworkers were the main victims.

The most common cause of death on the job was the car accident, accounting for 23 per cent of the total. Even police officers were slightly more likely to die behind the wheel than by homicide.

The single most dangerous specific job is said to be that of Alaskan crab fishermen working in the Bering Sea.

The risk of death can be calculated using the Duckworth scale, devised by Dr Frank Duckworth, editor of the Royal Statistical Society magazine. It measures the likelihood of dying as a result of any given activity. The safest kind of activity scores 0 and 8 will result in certain death.

One game of Russian Roulette carries a risk of 7.2. Twenty years of rock climbing weighs in at 6.3. The

90

chances of a man being murdered are 4.6. A 160-km (100-mile) car journey by a sober middle-aged driver scores 1.9: slightly more risky than a destructive asteroid impact (1.6).

On the Duckworth scale, 5.5 is particularly perilous. It's the risk of death by car crash or an accidental fall for men, as well as the chance of either sex dying while vacuuming, washing up or walking down the street.

WHAT KILLED MOST SAILORS IN AN EIGHTEENTH-CENTURY SEA BATTLE?

A nasty splinter.

Cannon balls fired from men o' war didn't actually explode (no matter what Hollywood thinks), they just tore through the hull of the ship causing huge splinters of wood to fly around the decks at high speed, lacerating anyone within range.

British naval ships of the period were often rotten and unseaworthy. Many of the officers had bought their commissions and had no idea how to sail, fight or control their men. Hernias caused by manhandling acres of wet canvas were so common that the navy was forced to issue trusses. To cap it all there wasn't a single pay rise for a century.

At close range, a 32-pound ball was capable of penetrating wood to a depth of 60 cm (2 feet). The best way to stop splinters (other than by building a metal ship) was to use a type of wood found in the south-eastern USA which resisted splintering.

As well as being one of the hardest of all woods, the Live Oak (*Quercus virginiana*) is the state tree of

Georgia and a symbol of strength and resistance for the southern states. It is the tree draped with long garlands of moss in films like *Gone with the Wind.*

WHICH WAR KILLED THE HIGHEST PROPORTION OF BRITISH SOLDIERS?

The English Civil War (or the 'War of the Three Nations' as historians now call it).

In the seven years between 1642 and 1649, a staggering one in ten of the adult male population died, more than three times the proportion that died in the First World War and five times the proportion who died in the Second World War.

The total UK population in 1642 is estimated at five million, of whom roughly two million were men of fighting age: 85,000 died on the battlefield, another 100,000 died of their wounds or of disease. The war was the biggest military mobilisation in English history with a quarter of those eligible to fight finding themselves in uniform.

In Ireland, things were even worse as the Civil War merged into a doomed battle for independence. Some historians calculate that half the Irish population had perished by the end of Cromwell's expedition in 1653.

In a 2004 poll organised by the BBC, it was revealed that 90 per cent of Britons cannot name a single battle of the English Civil War, 80 per cent do not know which English king was executed by Parliament in 1649 and 67 per cent of schoolchildren have never heard of Oliver Cromwell.

WHAT'S THE WORD FOR NAPOLEON'S MOST HUMILIATING DEFEAT?

Rabbits.

While Waterloo was no doubt Napoleon's most crushing defeat, it was not his most embarrassing.

In 1807, Napoleon was in high spirits having signed the Peace of Tilsit, a landmark treaty between France, Russia and Prussia. To celebrate, he suggested that the Imperial Court should enjoy an afternoon's rabbit-shooting.

It was organised by his trusted chief-of-staff, Alexandre Berthier, who was so keen to impress Napoleon that he bought thousands of rabbits to ensure that the Imperial Court had plenty of game to keep them occupied.

The party arrived, the shoot commenced, and the gamekeepers released the quarry. But disaster struck. Berthier had bought tame, not wild, rabbits, who mistakenly thought they were about to be fed rather than killed.

Rather than fleeing for their life, they spotted a tiny little man in a big hat and mistook him for their keeper bringing them food. The hungry rabbits stormed towards Napoleon at their top speed of 35 mph (56 kph).

The shooting party—now in shambolic disarray—could do nothing to stop them. Napoleon was left with no other option but to run, beating the starving animals off with his bare

I suppose nobody has ever been struck a direct blow by a rabbit. At least, not deliberately.
SIR WILLIAM CONNOR

93

hands. But the rabbits did not relent and drove the Emperor back to his carriage while his underlings thrashed vainly at them with horsewhips.

According to contemporary accounts of the fiasco, the Emperor of France sped off in his coach, comprehensively beaten and covered in shame.

WHO BLEW THE NOSE OFF THE SPHINX?

The Sphinx, which means 'strangler' in Greek, was a mythical beast with the head of a woman, the body of a lion and the wings of a bird. As you may have noticed, its giant 6,500-year-old statue beside the pyramids has no nose.

Over the centuries, many armies and individuals—British, German and Arab—have been accused of deliberately blowing it off for various reasons, but Napoleon generally gets the blame.

Almost none of these accusations is true. In fact, the only person that we can definitely say damaged it at all was an Islamic cleric named Sa'im al-dahr, who was lynched for vandalism in 1378.

The British and the German armies in either of the two World Wars are not guilty: there are photographs of the Sphinx without its nose dating from 1886.

As for Napoleon, there are sketches in existence of a nose-less Sphinx done in 1737, thirty-two years before he was even born. When he first clapped eyes on it as a twenty-nine-year-old general, it had probably been missing for hundreds of years.

Napoleon went to Egypt with a view to disrupting British communications with India. He fought two battles there: the battle of the Pyramids (which wasn't, as it happens, at the Pyramids), and the battle of the Nile (which wasn't at the Nile). As well as 55,000 troops, Napoleon brought with him 155 civilian experts known as 'savants'. It was the first professional archaeological expedition to the country.

When he returned to France after Nelson sank his fleet, the Emperor left behind his army and the savants, whose work continued. They produced the *Description de l'Egypte*, the first accurate picture of the country to reach Europe.

Despite all this, Egyptian guides at the Pyramids today still tell tourists that the Sphinx's nose was 'stolen by Napoleon' and taken back to the Louvre in Paris.

The most likely reason for the missing organ is the action of 6,000 years of wind and weather on the soft limestone.

WHAT'S THE NAME OF THE PICCADILLY CIRCUS STATUE IN LONDON?

a) Eros
b) The Angel of Christian Charity
c) Cupid
d) Anteros

The famous monument in Piccadilly Circus was erected in 1892 to commemorate the work of Lord Shaftesbury, the Victorian philanthropist.

Designed by the sculptor, Sir Alfred Gilbert, it represents Anteros and stands for, 'reflective and mature love, as opposed to Eros or Cupid, the frivolous tyrant'. Anteros was the younger brother of Eros.

95

This complicated idea never caught on. Because of the bow and the nudity, and people's generally shaky grasp of classical mythology, everyone assumed it was Eros (known to the Romans as Cupid), the Greek god of love.

As a result, a counter-rumour was spread by those wanting to protect Shaftesbury's reputation, claiming the memorial was, in fact, the Angel of Christian Charity (Greek, *agape*), a rather obscure, but less racy, alternative.

Whatever its name, the statue was technologically ground-breaking, as it was the first in the world to be cast in aluminium.

The use of a nude figure on a public monument was controversial, but it was generally well received. The *Magazine of Art* described it as '...a striking contrast to the dull ugliness of the generality of our street sculpture'.

Old London hands tell you that the memorial used to stand bang in the middle of Piccadilly Circus, aiming its bow down Shaftesbury Avenue ('he *buries* his *shaft* in Shaftes-bury'). During the Second World War the statue was removed for safe-keeping. When it was returned, so the story goes, the whey-faced bureaucrats of the London County Council decided to move it to one side and point it down Lower Regent Street instead.

This isn't so. It was certainly removed, but it has *always* pointed down Lower Regent Street, because Gilbert designed it to face the direction of Shaftesbury's home in Wimbourne St Giles, Dorset.

WHAT DID NERO DO WHILE ROME BURNED?

He certainly didn't play the fiddle, which wasn't invented until the fifteenth century.

The other charge was that Nero sang a song about the burning of Troy while Rome burned in AD 64, implying that he had set fire to the city himself in order to do so.

In fact, when the fire broke out, he was more than 56 km (35 miles) away at his seaside holiday home. When told the news, he raced back to Rome and took personal charge of the fire-fighting efforts.

The suspicion that he wanted to burn down Rome may have arisen from his stated ambition to redevelop the city. He eventually managed to shift the blame on to the Christians.

As to what Nero actually did: he was a transvestite who loved acting in women's clothes, singing, playing music and having orgies, and he had his mother killed. He was very proud of his musical abilities; his dying words are reported to have been 'What an artist the world is losing in me!'

According to some, he generally accompanied himself on the *kithara* (related to the lyre) but he also played the bagpipes.

Dio Chrysostom, a Greek writing around AD 100, noted: 'They say that he can write, carve statues, play the *aulos* both with his mouth, and also with the armpit, a bag being thrown under it.'

Early in the sixth century, Procopius, a Greek historian, mentions that the bagpipes were the instrument of choice of the Roman infantry while the trumpet was used in the cavalry.

Nero also invented ice cream (runners brought mountain snow flavoured with fruit juice) and his personal poisoner Locusta was history's first documented serial killer.

Locusta means 'lobster' or 'locust': Latin uses the same word for both.

WHAT'S MORE LIKELY: BEING KILLED BY LIGHTNING OR BY AN ASTEROID?

Absurd as it may seem, death by asteroid is almost twice as likely.

It is estimated that a large asteroid (nowadays known as a Near Earth Object or NEO) hits the Earth once every million years. Statistically, this event is now well overdue.

A 'dangerous' NEO is one more than 2 km (1.2 miles) in diameter. The shock of the impact would be equivalent to one million megatons of TNT. If it happened, the death toll would be in excess of a billion, so the chances of you personally dying in any given year are one in six million.

The chance of being killed by lightning in the UK in any given year is about one in ten million, roughly the same as being bitten by an adder.

Lightning is a giant electrical spark, with a brightness equivalent to 100 million light bulbs going on and off. Some strokes reach a peak current of 100,000 amps and 200 million volts creating a temperature of 30,000°C, five times hotter than the surface of the Sun. A bolt of lightning travels at speeds of up to 100 million feet per second, or over 115 million kph.

Each 'flash' is really composed of several strokes, each lasting less than a millionth of a second. Because they are so short, the energy value of lightning is limited—a single stroke would only generate enough energy to run an average household for a day. Lightning strikes the Earth more than 8 million times every day, or about fifty times every second.

Before the curse of statistics fell upon mankind we lived a happy, innocent life, full of merriment and go and informed by fairly good judgement.
HILAIRE BELLOC

Strikes are commonest in coastal areas, occurring at a rate of about two per square kilometre per year. They don't seem to do much damage: the electricity dissipates rapidly across the surface of the sea and whales have been observed to sing quite happily through ferocious electrical storms.

Human beings, on the other hand, are struck by lightning ten times more frequently than they ought to be under the laws of chance.

Men are struck by lightning six times more often than women.

Between three and six Britons and a hundred Americans are killed by lightning every year, many of them because they are carrying portable lightning conductors about their person—golf-clubs, carbon-fibre fishing rods and underwired bras.

If caught in a thunderstorm in the open, the safest position is well away from any trees, crouching down with your bottom sticking up in the air.

HOW MANY PEOPLE DIED IN THE GREAT FIRE OF LONDON?

Five.

Despite destroying 13,200 houses, 87 churches, 44 Livery Halls and over 80 per cent of the city, fewer than half a dozen deaths were recorded.

The dead were: the maid of the baker who started it; Paul Lowell, a Shoe Lane watchmaker; an old man who rescued a blanket from St Paul's but succumbed to the smoke; and two others who fell into their cellars in an ill-fated attempt to rescue goods and chattels.

The true death-toll may never be known. John Evelyn talks of the 'stench that came from some poor creatures' bodies', and modern forensic evidence suggests that, given the intense heat, some corpses would almost certainly have been vaporised and thus not recorded.

However, the leisurely pace of the fire (it burned for five days) made it relatively easy for people to evacuate, and the five cited remain the only definite casualties.

The authorities' response to the fire wasn't overly speedy. The Lord Mayor, Thomas Bludworth, went back to bed on the first night claiming 'a woman might piss it out' and Samuel Pepys found time to safeguard his valuables by burying a 'large parmazan cheese' in his back garden.

In the previous 'Great Fire' of London (in 1212), 3,000 people died, and in the two years prior to 1666, the plague had killed 65,000. The fire stopped the plague by destroying the black rats and their breeding grounds but the cost of the damage was estimated at

£10 million. With the entire annual income of the City of London running at £12,000, these costs would, theoretically, have taken 800 years to pay off.

Over 100,000 people lost their homes. Many of them camped out in a shanty town at Moorfields, or built shacks near their burned-out properties. But such was the speed of the rebuilding that by 1672 almost all had been rehoused.

The fire started in the King's bakery run by Thomas Farynor in Pudding Lane. Farynor denied this at the time and a deluded French watchmaker called Robert Hubert claimed he did it. Although it was evident to judge and jury that he couldn't have done, they hanged him anyway. His corpse was torn apart by an angry mob, suspecting a Popish plot.

Justice wasn't finally done until 1986, when the Worshipful Company of Bakers claimed official responsibility and apologised for the fire.

HOW DID ROMAN EMPERORS ORDER THE DEATH OF A GLADIATOR?

Thumbs up.

Neither Roman spectators calling for the death of a gladiator, nor Roman Emperors authorising one, ever gave a thumbs down. In fact, the Romans didn't use a 'thumbs down' sign at all.

If death was desired, the thumb was stuck up—like a drawn sword. For a loser's life to be spared, the thumb was tucked away inside the closed fist—as with a sheathed weapon. This is expressed in Latin as *pollice compresso favor iudicabatur*, 'goodwill is decided by the thumb being kept in'.

Before Ridley Scott agreed to direct *Gladiator*, Hollywood executives showed him the painting *Pollice Verso* by the nineteenth-century artist Jean-Léon Gérôme. In the painting, a Roman gladiator waits while the emperor stretches his thumb down to give the death sentence. Scott was captivated by the image, and decided on the spot that he must direct the film.

Little did Scott know that the source of his inspiration was utterly wrong. The painting is single-handedly responsible for one of the greatest fallacies of the last two centuries, namely that 'thumbs down' indicated death.

Historians agree that Gérôme wrongly assumed that the Latin *pollice verso*—'turned thumb'—meant 'turned down' when in fact it meant 'turned up'.

If further proof were needed, in 1997 a Roman medallion of the second or third century AD was discovered in southern France. It shows two gladiators at the end of a battle and a referee pressing his thumb against a closed fist. The inscription reads: 'Those standing should be released.'

The use of thumb signs can still be dangerously ambiguous in the modern world. In the Middle East, South America and Russia, a 'thumbs up' is considered to be a very rude insult, comparable to the Western V-sign. This has been problematic in Iraq, where American soldiers are unsure whether locals are welcoming them or about to blow them up.

Desmond Morris, author of *The Naked Ape*, traces the positive connotations of the 'thumbs up' in Britain to the Middle Ages, where it was used to close business deals. It found a new lease of life in World War Two when US airforce pilots adopted it as a signal to ground crews before take-off.

Ridley Scott was eventually told about the 'thumbs down' fallacy but felt obliged to have Commodus give the 'thumbs up' when sparing Maximus, in order 'not to confuse the audience'.

WHAT HAPPENED TO MOST PEOPLE ACCUSED OF WITCHCRAFT IN ENGLAND?

They were acquitted—and even if they had been found guilty they would have been hanged, not burned.

According to Malcolm Gaskill, in his detailed history of the seventeenth-century witch-hunting craze, *Witchfinders* (2005), the popular perception (encouraged by Dan Brown's *The Da Vinci Code*) that five million women were burned at the stake for witchcraft in Europe between 1450 and 1750 is a massive overestimate. He believes, like most historians of the period, that 40,000 is closer to the true figure, and that a quarter of those executed were men.

There are only 200 known executions in England directly resulting from an allegation of witchcraft. Nearly all of those were hangings. The Scots, French, Germans and Italians did all burn witches but, even then, it was more usual to strangle them at the stake and then burn the body afterwards, rather than burn them alive.

In Britain, from 1440 to 1650, only one 'witch' was burned per century.

Margery Jordemaine, the 'Witch of Eye', was burned at Smithfield on 27 October 1441; Isabella

Billington was burned at York in 1650 (although she was hanged first); and Isabel Cockie was burned in 1596.

An accusation of witchcraft in England by no means necessarily led to a death sentence. The Church—often blamed for persecuting witches—took no part in prosecutions. Accusers had to prove a witch had harmed them and English juries were surprisingly reluctant to convict. Seventy-five per cent of all witch trials ended in acquittal.

Contrary to the popular perception of baying mobs, it appears there was a good deal of resistance to the idea of witch-hunting, shared by both judges and ordinary people—the practice was regarded as superstitious, prejudicial to public order, and unnecessarily expensive.

Isabel Cockie's funeral pyre, for example, cost 105s. 4d.: the equivalent of more than £1,000 in today's money.

WHAT IS THE NUMBER OF THE BEAST?

616.

For 2,000 years, 666 has been the symbol of the dreaded Anti-Christ, who will come to rule the world before the Last Judgement. For many, it's an unlucky number: even the European Parliament leaves seat no. 666 vacant.

The number is from Revelation, the last and strangest book in the Bible: 'Let him that hath understanding count the number of the beast: for it is the number of a man; and his number is Six hundred threescore *and* six.'

But it's a wrong number. In 2005, a new translation of the earliest known copy of the Book of Revelation clearly shows it to be 616 not 666. The 1,700-year-old papyrus was recovered from the rubbish dumps of the city of Oxyrhynchus in Egypt and deciphered by a palaeographical research team from the University of Birmingham led by Professor David Parker.

If the new number is correct, it will not amuse those who have just spent a small fortune avoiding the old one. In 2003, US Highway 666—known as 'The Highway of the Beast'– was renamed Highway 491. The Moscow Transport Department will be even less amused. In 1999, they picked a new number for the jinxed 666 bus route. It was 616.

The controversy has been around since the second century AD. A version of the Bible citing the Number of the Beast as 616 was castigated by St Iranaeus of Lyon (c.130–200) as 'erroneous and spurious'. Karl Marx's friend Friedrich Engels analysed the Bible in his book *On Religion* (1883). He too calculated the number as 616, not 666.

Revelation was the first book of the New Testament to be written and it is full of number puzzles. Each of the twenty-two letters of the Hebrew alphabet has a corresponding number, so that any number can also be read as a word.

Both Parker and Engels argue that the Book of Revelation is a political, anti-Roman tract, numerologically coded to disguise its message. The Number of the Beast (whatever that may be) refers to either Caligula or Nero, the hated oppressors of the early Christians, not to some imaginary bogey-man.

The fear of the number 666 is known as *Hexakosioihexekontahexaphobia*. The fear of the number 616 (you read it here first) is *Hexakosioidekahexaphobia*.

The numbers on a roulette wheel added together come to 666.

WHICH CRIME DID BURKE AND HARE COMMIT?

Murder.

In the early nineteenth century, there was a big increase in the number of students of anatomy. The law in Britain specified that the only corpses that could be legally used for dissection were those of recently executed criminals. This was quite an advance on the anatomy lessons in Alexandria in the third century BC, where criminals were dissected while still alive.

The number of executions was inadequate to supply the demand and a brisk trade grew up in illicit grave robbing. Its practitioners were known as 'resurrection men'.

Burke and Hare were more proactive; they just murdered people and sold the bodies to an anatomist named Knox on an 'ask no questions' basis. In all, they killed sixteen people.

When suspicion fell on them, Burke and his wife Helen tried to get their story straight before they were separated to be interviewed by the police. They agreed to say that a missing woman had left their house at seven o'clock. Unfortunately, Mrs Burke said 7 p.m. and Mr Burke 7 a.m.

In return for his own immunity, Hare gave evidence against the Burkes. Burke was executed in

1829 but Helen got off 'not proven' and promptly vanished. Mr and Mrs Hare also disappeared, and Knox escaped prosecution altogether.

No man should marry until he has studied anatomy and dissected at least one woman.
HONORE DE BALZAC

The father of systematic dissection was a sixteenth-century Belgian anatomist called Andreas Vesalius. He published his findings in the classic seven-volume text *On the Fabric of the Human Body*.

In those days, dissection was forbidden by the Catholic Church, so Vesalius had to work in secret. At the University of Padua, he built an ingenious table in case of unexpected visitors. It could be quickly flipped upside down, dumping the human body underneath and revealing a splayed-open dog.

Over the last twenty years, dissection has fallen out of favour in medical schools—the victim of overly packed curriculums, a shortage of teachers and a general sense that it's an antiquated chore in a high-tech world.

It's now possible to qualify as a doctor without ever having dissected a body at all. To save time and mess, students study 'prosections'—bodies that have already been professionally dissected—or computer simulations that do away with cadavers entirely.

WHAT ARE CHASTITY BELTS FOR?

The idea of a crusader clapping his wife in a chastity belt and galloping off to war with the key round his neck is a nineteenth-century fantasy designed to titillate readers.

There is very little evidence for the use of chastity belts in the Middle Ages at all. The first known drawing of one occurs in the fifteenth century. Konrad Kyeser's *Bellifortis* was a book on contemporary military equipment written long after the crusades had finished. It includes an illustration of the 'hard iron breeches' worn by Florentine women.

In the diagram, the key is clearly visible—which suggests that it was the lady and not the knight who controlled access to the device, to protect herself against the unwanted attentions of Florentine bucks.

In museum collections, most 'medieval' chastity belts have now been shown to be of dubious authenticity and removed from display. As with 'medieval' torture equipment, it appears that most of it was manufactured in Germany in the nineteenth century to satisfy the curiosity of 'specialist' collectors.

The nineteenth century also witnessed an upturn in sales of new chastity belts—but these were not for women.

Victorian medical theory was of the opinion that masturbation was harmful to health. Boys who could not be trusted to keep their hands to themselves were forced to wear these improving steel underpants.

But the real boom in sales has come in the last fifty years, as 'adult' shops take advantage of the thriving bondage market.

There are more chastity belts around today than there ever were in the Middle Ages. Paradoxically, they exist to stimulate sex, not to prevent it.

WHAT WAS TUTANKHAMUN'S CURSE?

There wasn't one. It was made up by the papers.

The story of the 'pharaoh's curse' striking down all those who entered Tutankhamun's tomb when it was discovered by Howard Carter in 1922, was the work of the Cairo correspondent of the *Daily Express* (later repeated by the *Daily Mail* and the *New York Times*).

The article reported an inscription that stated: 'They who enter this sacred tomb shall swiftly be visited by wings of death.'

There is no such inscription. The nearest equivalent appears over a shrine dedicated to the god Anubis and reads: 'It is I who hinder the sand from choking the secret chamber. I am for the protection of the deceased.'

In the run-up to Carter's expedition, Sir Arthur Conan Doyle—who also famously believed in fairies—had already planted the seeds of 'a terrible curse' in the minds of the press. When Carter's patron, Lord Caernavon, died from a septic mosquito bite a few weeks after the tomb was opened, Marie Corelli, writer of sensational best-sellers and the Dan Brown of her day, claimed she had warned him what would happen if he broke the seal.

In fact, both were echoing a superstition that was less than a hundred years old, established by a young English novelist called Jane Loudon Webb. Her hugely popular novel *The Mummy* (1828) single-handedly invented the idea of a cursed tomb with a mummy returning to life to avenge its desecrators.

This theme found its way into all sorts of

subsequent tales – even Louisa May Alcott, author of *Little Women*, wrote a 'mummy' story—but its big break came with the advent of 'Tutankhamun-fever'.

No curse has ever been found in an ancient Egyptian tomb. Of the alleged twenty-six deaths caused by Tutankhamun's 'curse', thorough research published in the *British Medical Journal* in 2002 has shown that only six died within the first decade of its opening and Howard Carter, surely the number one target, lived for another seventeen years.

But the story just won't go away. As late as 1970, when the exhibition of artefacts from the tomb toured the West, a policeman guarding it in San Francisco complained of a mild stroke brought on by the 'mummy's curse'.

In 2005, a CAT scan of Tutankhamun's mummy showed that the nineteen-year-old was 1.7 m (5 feet 6 inches) and skinny, with a goofy overbite. Rather than being murdered by his brother, it seems he died from an infected knee.

WHAT DID FEMINISTS DO WITH THEIR BRAS?

No, they didn't.

Arguably the most influential feminist protest in history occurred at the 1968 'Miss America' beauty contest in Atlantic City, New Jersey.

A small group of protesters picketed the pageant with provocative slogans such as 'Let's Judge Ourselves as People' and 'Ain't she sweet; making profits off her meat'.

They produced a live sheep which they crowned 'Miss America' and then proceeded to toss their high-heeled shoes, bras, curlers and tweezers into a 'Freedom Trash Can'.

What they didn't do was burn their bras. They wanted to, but the police advised that it would be dangerous while standing on a wooden boardwalk.

The myth of the bra-burning began with an article by a young *New York Post* journalist called Lindsay Van Gelder.

In 1992, she told *Ms.* magazine: 'I mentioned high in the story that the protesters were planning to burn bras, girdles and other items in a freedom trash can... The headline writer took it a step further and called them "bra-burners".'

The headline was enough. Journalists across America seized on it without bothering to even read the story. Van Gelder had created a media frenzy.

Even scrupulous publications such as the *Washington Post* were caught out.

They identified members of the National Women's Liberation Group as the same women who 'burned undergarments during a demonstration at the Miss America contest in Atlantic City recently.'

The incident is now used as a textbook case in the study of how contemporary myths originate.

WHAT COLOUR IS THE UNIVERSE?

   a) Black with silvery bits
   b) Silver with black bits
   c) Pale green
   d) Beige

It's officially beige.

In 2002, after analysing the light from 200,000 galaxies collected by the Australian Galaxy Redshift Survey, American scientists from Johns Hopkins University concluded that the universe was pale green. Not black with silvery bits, as it appears. Taking the Dulux paint range as a standard, it was somewhere between Mexican Mint, Jade Cluster and Shangri-La Silk.

A few weeks after the announcement to the American Astronomical Society, however, they had to admit they'd made a mistake in their calculations, and that the universe was, in fact, more a sort of dreary shade of taupe.

Since the seventeenth century, some of the greatest and most curious minds have wondered why it is that the night sky is black. If the universe is infinite and contains an infinite number of uniformly distributed stars, there should be a star everywhere we look, and the night sky should be as bright as day.

This is known as Olbers' Paradox, after the German astronomer Heinrich Olbers who described the problem (not for the first time) in 1826.

Nobody has yet come up with a really good answer to the problem. Maybe there is a finite number of stars, maybe the light from the furthest ones hasn't reached us yet. Olbers' solution was that, at some time in the past, not all the stars had been shining and that something had switched them on.

It was Edgar Allan Poe, in his prophetic prose poem *Eureka* (1848), who first suggested that the light from the most distant stars is still on its way.

In 2003, the Ultra Deep Field Camera of the Hubble Space Telescope was pointed at what appeared to be the emptiest piece of the night sky and the film exposed for a million seconds (about eleven days).

The resulting picture showed tens of thousands of hitherto unknown galaxies, each consisting of hundreds of millions of stars, stretching away into the dim edges of the universe.

WHAT COLOUR IS MARS?

Butterscotch.

Or brown. Or orange. Maybe khaki with pale pink patches.

One of the most familiar features of the planet Mars is its red appearance in the night sky. This redness, however, is due to the dust in the planet's atmosphere. The surface of Mars tells a different story.

The first pictures from Mars were sent back from Viking I, seven years to the day after Neil Armstrong's famous Moon landing. They showed a desolate red land strewn with dark rocks, exactly what we had expected.

This made the conspiracy theorists suspicious: they claimed that NASA had deliberately doctored the pictures to make them seem more familiar.

The cameras on the two Viking rovers that reached Mars in 1976 didn't take colour pictures. The digital images were captured in grey-scale (the technical term for black and white) and then passed through three colour filters.

Adjusting these filters to give a 'true' colour image is extremely tricky and as much an art as a science. Since no one has ever been to Mars, we have no idea what its 'true' colour is.

In 2004, the *New York Times* stated that the early colour pictures from Mars were published slightly 'over-pinked', but that later adjustments showed the surface to be more like the colour of butterscotch.

NASA's Spirit rover has been operating on Mars for the past two years. The latest published pictures show a greeny-brown, mud-coloured landscape with grey-blue rocks and patches of salmon-coloured sand.

We probably won't know the 'real' colour of Mars until someone goes there.

In 1887, the Italian astronomer Giovanni Schiaparelli reported seeing long straight lines on Mars which he called *canali*, or 'channels'. This was mistranslated as 'canals', starting rumours of a lost civilisation on Mars.

Water is thought to exist on Mars in the form of vapour, and as ice in the polar ice caps, but since more powerful telescopes have been developed, no evidence of Schiaparelli's 'canals' has ever been found.

Cairo, or al-Qāhirah, is Arabic for Mars.

WHAT COLOUR IS WATER?

The usual answer is that it isn't any colour; it's 'clear' or 'transparent' and the sea only appears blue because of the reflection of the sky.

Wrong. Water really *is* blue. It's an incredibly faint shade, but it is blue. You can see this in nature when you look into a deep hole in the snow, or through the thick ice of a frozen waterfall. If you took a very large, very deep white pool, filled it with water and looked straight down through it, the water would be blue.

This faint blue tinge doesn't explain why water sometimes takes on a strikingly blue appearance when we look *at* it rather than *through* it. Reflected colour from the sky obviously plays an important part. The sea doesn't look particularly blue on an overcast day.

But not all the light we see is reflected from the surface of the water; some of it is coming from under the surface. The more impure the water, the more colour it will reflect.

In large bodies of water like seas and lakes the water will usually contain a high concentration of microscopic plants and algae. Rivers and ponds will have a high concentration of soil and other solids in suspension.

All these particles reflect and scatter the light as it returns to the surface, creating huge variation in the colours we see. It explains why you sometimes see a brilliant green Mediterranean sea under a bright blue sky.

WHAT COLOUR WAS THE SKY IN ANCIENT GREECE?

Bronze. There is no word for 'blue' in ancient Greek.

The nearest words—*glaukos* and *kyanos*—are more like expressions of the relative intensity of light and darkness than attempts to describe the colour.

The ancient Greek poet Homer mentions only four actual colours in the whole of the *Iliad* and the

Odyssey, roughly translated as black, white, greenish yellow (applied to honey, sap and blood) and purply red.

When Homer calls the sky 'bronze', he means that it is dazzlingly bright, like the sheen of a shield, rather than 'bronze-coloured'. In a similar spirit, he regarded wine, the sea and sheep as all being the same colour—purply red.

Aristotle identified seven shades of colour, all of which he thought derived from black and white, but these were really grades of brightness, not colour.

It's interesting that an ancient Greek from almost 2,500 years ago and NASA's Mars rovers of 2006 both approach colour in the same way.

In the wake of Darwin, the theory was advanced that the early Greeks' retinas had not evolved the ability to perceive colours, but it is now thought they grouped objects in terms of qualities other than colour, so that a word which seems to indicate 'yellow' or 'light green' really meant fluid, fresh and living, and so was appropriately used to describe blood, the human sap.

This is not as rare as you might expect. There are more languages in Papua New Guinea than anywhere else in the world but, apart from distinguishing between light and dark, many of them have no other words for colour at all.

Classical Welsh has no words for 'brown', 'grey', 'blue' or 'green'. The colour spectrum is divided in a completely different way. One word (*glas*) covered part of green; another the rest of green, the whole of blue and part of grey; a third dealt with the rest of grey and most, or part, of brown.

Modern Welsh uses the word *glas* to mean blue, but Russian has no single word for 'blue'. It has two—*goluboi* and *sinii*—usually translated 'light blue' and 'dark blue', but, to Russians, they are distinct, different colours, not different shades of the same colour.

All languages develop their colour terms in the same way. After black and white, the third colour to be named is always red, the fourth and fifth are green and yellow (in either order), the sixth is blue and the seventh brown. Welsh still doesn't have a word for brown.

HOW MUCH OF THE EARTH IS WATER?

Seven-tenths of the Earth's surface area may be covered in water, but water accounts for less than a fiftieth of one per cent of the planet's mass.

The Earth is big—it weighs about 6 million, billion, billion kg. Half of this is contained in the lower mantle, the massive semi-molten layer that begins 660 km (410 miles) below the crust. Even on the apparently watery crust, the mass of the land is forty times greater than that of the oceans.

How inappropriate to call this planet Earth when clearly it is Ocean.
ARTHUR C. CLARKE

A Japanese experiment reported in *Science* in 2002 suggests that there may be five times as much water dissolved in the lower mantle than sloshing around on the Earth's surface.

Using pressures of 200,000 kg per cm and temperatures of 1,600 °C, the researchers created four mineral compounds similar to those found in the lower mantle. They then added water and measured how much of it was absorbed.

If the Japanese are right, the proportion of the world that is water will have to be revised upwards—to 0.1 per cent.

WHICH WAY DOES THE BATHWATER GO DOWN THE PLUGHOLE?

a) Clockwise
b) Anti-clockwise
c) Straight down
d) It depends

It depends. The widely held belief that it is the Coriolis force, created by the Earth's spin, that drives bathwater into a spiral is untrue.

Although it does influence large, long-lasting weather patterns such as hurricanes and ocean currents, it is by orders of magnitude too weak to have an effect on domestic plumbing. The direction of drainage is determined by the shape of the basin, the direction from which it was filled and the vortices introduced into it by washing or when the plug is removed.

If a perfectly symmetrical pan, with a tiny plughole and a plug which could be removed without disturbing the water, were filled and left for a week or so, so that all the motion settled completely, then it might in principle be possible to detect a small Coriolis effect, which would be anti-clockwise in the northern hemisphere and clockwise in the south.

This myth was lent some credence by inclusion in

Michael Palin's *Pole-to-Pole* series. They showed film of a showman in Nanyuki, Kenya, who purports to demonstrate the effect on either side of the equator, but even supposing the effect existed, though, this particular demonstration got the direction of circulation the wrong way round.

WHAT DO CAMELS STORE IN THEIR HUMPS?

Fat.

Camels' humps don't store water, but fat, which is used as an energy reserve. Water is stored throughout their bodies, particularly in the bloodstream, which makes them very good at avoiding dehydration.

Camels can lose 40 per cent of their body-weight before they are affected by it, and can go up to seven days without drinking. When they do drink, they really go for it—up to 225 litres (around 50 gallons) at a time.

Here are a few quite interesting facts about camels, which have nothing to do with their humps.

Before elephants acquired their reputation for long memories, the ancient Greeks believed it was camels that didn't forget.

Persian hunting hounds—Salukis—hunted on camels. They lay on the camel's neck watching for deer, and then leapt off in pursuit when they saw one. A Saluki can jump up to 6 metres (20 feet) from a standing start.

In 1977 in *Zoo Vet*, David Taylor observed that

'camels may build up a pressure cooker of resentment toward human beings until the lid suddenly blows off and they go berserk.' The camel handler calms it down by handing the beast his coat. 'The camel gives the garment hell—jumping on it, biting it, tearing it to pieces. When the camel feels it has blown its top enough, man and animal can live together in harmony again.'

Camel-racing in the United Arab Emirates has started to use robot riders in place of the traditional child jockeys. The remotely operated riders were developed following a ban on the use of jockeys under sixteen years of age, imposed by the UAE Camel Racing Association in March 2004.

These laws are regularly flouted and there is a brisk child-slave trade, with children as young as four being kidnapped in Pakistan and kept in Arab camel camps. The only qualifications needed to become a jockey are not to weigh much and be able to scream in terror (this encourages the camels).

The famous line from the Gospels of Matthew, Mark and Luke, 'it is easier for a camel to pass through the eye of a needle than for a rich man to enter the kingdom of God', is possibly a mistranslation, where the original Aramaic word *gamta*, 'sturdy rope', was confused with *gamla*, 'camel'.

This makes more sense, and is a comforting thought for the well-off.

WHERE DO CAMELS COME FROM?

North America.

The icons of the African and Arabian deserts are American in origin.

Like horses and dogs, camels evolved in the grasslands of America, 20 million years ago. In those days they were more like giraffes or gazelles than the humped beasts of burden we know and love. It wasn't until four million years ago that they crossed the Bering land bridge into Asia.

They became extinct in North America during the last Ice Age and, unlike horses and dogs, haven't made it back.

It is not clear why the North American camel species died out. Climate change is the obvious culprit. More specifically it may have been due to a change in the silica content of grass. As the North American climate got cooler and drier, silica levels in grass tripled. This new super-tough grass wore out the teeth of even the longest-toothed grazers and the horses and camels gradually died of starvation, as a result of being unable to chew.

There is also some evidence that these already weakened species, their escape-route to Asia blocked by the disappearance of the Bering land bridge 10,000 years ago, were 'finished off' by human hunters.

WHO IS AMERICA NAMED AFTER?

Not the Italian merchant and cartographer Amerigo Vespucci, but Richard Ameryk, a Welshman and wealthy Bristol merchant.

Ameryk was the chief investor in the second transatlantic voyage of John Cabot—the English name of the Italian navigator Giovanni Caboto whose voyages in 1497 and 1498 laid the groundwork for the later British claim to Canada. He moved to London from Genoa in 1484 and was authorised by King Henry VII to search for unknown lands to the West.

On his little ship *Matthew*, Cabot reached Labrador in May 1497 and became the first recorded European to set foot on American soil, pre-dating Vespucci by two years.

Cabot mapped the North American coastline from Nova Scotia to Newfoundland. As the chief patron of the voyage, Richard Ameryk would have expected discoveries to be named after him. There is a record in the Bristol calendar for that year: '...on St John the Baptist's day [24 June], the land of America was found by the merchants of Bristowe, in a ship of Bristowe called the *Mathew*', that clearly suggests this is what happened.

Although the original manuscript of this calendar has not survived, there are a number of references to it in other contemporary documents. This is the first use of the term 'America' to refer to the new continent.

The earliest surviving map to use the name is Martin Waldseemüller's great map of the world of

1507, but it only applied to South America. In his notes Waldseemüller makes the assumption that the name is derived from a Latin version of Amerigo Vespucci's first name, because Vespucci had discovered and mapped the South American coast from 1500 to 1502.

This suggests he didn't know for sure, and was trying to account for a name he had seen on other maps, possibly Cabot's. The only place where the name 'America' was known and used was Bristol—not somewhere the French-based Waldseemüller was likely to visit. Significantly, he replaced 'America' with 'Terra Incognita' in his world map of 1513.

Vespucci never reached North America. All the early maps and trade were British. Nor did he ever use the term 'America' for his discovery.

There's a good reason for this. New countries or continents were never named after a person's first name, but always after the second (as in Tasmania, Van Diemen's Land or the Cook Islands).

America would have become 'Vespucci Land' (or Vespuccia) if the Italian explorer had consciously given his name to it.

HOW MANY STATES ARE THERE IN THE USA?

Technically, there are only forty-six.

Virginia, Kentucky, Pennsylvania and Massachusetts are all officially Commonwealths.

This grants them no special constitutional powers. They simply chose this word to describe themselves at the end of the War of Independence. It made clear they were no longer 'royal colonies' answering to the King, but states governed by the 'common consent of the people'.

Virginia (named after the 'Virgin' Queen Elizabeth I) was one of the thirteen original states (hence the thirteen red stripes on the American flag) and the first of the states to declare itself a Commonwealth in 1776.

Pennsylvania and Massachusetts followed suit shortly afterwards, and Kentucky, which was originally a county of Virginia, became a Commonwealth in 1792.

There are also two American Commonwealths overseas. In July 1952, the Caribbean island of Puerto Rico drew up its own constitution which declared itself a Commonwealth of the United States. The Northern Mariana Islands in the Pacific Ocean did the same in 1975. Neither are US states.

WHO WAS THE FIRST AMERICAN PRESIDENT?

Peyton Randolph.

He was the first of fourteen pre-Washington Presidents of the Continental Congress, or the 'United States in Congress Assembled'.

The Continental Congress was the debating body formed by the thirteen colonies to formulate their complaints to the British Crown. In its second meeting, under Randolph, it resolved that Britain had declared war on the colonies, and, in response, created the Continental Army, appointing George Washington as its Commander-in-Chief.

Randolph's successor, John Hancock, presided over the declaration of independence from Great Britain, where the Congress asserted its right to govern the thirteen colonies.

Peyton was followed by thirteen other Presidents until, on 30 April 1789, the triumphant George Washington was sworn in as the President of the independent United States of America.

Democracy is two wolves and a lamb voting on what to have for lunch. Liberty is a well-armed lamb contesting the vote.
BENJAMIN FRANKLIN

WHAT WERE GEORGE WASHINGTON'S FALSE TEETH MADE FROM?

I DON'T KNOW

Mostly hippopotamus.

Washington was a martyr to his teeth. According to John Adams he lost them because he used them to crack Brazil nuts, although modern historians suggest it was probably the mercury oxide he was given to treat illnesses such as smallpox and malaria.

He lost his first tooth when he was twenty-two and had only one left by the time he became President. He had several sets of false teeth made, four of them by a dentist called John Greenwood.

Contrary to traditional wisdom, none of these sets was made of wood. The set made when he became President was carved from hippopotamus and elephant ivory, held together with gold springs. The hippo ivory was used for the plate, into which real human teeth and also bits of horses' and donkeys' teeth were inserted.

Dental problems left Washington in constant discomfort, for which he took laudanum, and this distress is apparent in many of the portraits of him painted while he was in office—including the one still used on the $1 bill.

The awkward look of a man with a mouth full of hippopotamus teeth is thought to have been deliberately exaggerated by the portraitist Gilbert Stuart, who didn't get on with the President.

Until the invention of modern synthetic materials, the false tooth of choice was another human tooth, but these were hard to come by. In addition, they could fall out if they were rotten, or if their previous owner had syphilis.

The best source for decent false teeth was dead (but otherwise healthy) young people and the best place to find them was a battlefield.

One such was Waterloo; 50,000 men died in the battle and their teeth were plundered wholesale for the denture market. For years afterwards dentures were known as 'Waterloo teeth', even when they came from other sources.

Real human teeth continued to be used in dentures until the 1860s, when the American Civil War provided a plentiful supply.

Artificial false teeth came in at the end of the nineteenth century. Celluloid was one of the first materials to be tried, though not with conspicuous success.

Celluloid teeth tasted of ping-pong balls and melted if you drank hot tea (see p. 152).

126

WHAT DID BUFFALO BILL DO TO BUFFALOES?

Nothing. There are no buffaloes in North America. However, he did kill a lot of *bison*—4,280 of them in fewer than eighteen months.

The word 'buffalo' is frequently misapplied to bison. The North American Plains Bison (*Bison bison*) is related to neither genus of true buffalo—the water buffalo *Bubalus* and the African buffalo *Synceros*. Their most recent common ancestor died out six million years ago.

The bison population fell from 60 million in the seventeenth century to just a few hundred by the late nineteenth. There are about 50,000 bison roaming the range today. Bison/cattle crosses are bred for meat, called 'cattalo' or 'beefalo'. They have cattle fathers and bison mothers. Offspring of a male bison and female cattle are too broad-shouldered for the cow to deliver safely.

William Frederick 'Buffalo Bill' Cody, hunter, Indian-fighter and showman, joined the Pony Express—the West's legendary mail service—at the age of fourteen, in response to an ad which ran: 'WANTED young skinny wiry fellows not over eighteen. Must be expert riders willing to risk death daily. Orphans preferred. Wages $25 a week.'

The Pony Express only lasted nineteen months and was superseded by the railroad. In 1867, Cody was hired to hunt bison to feed the construction crews of the Kansas Pacific Railroad, which is where he notched up his astounding total.

He ran his Wild West Show from 1883 to 1916.

The show was hugely popular; its European tour was attended by Queen Victoria. On his death in 1917—and despite the fact there was a war going on—Cody received tributes from the King of England, the German Kaiser and President Woodrow Wilson.

Although he had specified in his will that he should be buried near the town of Cody, Wyoming (which he had founded), his wife stated that he had converted to Catholicism on his deathbed and asked for him to be buried on Lookout Mountain, near Denver.

In 1948, the Cody branch of the American Legion offered a $10,000 reward for the 'return' of the body, so the Denver branch mounted a guard over the grave until a deeper shaft could be blasted into the rock.

Hatchets weren't buried until 1968, when there was an exchange of smoke signals between Lookout Mountain (Denver) and Cedar Mountain (Cody), while the spirit of Buffalo Bill was transported symbolically from one mountain to the other on a riderless white horse.

WHERE WAS BASEBALL INVENTED?

England.

Baseball (originally base ball) was invented in England and first named and described in 1744 in *A Little Pretty Pocket Book*. The book was very popular in England and was reprinted in America in 1762.

Baseball is not based on rounders, the first description of which didn't appear in print until 1828, in the second edition of *The Boy's Own Book*. The first US mention of rounders is in 1834 in *The Book of Sports* by Robin Carver. He credited *The Boy's Own Book* as his source, but called the game 'base ball' or 'goal ball'.

In the first chapter of *Northanger Abbey*, written in 1796, the young heroine Catherine Morland is described as preferring 'cricket, baseball, riding on horseback and running about the country to books'.

The baseball authorities were so paranoid about the non-American origin of the game that in 1907 they carried out a shameless fraud. In a report into the game's origins commissioned by the major league's executive board, they advanced the story that the game was invented by the Civil War general and hero Abner Doubleday in Cooperstown, New York, in 1839.

A legend was born. Despite the evidence of numerous bat-and-ball games being played all over early Puritan America, and the fact that Doubleday never visited Cooperstown, or ever mentioned baseball in his diaries, it stuck firm in the American psyche. As one wag put it, 'Abner Doubleday didn't invent baseball, baseball invented Abner Doubleday.'

If any one person should be credited with inventing the modern US game, it is Alexander Cartwright, a Manhattan bookseller. He had been a volunteer fireman and in 1842 founded the Knickerbocker Baseball Club (after the Knickerbocker Fire Engine Company).

He and other firemen played on a field at 47th and 27th Streets. The rules of the modern game are based on their by-laws and Cartwight was the first to draw a diagram of the diamond-shaped field.

He was finally inducted into the Baseball Hall of Fame in 1938.

WHAT WAS BILLY THE KID'S REAL NAME?

a) William H. Bonney
b) Kid Antrim
c) Henry McCarty
d) Brushy Bill Roberts

Billy the Kid was born Henry McCarty in New York City. William H. Bonney was just one of his aliases, the one he was using when he was sentenced to death.

Born in New York City, his mother Catherine was a widow who resettled with Henry and his brother Joe in Wichita, Kansas in 1870. It was a wild place, the centre of the cattle trade. 'In Wichita', according to a contemporary newspaper, 'pistols are as thick as blackberries.'

By November 1870, the town had 175 buildings and a population of nearly 800. Mrs McCarty was well known in town for the hand laundry she ran on North Main Street. The family later moved to Santa Fe, New Mexico, where Billy's mother was married to William Antrim, a homesteader.

It was in the deserts of New Mexico that Billy began to rustle cattle and make a name for himself as a gunslinger. By 1879, with perhaps seventeen deaths to his name, he was offered an amnesty by the Governor of New Mexico, Lew Wallace, best remembered today as the author of *Ben Hur*, the best-selling American novel of the nineteenth century.

You can get much further with a kind word and a gun than you can with a kind word alone.
AL CAPONE

130

Billy turned himself in, then had second thoughts and broke jail. He was pursued and finally killed by Pat Garrett in 1881, but not before he had sent a series of letters imploring Wallace to honour his promise of an amnesty. They went unacknowledged.

Despite the official death warrant, there were persistent stories that the Kid had survived. In 1903, Wallace's successor as Governor of New Mexico had the case reopened to establish whether he had really died and whether he deserved to be pardoned. The investigation was never concluded.

In 1950, a member of Buffalo Bill the bison-killer's Wild West Show known as 'Brushy Bill Roberts' died claiming that he was in fact Billy the Kid.

Billy the Kid is said to be the real-life person who has been most depicted in films; he's portrayed in at least forty-six movies.

Carty/Antrim/Bonney didn't become known as Billy the Kid until the end of the last full year of his life. Until then, he was known, simply, as 'the Kid'.

WHAT DO WE HAVE THOMAS CRAPPER TO THANK FOR?

    a) The manhole cover
    b) The bathroom showroom
    c) The ballcock
    d) The flush toilet

All of them except the last one.

Thomas Crapper (1836–1910) was a London plumber who held nine patents: for manhole covers, drains, pipe joints, and, most notably, the ballcock.

His innovative Chelsea showroom was a big hit, though ladies were said to faint at the sight of the unmentionables on display. Crapper's, on the King's Road, started by his nephew George, only closed in 1966.

Crapper & Co. held four royal warrants. When the Prince of Wales (later Edward VII) bought Sandringham in 1880, they did all the plumbing.

In *Flushed with Pride* (1969), the author Wallace Reyburn claimed Crapper invented the flush toilet, and was knighted and cited in the *Encyclopaedia Britannica*. As any plumber will tell you, none of these things is true.

Though Crapper's 'Silent Valveless Waste Water Preventer' was a flush toilet, the patent was not his: it was filed by a Mr Alfred Giblin in 1819.

The first flush toilet was discovered in China in 2000 in the palace of a king of the Han Dynasty (206 BC–AD 220). It is a stone latrine with a seat, armrest and a system of pipes for flushing the pan. Arguably, the first modern WC was invented in 1592 by Sir John Harington, a godson of Queen Elizabeth I.

As for Crapper's surname being the origin of the slang for a lavatory, this is just possible. The word doesn't appear in print until the 1930s. 'Crap' dates from 1440, but it meant 'chaff' and had fallen out of use by 1600. Victorians would not have understood the word 'crapper', let alone found it funny.

The story goes that English settlers took the word with them to America, where it was vulgarised to its present meaning. When American GIs came to

132

Britain in the First World War, they found the name Crapper engraved on all the lavatories hilarious, and the name stuck.

Wallace Reyburn went on to publish *Bust-Up: The Uplifting Tale of Otto Titzling* (1971), a ludicrous fiction about the supposed inventor of the bra.

WHAT WAS MOZART'S MIDDLE NAME?

Wolfgang.

His full name was Johann Chrysostomus Wolfgangus Theophilus Mozart. He usually called himself Wolfgang Amade (not Amadeus) or Wolfgang Gottlieb. 'Amadeus' is Latin for Gottlieb and means 'God's love'.

Other memorable middle names include Richard Tiffany Gere, Rupert Chawney Brooke, William Cuthbert Faulkner and Harry S. Truman, where the S stands for nothing, despite the full stop.

Apparently Truman's parents couldn't agree whether he should be named after Anderson *Shipp* Truman or *Solomon* Young, his grandfathers.

For punctuation fiends, we draw your attention to *The Chicago Manual of Style*: 'all initials given with a name should for convenience and consistency be followed by a period even if they are not abbreviations of names.'

HOW DID NOME IN ALASKA GET ITS NAME?

a) By mistake
b) To attract good luck: 'Nomes' are a type of Alaskan pixie
c) After Sir Horace Nome (1814–72), Scottish explorer
d) After an Inuit greeting: *Nome nome* ('Here you belong')

It was a spelling mistake.

In the 1850s, a British ship noted the existence of a prominent but unnamed point of land in Alaska. A ship's officer scribbled 'Name?' next to the point on a manuscript map. When the map was being copied at the Admiralty, a cartographer misread the scribble, and wrote in the new point's name as 'Cape Nome'.

In 1899 the burghers of Nome tried to change the name of their town to Anvil City, but the US Postal service objected on the grounds that it risked confusion with the nearby settlement of Anvik, so the name stuck.

As the city's community website www.nomealaska.org reminds us: 'There's no place like Nome.'

WHAT IS THE NAME OF THE CAPITAL CITY OF THAILAND?

Grung Tape.

The city's day-to-day name, which means 'City of

Angels' (the same as Los Angeles), is an abbreviation for the official name, which is the longest place name in the world.

Only ignorant foreigners call it Bangkok, which hasn't been used in Thailand for more than 200 years. For Europeans (and every single one of their encyclopaedias) to go on calling the capital of Thailand Bangkok is a bit like Thais insisting that the capital of Britain is called Billingsgate or Winchester.

Grung Tape (the rough pronunciation) is usually spelt Krung Thep.

Bangkok was the name of the small fishing port that used to exist before King Rama I moved his capital there in 1782, built a city on the site and renamed it.

The full official name of Krung Thep is Krungthep Mahanakhon Amorn Rattanakosin Mahintara Yudthaya Mahadilok Pohp Noparat Rajathanee Bureerom Udomrajniwes Mahasatarn Amorn Pimarn Avaltarnsatit Sakatattiya Visanukram Prasit.

In Thai, this is written as a single word of 152 letters or 64 syllables.

It translates roughly as 'Great City of Angels, the supreme repository of divine jewels, the great land unconquerable, the grand and prominent realm, the royal and delightful capital city full of nine noble gems, the highest royal dwelling and grand palace, the divine shelter and living place of the reincarnated spirits.'

The front part of the name Bangkok is the common Thai word *bang* meaning village. The second part is supposed to have come from an old Thai word *makok* which means some kind of fruit (either olives or plums or some sort of mixture of the two). So it could be 'Village of Olives' or 'Village of Plums'. Nobody seems to be quite sure which—or to care.

Krung Thep (or Bangkok if you insist) is the only city in Thailand. It is almost forty times bigger than the next largest town.

WHAT'S THE WORLD'S LARGEST CITY?

a) Mexico City
b) São Paolo
c) Mumbai
d) Honolulu
e) Tokyo

Honolulu, although it's a bit of a trick question.

Under a Hawaiian state law established in 1907, the City and County of Honolulu are one and the same. The county not only includes the rest of the main island of Oahu but also the rest of the north-western Hawaiian islands which stretch 2,400 km (1,500 miles) into the Pacific.

This means that Honolulu covers the largest area of any city—5,509 square km (2,127 square miles)— despite only having a population of 876,156. Seventy-two per cent of the city is covered in seawater.

The world's most populous city is Mumbai (formerly Bombay) with 12.8 million people living in 440 square km (170 square miles): an astonishing 29,042 people per square kilometre. If the whole metropolitan area is included, the most populous city is Tokyo with 35.2 million living in 13,500 square km (5,200 square miles).

Honolulu is the state capital of Hawaii, but it is not

on the island of Hawaii. It is on Oahu, which is much smaller but much more densely populated. Hawaii is the most isolated major population centre on earth.

The islands of the Hawaiian Archipelago are the projecting tips of the world's biggest mountain range. Hawaii is the only US state that grows coffee. More than a third of the world's pineapples come from Hawaii and Hawaiians are the world's largest per capita consumers of Spam, getting through seven million cans a year.

Spam's popularity is mysterious but is probably due to the heavy US military presence during the war and the fact that tinned meat is handy during a hurricane. Spam fried rice is a Hawaiian classic.

Captain Cook discovered the Hawaiian islands in 1778 and renamed them the Sandwich Islands in memory of his patron, the Earl of Sandwich. Cook was murdered on Hawaii in 1779.

By the early nineteenth century the islands were known as the Kingdom of Hawaii. Although it became an American territory in 1900, and the 50th state in 1959, Hawaii is the only US state that still uses the Union Jack on their flag.

WHAT'S THE SINGLE LARGEST MAN-MADE STRUCTURE ON EARTH?

Wrong answers include the Great Pyramid, the Great Wall of China and (for clever-dicks) Mubarak al-Kabir Tower, Kuwait.

Our answer is Fresh Kills, the rubbish dump on Staten

There is always something larger or smaller.
ANAXAGORAS

Island, New York, though we quite like Jimmy Carr's alternative suggestion—Holland.

Opened in 1948, the Fresh Kills landfill site (named after the Dutch word *kil* meaning 'small river') soon became one of the largest projects in human history, eventually trumping (by volume) the Great Wall of China as the world's largest man-made structure.

The site is 12 square km (4.6 square miles) in area and, when operational, twenty barges, each carrying 650 tons of rubbish, were shipped in every day. Had Fresh Kills continued to stay open as planned, it would have grown to be the highest point on the Eastern Seaboard. At its peak the dump was already 25 m (over 80 feet) higher than the Statue of Liberty.

Under local pressure, the landfill closed in March 2001, only to be opened again to cope with the enormous amount of debris created by the destruction of the World Trade Center.

It is now completely shut down, and new restrictions mean it can't reopen (no landfill is allowed within NYC limits). The site is currently being flattened and landscaped into parkland and a wildlife facility. Nice.

Arguably, there are structures which are spread across more space—the US road network, perhaps? The internet? The GPS satellite network?—but the Fresh Kills landfill is the largest single cohesive structure.

WHERE'S THE COOLEST PLACE IN THE UNIVERSE?

It's in Finland.

In 2000, a team from Helsinki University of Technology cooled a piece of rhodium to a tenth of a billionth of a degree above absolute zero (–273 °C).

Rhodium is a rare metal, whose main use is in catalytic converters for cars.

The next coldest spot is in the Massachusetts Institute of Technology. In 2003, a team led by Wolfgang Ketterle produced extremely cool sodium gas.

Ketterle won the Nobel Physics Prize in 2001 for his work on Bose-Einstein condensate, a new state of matter that only exists close to absolute zero. As a child, his interest in science was sparked by playing with Lego.

These extremely cold temperatures produced in laboratories are remarkable. Even in deep space, the temperature rarely falls below –245 °C.

The only known exception to this is the Boomerang Nebula, identified by Australian astronomers in 1979. It looks like a boomerang (or possibly a bow tie). At its core is a dying star, three times heavier than our own sun.

The Boomerang Nebula has been spraying out gas at a speed of 500,000 kph (over 300,000 mph) for the last 1,500 years. Just as our breath cools when we force it through the narrow hole of our mouths, the gas squeezed out of the nebula is two degrees lower than the space it is expanding into. It reaches –271 °C, the lowest natural temperature so far recorded.

The coldest temperature in the solar system, −235 °C, measured in 1989 by Voyager II on the surface of Triton, one of Neptune's moons—is barely chilly by comparison; and the coldest temperature ever recorded on Earth, −89.2 °C in Antarctica in 1983, is positively tropical.

Low temperature research is important in the study of superconductors, materials which have zero electrical resistance but which so far have only been found to work at very low temperatures.

If superconductors can be harnessed they will totally transform the world.

They will massively increase the power of computers, while hugely reducing the cost of electricity and the emission of greenhouse gases. They will provide fuel-free transport, an alternative way of seeing inside the human body without the use of dangerous X-rays, and the E-bomb—a weapon which destroys the enemy's electronics without the need to kill anyone.

WHEN DID THE MOST RECENT ICE AGE END?

We're still in it.

Geographers define an ice age as a period in the Earth's history when there are polar ice caps. Our current climate is an 'interglacial' period. This doesn't mean 'between ice ages'. It is used to describe the period within an ice age when the ice retreats because of warmer temperatures.

'Our' interglacial started 10,000 years ago, in what we think is the Fourth Ice Age.

When it will end is anyone's guess; ideas about the duration of the interglacial period range from 12,000 to 50,000 years (without allowing for man-made influences).

The causes of the fluctuations are not well understood. Possible factors include the position that the land masses happen to be in, the composition of the atmosphere, changes in the Earth's orbit around the Sun and possibly even the Sun's own orbit around the galaxy.

The 'Little Ice Age', which began in 1500 and lasted for 300 years, saw the average temperature in northern Europe drop by 1 °C. It also coincided with a period of extremely low sunspot activity, though whether the two were linked is still being argued over.

During this period, the Arctic ice sheet extended so far south that Eskimos are recorded as reaching Scotland in kayaks on six different occasions and the inhabitants of the Orkneys had to fight off a disorientated polar bear.

Recent research at Utrecht University has linked the Little Ice Age with the Black Death.

The catastrophic decline in population across Europe meant that abandoned farmland was gradually covered by millions of trees. This would have led to a significant absorption of carbon dioxide from the atmosphere, forcing the average temperature down in an 'anti-greenhouse effect'.

WHO LIVES IN IGLOOS?

Probably no one any more.

The word 'igloo' (or *iglu*) means 'house' in Inuit. Most igloos are made of stone or hide.

Snow-block igloos were part of the lifestyle of the Thule, the precursors of the Inuit, and were used until fairly recent history in central and eastern Canada.

But only Canadian Eskimos build igloos from snow. They are completely unknown in Alaska and, according to a 1920s census of 14,000 Eskimos living in Greenland, only 300 had ever seen one. Few remain anywhere today.

The first igloos seen by Europeans were encountered by Martin Frobisher on Baffin Island in 1576 during his search for the North-West Passage. He was shot in the bottom by an Eskimo. In return, Frobisher's men killed a few Inuit, captured one of them and took him to London where he was exhibited like an animal.

In the 1920s, a newspaper in Denver, Colorado erected a snow igloo at the municipal buildings near where some reindeer were kept, and hired an Alaskan Eskimo to explain to visitors that he and the other reindeer herders of Alaska lived in that type of house when they were at home. In fact, he had never seen one before except in the movies.

In Thule, in north-eastern Greenland, by contrast, the locals were such expert igloo-builders that they built vast halls of ice for dancing, singing and wrestling competitions during the long dark winters.

The community was so remote that, until the start of the nineteenth century, they believed themselves to be the only people in the world...

WOULD YOU CALL SOMEONE AN ESKIMO?

The term 'Eskimo' covers a range of distinct groups and is not necessarily (as is sometimes asserted) insulting.

Eskimo describes those who live in the high Arctic regions of Canada, Alaska and Greenland. Bestowed by Cree and Algonquin Indians, the name has several possible meanings, including 'one who speaks another language', 'one who is from another country' or 'one who eats raw meat'.

In Canada (where the politically correct term is 'Inuit'), it is regarded as rude to describe someone as an 'Eskimo' but Alaskan Eskimos are perfectly happy about it. In fact, many prefer 'Eskimo' because they are emphatically *not* Inuit, a people who live mainly in northern Canada and parts of Greenland.

To call the Kalaallit in Greenland, the Inuvialuit in Canada and the Inupiat, Yupiget, Yuplit and Alutiit in Alaska 'Inuit' is like calling all black people 'Nigerians', or all white people 'German'. The Yupik of south-western Alaska and Siberia don't even know what the word Inuit means. As it happens, *Inuit* means 'the people'; *Yupik* goes one better: it means 'real person'.

The languages of the Eskimo-Aleut family are related to each other but to no other languages on earth.

Inuit, which is thriving, is spoken in northern Alaska and Canada as well as in Greenland, where it is now the official language and the one used in schools. Also known as Inupiaq or Inuktitut, it has only three vowels and no adjectives. The Inuit language was banned in the USA for seventy years.

Eskimos buy refrigerators to stop their food from getting too cold and if they need to count to more than twelve, they have to do it in Danish.

They do not 'rub noses' when greeting each other. Most get annoyed at this suggestion. The *kunik* is a sort of affectionate (rather than sexual) snuffling, mostly practised between mothers and infants but also between spouses.

In some Eskimo languages the words for 'kiss' and 'smell' are the same.

In 1999, Canadian Eskimos were given one-fifth of the land of Canada (the second largest country in the world) as their own territory. Nunavut is one of the world's newest nation states: it means 'our land' in Inuit.

At five to a car, all the Eskimos in the world could park at Los Angeles International Airport. More people use computers in Iqualuit, capital of Nunavut, than in any other town in Canada. It also has the highest suicide rate of any town in North America.

The average Eskimo is 1.62 m (5 feet 4 inches) tall with a life expectancy of thirty-nine.

HOW MANY WORDS DO ESKIMOS HAVE FOR SNOW?

No more than four.

It's often said that Eskimos have 50, 100 or even 400 words for snow, compared to English's one, but this is not so. In the first place, there is more than one English word for snow in various states (ice, slush, crust, sleet, hail, snowflakes, powder, etc.).

Second, most Eskimo groups will admit to only two words equivalent to 'snow'. It seems that out of all of the languages of Eskimo groups, there are no more than four root-words for snow all together.

Eskimo-Aleut tongues are agglutinative languages, in which the word 'word' itself is virtually meaningless. Adjectival and verbal bits are added in strings on to basic stems, so that many 'word-clumps' are more like our equivalent of sentences. In Inupiaq, *tikit-qaag-mina-it-ni-ga-a* means 'he (A) said that he (B) would not be able to arrive first' (literally 'to arrive first be able would not said him he').

The number of basic word stems is relatively small but the number of ways of qualifying them is virtually unlimited. Inuit has more than 400 affixes (bits added at the end or in the middle of stems) but only one prefix. Thus, it has many 'derived words' as in the English 'anti-dis-establish-ment-ari-an-ism'.

Sometimes these appear to be unnecessarily complicated renderings of what is a simple concept in English. *Nalunaar-asuar-ta-at* ('that by which one communicates habitually in a hurry') is an 1880s Greenlandic coinage for 'telegraph'.

If you were looking beyond the 'words for snow' for something which really sets Eskimo-Aleut languages apart it is demonstrative pronouns.

English has only four (*this, that, these* and *those*). Eskimo-Aleut languages—notably Inupiaq, Yupik and Aleut—have more than thirty such words. Each of the words for 'this' and 'that' can take eight different cases and there is a wealth of ways of expressing distance, direction, height, visibility and context in a single such demonstrative pronoun.

For example, in Aleut, *hakan* means 'that one high

145

up there' (as in a bird in the air), *qakun* is 'that one in there' (as in another room) and *uman* means 'this one unseen' (i.e. smelled, heard, felt).

WHAT DID HUMAN BEINGS EVOLVE FROM?

Not apes. And certainly not monkeys.

Homo sapiens sapiens and apes both evolved from a common ancestor, though this elusive chappie has not been found yet. He lived in the Pliocene era, more than five million years ago.

This creature descended from squirrel-like tree-shrews, which in turn evolved from hedgehogs, and before that, starfish.

The latest comparison of genomes of humans and our closest relative, the chimpanzee, shows that we split much later than was previously assumed. This means we quite possibly interbred to produce unrecorded and now extinct hybrid species before the final separation 5.4 million years ago.

Stephen Jay Gould once remarked that *Homo sapiens sapiens* is a recent African twig on the bushy tree of human evolution. While none of the evidence completely rules out the evolution of humans in other locations, the spread of humans from Africa remains the most plausible theory.

Genetic evidence suggests that one of the first populations outside Africa were the Andaman islanders, off the coast of India. They have been isolated for 60,000 years—longer even than the Australian aborigines.

There are fewer than 400 Andamanese left. Half of these belong to two tribes: the Jarawa and the

Sentinelese, who have almost no contact with the outside world. So isolated are the 100 or so Sentinelese that no one has ever studied their language. The other Andamanese languages have no known relatives. They have five numbers: 'one', 'two', 'one more', 'some more' and 'all'. On the other hand, they have twelve words to describe the different stages of ripeness of fruit, two of which are impossible to translate into English.

The missing link between animals and the real human being is most likely ourselves.
KONRAD LORENZ

The Andamanese are one of only two tribal groups in the world who are not able to make fire (the other are the Ake pygmies of central Africa). Instead they have elaborate procedures for keeping and transporting embers and smouldering logs in clay containers. These have been kept alight for millennia, probably having originated in lightning strikes.

Though this seems strange to us, they have a rather familiar idea of God. Their supreme deity, Puluga, is invisible, eternal, immortal, all-knowing, the creator of everything except evil; he is angered by sin and offers comfort to those in distress. To punish men for their wrongdoing he sent a great flood.

The *tsunami* of 2004 hit the Andamans with its full force but, as far as we are able to tell, it left its ancient tribes unharmed.

WHO COINED THE PHRASE 'THE SURVIVAL OF THE FITTEST'?

Herbert Spencer

Spencer was an engineer, philosopher and psychologist, who in his day was as famous as Darwin.

He first coined the phrase 'survival of the fittest' in his *Principles of Biology* (1864), having been inspired by Darwin's theory of 'natural selection'.

Darwin paid him the compliment of using it himself in the 5th edition of *The Origin of Species* in 1869, commenting: 'I have called this principle, by which each slight variation, if useful, is preserved, by the term natural selection, in order to mark its relation to man's power of selection. But the expression often used by Mr Herbert Spencer, of the Survival of the Fittest, is more accurate, and is sometimes equally convenient.'

Herbert Spencer (1820–1903) was the eldest of nine children, all the rest of whom died in infancy. Trained as a civil engineer, he became a philosopher, psychologist, sociologist, economist and inventor. He sold more than a million books in his lifetime and was the first to apply evolutionary theory to psychology, philosophy and the study of society.

He also invented the paperclip. The device was called Spencer's Binding Pin and was produced on a modified hook-and-eye machine by a manufacturer called Ackermann whose offices were on the Strand in London.

It did well in its first year, making Spencer £70, but demand dried up, Ackermann shot himself and the invention had entirely disappeared by 1899 when the Norwegian engineer Johann Vaaler filed his patent for the modern paperclip in Germany.

During the Second World War, paperclips were an emotive symbol of Norwegian resistance to the German occupation, worn on the lapel in place of the forbidden badges of the exiled King Haakon VII. A giant paperclip was later erected in Oslo in Johann Vaaler's memory.

Today, more than 11 billion paperclips are sold annually, but a recent survey claimed that of every 100,000 sold, only five are actually used to hold papers together. Most are adapted as poker-chips, pipe-cleaners, safety pins and toothpicks. The rest are dropped and lost, or bent out of shape during dull or awkward phone calls.

WHO INVENTED THE BALL-POINT PEN?

a) Mr Biro
b) Mr Bich
c) Mr Quiet
d) Mr Loud

Writing was a hazardous activity before the advent of the ballpoint pen. Fountain pens had to be regularly dipped into an ink pot and were prone to leakages, and Indian ink (invented in China) was slow to dry on the page.

These problems were first recognised in a patent registered on 30 October 1888 by a leather tanner called John J. Loud. He created a pen with a small rotating ball for a nib that was constantly fed by an ink reservoir. Although the pen still leaked, it was much more effective for writing on leather than a fountain pen. Loud failed to exploit his patent. If he had, we might be talking about disposable 'louds' instead of 'biros'.

The Hungarian László Biró (1899–1985) originally trained as a doctor but never graduated. He had brief stints as a hypnotist and a racing driver before taking up journalism.

Puzzled by the difference in drying times between newspaper ink and the slow-drying substance in his fountain pen, Biró and his chemist brother, György, fitted a pen with a small ball-bearing which successfully drew down the printing ink as it rotated. The biro was born.

The pair patented the pen in Hungary in 1938, and emigrated to Argentina in 1940 to avoid the Nazis, re-patenting it there in 1943. An early customer was the RAF, encouraged by the pen's performance at high altitude. This ensured the name 'biro' became synonymous with the ballpoint in Britain.

The first biros sold to the public were manufactured in 1945. At the same time, Biró licensed his pen to Frenchman Marcel Bich.

Bich called his company BiC and, by modifying Biró's design, set up a mass-production process that meant the pens could be sold incredibly cheaply.

BiC remains the world's ballpoint market-leader with annual sales of 1.38 billion euros. In 2005, they sold their 100 billionth pen. The best-selling BiC Cristal sells 14 million units a day.

As a mark of respect to Biró, the Argentines—who call the pens *birome*—celebrate Argentinian Inventors Day on 29 September, his birthday.

WHAT DO WE USE TO WRITE ON A BLACKBOARD?

Gypsum.

School 'chalk' is not chalk. Chalk is made of calcium carbonate—as is coral, limestone, marble, the skeletons of humans and fish, the lenses of eyes, the limescale in kettles and the indigestion pills Rennies, Setlers and Tums.

Gypsum is made of calcium sulphate. You may think it's a picky distinction but though the two *look* similar they are in fact quite different and are not even made of the same chemical elements.

Many substances that *appear* to be radically different are actually made of exactly the *same* chemical elements. Take carbon, hydrogen and oxygen. Combined in different proportions, they make stuff as wildly different as testosterone, vanilla, aspirin, cholesterol, glucose, vinegar and alcohol.

Technically known as hydrated calcium sulphate, gypsum is one of the most widely available minerals in the world. It has been mined for at least 4,000 years—the plasterwork inside the Pyramids is made of gypsum—and it is used today in a huge range of industrial processes, the commonest of which is ordinary building plaster.

About 75 per cent of all gypsum is used for plaster and products such as plasterboard, tiles and plaster of Paris. Gypsum is a key ingredient of cement and is used in the manufacture of fertiliser, paper and textiles. A typical new American home contains more than seven tons of gypsum.

Plaster of Paris is so called because there are large

deposits of gypsum in the clay soil in and around Paris, especially in Montmartre.

Gypsum also occurs naturally in the form of alabaster, a snow-white, translucent material used to make statues, busts and vases.

Alabaster can be artificially dyed any colour and, if heated, can be made to resemble marble. Powdered alabaster made into a salve was traditionally believed to be a cure for bad legs. It was common for people to chip pieces off church statues to make the ointment.

Ironically, the word gypsum comes from the Greek *gypso*s, meaning 'chalk'.

WHAT'S MADE OF CELLULOID?

Ping-pong balls and collar stiffeners.

Film isn't made of celluloid any more. The main ingredient of celluloid is cellulose nitrate; modern film is made from cellulose acetate.

Celluloid is generally regarded as the first plastic. In technical terms, it is a thermoplastic, which means it can be moulded each time it is re-heated.

It is made from cellulose nitrate and camphor. Cellulose occurs naturally in the cell walls of plants. Camphor comes from the camphor tree and smells distinctively of the mothballs into which it is also made.

Celluloid was first manufactured in Birmingham, England by Alexander Parkes who patented it for use in waterproofing clothing in 1856. Another early use was as a cheap ivory substitute: for billiard balls and false teeth.

Celluloid made the movies possible because of its flexibility. Rigid glass plates don't run through projectors. But it is both highly flammable and quick to decompose, so it is difficult to store and is now rarely used.

It has largely been replaced by more stable plastics such as cellulose acetate (made from wood pulp) and polyethylene (a by-product of petroleum).

Cellulose nitrate (or nitrocellulose) was invented by accident in 1846 by Christian Schönbein, the man who, six years earlier, had discovered ozone.

Experimenting in his kitchen with nitric and sulphuric acid, he broke a bottle, wiped up the mess with his wife's cotton apron, and put it on the stove to dry. It immediately burst into flames: Schönbein had discovered the first new explosive since gunpowder was invented by the ancient Chinese.

The new explosive was called 'guncotton'. It was smokeless and four times as powerful as gunpowder. Schönbein patented it at once and sold the exclusive manufacturing rights to John Hall and Sons. The next year, it blew up their factory in Faversham, Kent, killing twenty-one people.

Lethal explosions followed in France, Russia and Germany. It was forty years before a stable use was found for cellulose nitrate when James Dewar and Frederick Abel created cordite in 1889.

Seven years earlier, Dewar had invented the Thermos flask.

WHO INVENTED RUBBER BOOTS?

a) Amazonian Indians
b) The Duke of Wellington
c) Charles Goodyear
d) Charles Macintosh

Amazonian Indians have been making instant gumboots since time immemorial by standing knee-deep in liquid latex until it dries.

The boots designed for, and named after, the Duke of Wellington in 1817 were made of leather. The first rubber boots didn't appear until 1851, the year before the Duke died.

Rubber was a disastrous failure for clothing when first tried because it either melted all over you in hot weather or set as hard as granite in winter. The breakthrough came in 1839 when Charles Goodyear heated rubber mixed with sulphur and accidentally spilt some on the family stove.

Goodyear's story is inspiring and tragic by turns. He struggled in desperate poverty all his life—six of his twelve children died of malnutrition—but rubber was his obsession and he never gave up trying to improve the qualities of what he called 'vegetable leather'.

The process he had inadvertently discovered solved the rubber problem by giving it a stable consistency. In his excitement Goodyear shared his samples with Thomas Hancock and Charles Macintosh, who became successful British rubber merchants.

The greatest of all inventors is accident.
MARK TWAIN

154

After analysing them, they were able to reproduce the process and patented it in 1843, calling it 'vulcanisation' after the Roman god of fire. Goodyear sued, unsuccessfully, and not for the first time was forced to spend time in a debtor's prison—or his 'hotel' as he liked to call it.

He died, still deep in debt, although widely acclaimed for his vision and perseverance. He once wrote: 'Life should not be estimated exclusively by the standard of dollars and cents. I am not disposed to complain that I have planted and others have gathered the fruits. A man has cause for regret only when he sows and no one reaps.'

Forty years after he died, his immortality was assured when the founders of the Goodyear Rubber Company, now the world's largest, named their business in his honour. Their turnover in 2005 was $19.7 billion.

WHAT EDISON INVENTION DO ENGLISH SPEAKERS USE EVERY DAY?

The word 'Hello'.

The first written use of hello spelt with an 'e' is in a letter of Edison's in 1887 suggesting that the best way of starting a conversation by telephone was to say 'hello' because it 'could be heard ten or twenty feet away'.

Edison discovered this while testing Alexander Graham Bell's prototype telephone. Bell himself preferred the rather nautical 'Ahoy, hoy!'

Edison used to shout 'hello!' into telephone receivers at Menlo Park Labs while he was working on improvements to Bell's design. His habit spread to the rest of his co-workers and then to telephone exchanges until it became common usage. Before 'hello' was used, telephone operators used to say, 'Are you there?' or 'Who are you?' or 'Are you ready to talk?'

Once 'hello' became standard the operators were called 'hello girls'.

'Hullo' was used at the time purely to express surprise. Charles Dickens used the word in this way in *Oliver Twist* (1839) when the Artful Dodger first notices Oliver with a 'Hullo, my covey! What's the row?'

'Halloo' was used to call hounds and ferrymen and was also a favourite word of Edison's. When he first discovered how to record sound (18 July 1877) the word he shouted into the machine (the strip phonograph) was 'Halloo': 'I tried the experiment, first on a strip of telegraph paper, and found that the point made an alphabet. I shouted the word "Halloo! Halloo!" into the mouthpiece, ran the paper back over the steel point and heard a faint "Halloo! Halloo!" in return! I determined to make a machine that would work accurately, and gave my assistants instructions, telling them what I had discovered.'

The earliest recorded use of delegate badges saying 'Hello, my name is ...' was at the first telephone operators' convention in Niagara Falls in 1880.

WAS THE FIRST COMPUTER
BUG A REAL INSECT?

Yes and no.

First, the 'yes'. In 1947, at Harvard University, the US Navy's Mark II computer, housed in a large un-air-conditioned room, was brought to a standstill by a moth getting itself jammed in a relay switch. The operators removed the battered corpse of the insect and taped it next to the entry in the log book before restarting the machine.

The mechanical nature of this computer made it particularly vulnerable to insect interference. Most of the early computers, like ENIAC (Electronic Numerical Integrator and Computer) at the University of Pennsylvania were electronic and used moth-proof vacuum tubes.

But was this the origin of the term 'bug'? No. Used to mean an error or fault in a piece of machinery, the word 'bug' dates from the nineteenth century. The *OED* cites a newspaper report from 1889, in which Thomas Edison 'had been up the two previous nights searching for a bug in his phonograph'. Webster's dictionary also gives the modern meaning of 'bug' in its 1934 edition.

And regardless of what numerous books and websites say, 'de-bugging' was also being used before the moth brought things to a standstill at Harvard.

This is a rather satisfying example of life imitating language: a metaphor that, literally, came to life.

WHAT IS THE MOST LIKELY SURVIVOR OF A NUCLEAR WAR?

Cockroaches is the wrong answer.

Quite why so many of us persist in the belief that cockroaches are indestructible is an interesting subject in its own right.

They have been around a lot longer than we have (about 280 million years) and are almost universally hated as hard-to-control carriers of disease. Plus, they can live for a week without their heads. But they aren't invincible and, since the groundbreaking research of Drs Wharton and Wharton in 1959, we have known they would be one of the *first* insects to die in a nuclear war.

The two scientists exposed a range of insects to varying degrees of radiation (measured in 'rads'). Whereas a human will die at exposure to 1,000 rads, the Whartons concluded that the cockroach dies at a dose of 20,000 rads, a fruit fly dies at a dose of 64,000 rads, while a parasitic wasp dies at a dose of 180,000 rads.

The king of radiation resistance is the bacterium *Deinococcus radiodurans* which can tolerate a whopping 1.5 million rads, except when frozen, when its tolerance doubles.

The bacterium—fondly known by its students as 'Conan the Bacterium'—is pink and smells of rotten cabbage. It was discovered happily growing in a can of irradiated meat.

Since then it's been found to occur naturally in elephant and llama dung, irradiated fish and duck meat and even in granite from Antarctica.

Conan the Bacterium's resistance to radiation and cold, and its ability to preserve its DNA intact under these extreme conditions, have led NASA scientists to believe it might hold the clue to finding life on Mars.

WHAT'S THE BEST USE FOR MARMITE?

Solving the Arab–Israeli conflict in the Middle East

No less a person than the inventor of lateral thinking himself, Edward de Bono, advised a Foreign Office committee in 2000 that the whole sorry business might be due, in part, to low levels of zinc found in people who eat unleavened bread, a known side-effect of which is aggression. He suggested shipping out jars of Marmite to compensate.

The popular belief that eating Marmite will keep mosquitoes at bay has no basis in scientific fact. Sadly, the B group vitamins present in Marmite (and beer for that matter) don't appear to have any effect on mosquito behaviour.

Marmite, the love-it-or-hate-it spread, was invented in 1902 in Burton-on-Trent by the Marmite Food Extract Company and contains yeast extract, salt, wheatgerm extract, niacin, thiamine, spices, riboflavin and folic acid.

The exact recipe is—you guessed it—'a closely guarded secret'. Since 2000 it's been owned by Unilever,

The simple process of focusing on things that are normally taken for granted is a powerful source of creativity.
EDWARD DE BONO

159

proprietors of Persil, Domestos, Colman's, Cif, Cornetto and Impulse. Its annual sales exceed 24 million jars.

Marmite exerts a strange hold on British popular consciousness—its taste is one of the things that expats claim they miss most about home. Bill Bryson has described it as 'an edible yeast extract with the visual properties of an industrial lubricant'.

A *marmite* is a traditional French lidded cooking pot, the shape of which is echoed by that of the Marmite jar. The word originally meant 'hypocrite', deriving from *marmouser* or *marmotter*, 'to murmur' (perhaps because both hypocrites and cooking pots hide things from view and bubble away quietly).

WHICH IS THE HOTTEST PART OF A CHILLI?

A generation of television chefs have had us believe that the hottest bit of the chilli pepper is its seeds. Not so.

It is the central membrane to which the seeds are attached. The membrane contains the highest levels of capsaicin, the colourless, odourless compound that gives chillies their distinctive heat.

Chilli heat is measured using the Scoville Scale, created by American pharmacist Wilbur L. Scoville in 1912. In his early tests, Scoville mixed a range of chilli extracts dissolved in alcohol and diluted in sugar water. He asked a panel of testers to consume a range of concentrations of various chillies until they ceased to taste hot. A numerical scale was then devised according to the heat of the chillies.

A jalapeño pepper, for example, is said to have

4,500 Scoville Heat Units (SHU), because it has to be diluted 4,500-fold before it loses its heat.

The hottest chilli in the world is from Dorset, on the south-west coast of England. Michael and Joy Michaud's Dorset Naga—*naga* is Sanskrit for 'serpent'—was grown on a plant from Bangladesh.

It was tested by two American laboratories in 2005, and came in at a palate-torching 923,000 SHU. Even half a small Naga would render a curry inedible, and consuming a whole one would mean a trip to hospital. Despite this, 250,000 Nagas were sold last year.

To put it in perspective, pure capsaicin powder delivers 15–16 million SHU. It is so hot that pharmacists who experiment with it must work in a filtered 'tox room' wearing a full protective body-suit with a closed hood to prevent inhalation.

There are an estimated 3,510 varieties of chilli.

WHERE DO TULIPS COME FROM?

Whether from Amsterdam or elsewhere, tulips are as famous a symbol of Holland as windmills and clogs, but they are not native to the Netherlands.

The natural habitat of the tulip is mountainous terrain.

It was only in 1554 that the first tulips were imported from Constantinople (now Istanbul) into the Netherlands. Wild tulips can be found in southern Europe, North Africa, and parts of Asia up to north-east China. The tulip is the national flower of both Turkey and Iran.

The name of the flower comes from the word

tülbent which is the Turkish pronunciation of the Persian word *dulband*, meaning turban. This is because of what etymologists call a 'fancied resemblance' of the shape of the flower when not in full blossom to a turban (or perhaps because the Turks traditionally wore the bloom in their headwear).

Tulips did become exceedingly popular in the Netherlands (as it should be called: 'Holland' only describes two of the country's twelve provinces) but the stories of the great 'tulipomania' bubble of the early seventeenth century now look rather overcooked.

According to Professor Peter Garber, Head of Global Strategy at Deutsche Bank, the most lurid tales of people being ruined by the collapse of tulip prices stem mainly from a single book— *Extraordinary Popular Delusions & the Madness of Crowds* by Charles Mackay published in 1852—and were the result of a moralistic campaign by the Dutch government to spread scare stories to discourage tulip speculation.

It's true that the price of tulips was inflated (and that one bulb of the most valuable plants could cost as much as a house) but there are many instances of even higher values being achieved in other countries for other plants, for example, orchids in nineteenth-century England.

At its wildest, Garber says that the Dutch speculation 'was a phenomenon lasting one month in the dreary Dutch winter of 1637… and was of no real economic consequence'.

Today, Holland produces about three billion tulip bulbs a year, of which two billion are exported.

HOW MANY CROCUSES DOES IT TAKE TO MAKE A KILO OF SAFFRON?

Between 85,000 and 140,000. Which is why, even today, top-grade Spanish '*mancha*' saffron retails at £3,750 per pound.

There are frescoes in Minoan Crete dated to 1600 BC showing saffron being gathered. Alexander the Great washed his hair in saffron to keep it a lovely shiny orange colour. It was a seriously upmarket shampoo: at that time saffron was as rare as diamonds, and more expensive than gold.

In fifteenth-century Nuremberg and during the reign of Henry VIII in England, adulterating saffron by mixing it with something else was a capital offence. Culprits were burned at the stake, or buried alive with their illegal wares.

The town of Saffron Walden in Essex takes its name from the spice: it was the centre of the English saffron trade. Legend has it that this dates from the fourteenth century when a pilgrim from the Middle East arrived with a stolen bulb of a saffron crocus hidden in his stick. Until then, the town was simply called Walden.

Only the arrival of tea, coffee, vanilla and chocolate saw its cultivation decline, although it remained an important crop in Italy, Spain and France.

The word saffron comes from the Arabic *asfar*, meaning 'yellow'.

WHAT WAS THE FIRST INVENTION TO BREAK THE SOUND BARRIER?

The whip.

Whips were invented in China 7,000 years ago but it wasn't until the invention of high-speed photography in 1927 that the 'crack' of the whip was seen to be a mini sonic-boom and not the leather hitting the handle.

The whip's crack is caused by a loop that forms in the whip as you flick it. The loop travels along the length of the whip and, because the leather tapers to a fine tip, the loop speeds up as it travels, reaching over ten times its original speed. The 'crack' is when the loop breaks the sound barrier at about 1,194 kph (742 mph).

The Bell X1 was the first aircraft to break the sound barrier, piloted by Chuck Yeager in 1947. In 1948 it reached 1,540 kph (957 mph) at 21,900 metres (71,850 feet).

The record for the fastest manned flight is still held by the X-15A which reached 6,389 kph (3,970 mph) at 31,200 metres (102,360 feet) in 1967.

Light travels faster than sound – isn't that why some people appear bright until you hear them speak?
STEVEN WRIGHT

The fastest any human has ever travelled was on the re-entry of Apollo 10 in 1969. This was recorded at 39,897 kph (24,791 mph).

WHAT KIND OF MUSIC CHARMS SNAKES MOST?

They don't care, it's all the same to them.

Cobras in snake-charming acts are responding to the *sight* of the flute, not its sound.

Snakes don't really 'hear' music though they are certainly not deaf. They have no external ears or eardrums, but can sense vibrations transmitted up from the ground into their jaw and the belly muscles. They also seem to be able to detect airborne sounds via an inner ear.

It used to be thought that snakes could not hear at all because they don't respond to loud noises but research at Princeton has shown that they have acute hearing.

The key discovery was how the snake's inner ear functions. Snakes were wired to voltmeters and the effect of airborne sound on their brains measured. It appears that their hearing is 'tuned' to the frequency range of noises and vibrations made by the movement of larger animals, so music would be meaningless to them.

'Charmed' cobras stand upright if threatened and sway in response to the movement of the instrument. If they strike at the flute, they hurt themselves, so they don't do it again.

Most cobras have had their fangs removed but, even so, they can only strike at a distance within their own length, rather as if you put your elbow on a table and strike downward with your hand.

The cobra's natural attitude is defensive, not aggressive.

WHAT ARE VIOLIN STRINGS MADE FROM?

Violin strings are *not* made of catgut, and never have been.

This is a myth started by medieval Italian violin-makers who had discovered that sheep intestines made good strings for their instruments. Killing a cat brought terribly bad luck, so they protected their invention by telling everyone else their strings were made from the intestines of cats.

The legend was that a saddle-maker called Erasmo, in the Abruzzi mountain village of Salle, near Pescara, heard the wind blowing through the strands of drying sheep's gut one day and thought that they might make a good string for the early violin known as the renaissance fiddle.

Salle became the centre of violin string production for 600 years and Erasmo was canonised as the patron saint of string-makers.

Bad earthquakes in 1905 and 1933 brought an end to the industry in Salle itself, but two of the world's leading string makers—D'Addario and Mari—are still run by Sallese families.

Until 1750 all violins used sheep's-gut strings. The gut must be removed from the animal when warm, stripped of fat and waste and soaked in cold water. The best sections are then cut into ribbons and twisted and scraped until a string of the required thickness is made.

Today a combination of gut, nylon and steel are used, although most aficionados still believe that gut produces the warmest tone.

Richard Wagner circulated a terrible story to discredit Brahms, whom he loathed. He claimed Brahms had received a gift from Czech composer Antonín Dvořák of a 'Bohemian sparrow-slaying bow'. With this he allegedly took pot-shots at passing cats from his Viennese apartment window.

Wagner went on: 'After spearing the poor brutes, he reeled them in to his room after the manner of a trout-fisher. Then he eagerly listened to the expiring groans of his victims and carefully jotted down in his notebook their *ante mortem* remarks.'

Wagner had never visited Brahms or seen his apartment; there seems to be no record of such a 'sparrow bow' existing, let alone being sent by Dvořák.

Cats tend to die, like most other species, in silence.

Despite this, the rumours of felicide have stuck to Brahms and the claim has been reproduced as fact in several biographies.

WHAT'S THE BEST FLOOR OF A BUILDING TO THROW A CAT FROM?

Any of them above the seventh floor.

Higher than the seventh floor, it doesn't really matter how far the cat falls, as long as its oxygen holds out.

Like many small animals, cats have a non-fatal terminal velocity—in cats this is about 100 kph or 60 mph. Once they relax, they orientate themselves, spread out, and parachute to earth like a squirrel.

Terminal velocity is the point at which a body's

Cats are intended to teach us that not everything in nature has a function.
GARRISON KEILLOR

weight equalises against the resistance of the air and it stops accelerating—in humans it's nearly 195 kph (about 120 mph), reached in free fall at about 550 metres (1,800 feet).

There are cats on record that have fallen thirty storeys or more without ill effects. One cat is known to have survived a forty-six-storey fall, and there is even evidence of a cat deliberately thrown out of a Cessna aircraft at 244 metres (800 feet) that survived.

A 1987 paper in the *Journal of the American Veterinary Medical Association* studied 132 cases of cats that had fallen out of high-rise windows in New York. On average they fell 5.5 storeys. Ninety per cent survived, though many suffered serious injuries. The data showed that injuries rose proportionally to the number of storeys fallen—up to seven storeys. Above seven storeys, the number of injuries per cat sharply declined. In other words, the further the cat fell, the better its chances.

The most famous human free-falls are Vesna Vulović, who fell 10,600 metres (34,777 feet) when a terrorist bomb destroyed her Yugoslavian airlines DC-10 in 1972, and Flight Sergeant Nicholas Alkemade, an RAF tailgunner who leaped from his burning Lancaster in 1944, falling 5,800 metres (19,000 feet).

Vulović broke both legs, and suffered some spinal damage, but was saved by the fact that her seat and the toilet booth it was attached to took the impact.

Alkemade's fall was broken by a pine tree and then a snowdrift. He escaped unharmed and remained sitting in the snow, quietly smoking a cigarette.

WHY DID THE DODO DIE OUT?

a) Hunted for food
b) Hunted for sport
c) Loss of habitat
d) Competition with other species

The dodo (*Raphus cucullatus*) has the unenviable double distinction as a byword for being both dead and stupid.

A flightless native of Mauritius, it evolved in an environment free of ground-based predators and was wiped out in less than a hundred years by the destruction of its forest habitat and the introduction of pigs, rats and dogs to the island.

Improbably enough, the dodo was a species of pigeon, but, unlike the other famous extinct fowl, the passenger pigeon, it was not hunted for food as it was barely edible—the Dutch called it *walgvogel*, the disgusting bird.

The Portugese name *dodo* is also unkind; it means 'simpleton' (as in 'durrr-durrr'), a reference to the fact that it had no fear of humans so didn't run away, making it of limited value as a sporting bird. It was extinct by 1700.

In 1755, the director of the Ashmolean Museum in Oxford decided that their specimen was too moth-eaten to keep and threw it on a bonfire. It was the only preserved dodo in existence. A passing employee tried to rescue it, but could only save its head and part of one limb.

For a long time, all that was known about the dodo derived from these remains, a handful of

169

descriptions, three or four oil paintings and a few bones. We knew more about some dinosaurs. In December 2005, a large cache of bones was found on Mauritius which has allowed for a much more accurate reconstruction.

From the time of its extinction until the publication of *Alice in Wonderland* in 1865 the dodo was pretty thoroughly forgotten. Charles Dodgson (better known as Lewis Carroll) was an Oxford maths lecturer who must have seen it in the Ashmolean.

The dodo appears in *Alice in Wonderland* in the Caucus Race, a 'race' with no precise start or end, in which everyone gets a prize. Each of the birds corresponds to a member of the boating party present when Dodgson first told the story and the dodo is said to be based on himself.

Sir John Tenniel's illustrations in the book quickly made the bird famous. The phrase 'dead as a dodo' also dates from this period.

WHAT BURIES ITS HEAD IN THE SAND?

Wrong.

No ostrich has ever been observed to bury its head in the sand. It would suffocate if it did. When danger threatens, ostriches run away like any other sensible animal.

The myth about ostriches may have arisen because they sometimes lie down in their nest (which is a shallow hole in the ground) with their necks stretched out flat and scan the horizon for trouble. If the predator gets too close they get up and leg it. They can run at speeds up to 65 kph (40 mph) for thirty minutes.

The ostrich is the largest bird in the world: a male can reach 2.7 m (9 feet) tall, but their brains are the size of a walnut, smaller than their eyeballs.

The ostrich was classified by Linnaeus as *Struthio camelus* or 'sparrow camel', presumably because they live in the desert and have long, camel-like necks. The Greek for ostrich was *ho megas strouthos*, 'the big sparrow'.

The head-burying myth was first reported by the Roman historian Pliny the Elder, who also thought ostriches could hatch their eggs by looking at them aggressively.

He didn't mention their ability to swallow odd things.

As well as the stones they use to aid digestion, ostriches will eat iron, copper, brick or glass. One ostrich in London Zoo was found to have eaten a metre-length of rope, a spool of film, an alarm clock, a cycle valve, a pencil, a comb, three gloves, a handkerchief, pieces of a gold necklace, a watch and a number of coins.

Ostriches in Namibia have been known to eat diamonds.

WHERE DO GORILLAS SLEEP?

In nests.

These large, muscular primates build new nests every evening (and sometimes after a heavy lunch) either on the ground or in the lower branches of trees.

Aside from the very young, it's strictly one gorilla, one nest.

They aren't works of art—bent branches woven

together, with softer foliage as a mattress—and usually take ten minutes to make. Females and young animals prefer to sleep in trees; males or 'silverbacks' sleep on the ground.

According to some accounts, lowland gorillas are hygienic and houseproud, whereas mountain gorillas regularly foul their nests and sleep on a mound of their own dung.

Gorillas cannot swim. They have forty-eight chromosomes, two more than people.

More gorillas are eaten by people in the form of 'bushmeat' every year than there are in all the zoos in the world.

WHAT'S THE COMMONEST BIRD IN THE WORLD?

The chicken, by miles.

There are about 52 billion chickens in the world: that's almost nine for every human. Seventy-five per cent of them will be eaten but, for almost 3,000 years, they were farmed primarily for their eggs. Until the Romans came to Britain it had never occurred to anyone to eat the bird itself.

All the chickens in the world are descended from a kind of pheasant called the Red Jungle Fowl (*Gallus gallus gallus*), native to Thailand. Its nearest modern relative is the gamecock used in cockfighting.

Mass production of chickens and eggs started in about 1800. Eating chicken began as a by-product of egg production. Only chickens too old to produce enough eggs were killed and sold for meat. In 1963, chicken meat was still a luxury. It wasn't until the

1970s that it became the meat of choice for most families. Today it accounts for almost half of all meat eaten in the UK.

As a result of selective breeding and hormone treatment, it now takes less than forty days to grow a chicken to maturity, which is twice as fast as allowing nature to take its course.

Ninety-eight per cent of all chickens raised anywhere in the world—even organic ones—come from breeds developed by three American companies. Over half the world's 'broilers' (eating chickens) are Cobb 500s, developed in the 1970s by the Cobb Breeding Co.

There were no chickens at all in the Americas before 1500. They were introduced by the Spanish.

More than a third of all UK chicken is produced by one Scottish company, the Grampian Country Foods Group. They supply all the major supermarket chains, and are a major donor to the Conservative Party. They process 3.8 million chickens a week through their eight vast Integrated Chicken Units, one of which is in Thailand. Their motto is 'Traditional Goodness'.

Most chickens sold for eating are female. Male ones for eating are castrated cocks and are called capons. Nowadays castration is done chemically with hormones that cause the testicles to atrophy.

A hen is only an egg's way of making another egg.
SAMUEL BUTLER

The industry term for chicken feet is 'paws'. Most of America's 'paws' get exported to China even though three billion chickens already live there.

Danish chickens go *gok-gok*; German chickens go *gak gak*; Thai chickens go *gook gook*; Dutch

173

chickens go *tok tok*; Finnish and Hungarian chickens go *kot kot*. The rather superior French hen goes *cotcotcodet*.

WHAT'S THE 'SPORT OF KINGS'?

At various times this phrase has been applied to chariot racing, jousting, falconry, bowls, polo, and, most recently, horse-racing.

However, for the best part of 2,000 years there was one 'sport' which earned the 'royal' tag above all others: cock-fighting.

Until it was banned in 1835 it was Britain's national sport, with every village boasting at least one cockpit. Everyone from royalty to schoolboys joined in: there were even cockpits in the palace of Westminster and on Downing Street. On Shrove Tuesday, for a fee of one 'cock-penny', boys could bring their gamecocks to school and fight them for the day.

No one knows how or when the Old English Game fowl (OEG) arrived in Britain. There is a legend that Phoenician tradesmen introduced them but it seems likely they were carried here by Iron Age tribes migrating from the East. In 54 BC Julius Caesar was impressed that the ancient Britons bred birds for fighting rather than meat.

OEGs are universally acknowledged as the most aggressive of all fowl. A good gamecock will fight to the death with no special encouragement, hence their pre-eminence as fighting birds.

Competition among their breeders was intense. Recipes for special bread to 'build courage' were

174

jealously guarded, though the practice of soaking it in warm urine was universal. The cock had his comb and wattles removed (dubbed) and steel spurs (gavelocks) attached.

A good cocker would think nothing of cleaning his cock's wounded head by sticking it in his mouth and sucking it clean. Racing and cockfighting often took place together, as both involved gambling.

Some bloodlines were legendary; the White Piles bred by Dr Bellsye near Chester were famous for the 'Chesire drop', a sudden burst of murderous violence just when the cock looked finished.

Cockfighting is still legal in Louisiana and New Mexico, and only classed as a 'misdemeanour' in sixteen other states such as Tennessee and Arkansas.

A cock is a male bird over a year old; under a year he's a cockerel, or 'stag' in cocker-speak. Other words and phrases deriving from the 'sport of kings' include 'game' (i.e. up for it), 'pitted against', 'turn tail', 'show the white feather' (cowardice), 'show a clean pair of heels', 'well-heeled' (which originally meant possessing sharp natural spurs), 'cocksure' and 'cock-eyed' (to squint).

WHAT'S BRITAIN'S SMALLEST BIRD?

The goldcrest and the firecrest tie for the title of the smallest bird in Britain. Both are a mere 9 cm (3.5 inches) long, whereas the wren measures in at 9.5–10 cm (3.75–4 inches), making it the *third* smallest British bird.

However, the wren is Britain's commonest wild bird and can be found in every kind of habitat. There are currently ten million breeding pairs.

Its name, *Troglodytes troglodytes,* means 'cave dweller'. Wrens build their dome-like nest in the most unlikely places: caves, burrows, inside the carcasses of dead animals, the folds of church curtains, watering cans.

The male usually builds six nests in his territory for the female to choose from, although there are records of them building five times that number.

Despite their size, the piercing 'squitter' of the wren can carry for half a mile and is one of the few bird songs that can be heard all year round. Wrens are susceptible to cold, and communal roosts of anything up to thirty birds can be found, as they huddle together for warmth.

The word wren comes from the Old English *wrenna*, which also meant 'horny', perhaps referring to the bird's cocked tail. The wren is still called a 'stag' in Norfolk, from the Danish *stag* meaning 'spike'.

On St Stephen's Day (26 December) in the west of Britain and Ireland, 'Hunting the Wren' was an important Hallowe'en-style custom. A wren was captured, nailed to a pole, and paraded from door to door by children and adults wearing masks. In return for a song and a feather from the bird, householders offered food and drink, preferably beer.

The goldcrest's Latin name, *Regulus regulus*, means 'little king', presumably because of its 'crowning' gold stripe. A fully grown goldcrest weighs about the same as a five-pence piece (5 g, less than a fifth of an ounce). There are stories of hungry goldcrests latching on to dragonflies and being 'towed' by the heavier insect.

Goldcrests are tough, regularly migrating across

the North Sea to overwinter in Britain. They nest in conifers and the spread of British conifer plantations over the last fifty years means they are much less rare than they used to be.

The firecrest, on the other hand, remains elusive. It was only added to the list of British breeding birds in 1962 and there are still probably fewer than 100 breeding pairs.

WHAT ANIMAL ARE THE CANARY ISLANDS NAMED AFTER?

Dogs. Canary birds are named after the islands (where they are indigenous), not the other way round.

The archipelago gets its name from the Latin name for the largest of the islands, which the Romans named 'Isle of Dogs' (*Insula Canaria*) after the large numbers of dogs there, both wild and domesticated.

The volcano on La Palma in the Canaries is said to have the potential to cause a catastrophic collapse of the western half of the island, creating a *tsunami* that could cross the Atlantic and hit the eastern seaboard of the United States of America eight hours later with a wave as high as thirty metres.

In 'Canarian Wrestling' the participants confront each other in a sand circle called a *terrero*; the aim is to make your opponent touch the sand with any part of his body other than the feet. No hitting is permitted. The sport originated with the Guanches, the islands' pre-Spanish indigenous people.

The *Silbo Gomero* ('Gomeran Whistle') is a whistled language used in the Canary island of La Gomera to communicate across its deep valleys. Its speakers are called 'silbadors'. Although it was originally a Guanche language, it has been adapted so that modern silbadors are, effectively, whistling in Spanish. It's a compulsory subject for Gomeran schoolchildren.

Canaries are a kind of finch. For centuries, British mining regulations required the keeping of a small bird for gas detection. They were used in this way until 1986, and the wording wasn't removed from the regulations until 1995. The idea was that toxic gases like carbon monoxide and methane killed the birds before they injured the miners. Canaries were favoured because they sing a lot, so it's noticeable when they go quiet and fall over.

Only the male canaries sing; they can also mimic telephones and other household devices. 'Tweety' in the Warner cartoons is a canary.

Canaries were originally a mottled greeny-brown, but 400 years of cross-breeding by human beings produced their familiar yellow colour. No one has ever bred a red canary but a diet of red peppers turns them orange.

London's Isle of Dogs was first so-called on a map dated 1588: perhaps because it was home to the royal kennels, though it may simply have been a term of abuse. It's an odd coincidence that Canary Wharf is located there.

WHAT'S THE SMALLEST DOG IN THE WORLD?

The smallest dog on record was a Yorkshire terrier owned by Arthur

Marples of Blackburn. It was 6.5 cm (2.5 inches) high at the shoulder, 9.5 cm (3.75 inches) long from the tip of its nose to the root of its tail, weighed 113 g (4 oz), and died in 1945.

The world's smallest breed of dog is usually said to be the chihuahua. Nonetheless, according to the *Guinness Book of World Records*, the record for today's smallest living dog is not necessarily held by one.

It depends what you mean by 'smallest'. The current record is shared by a chihuahua (shortest in length) and a Yorkshire terrier (shortest in height).

Whitney, the Yorkshire terrier, lives in Shoeburyness, Essex and is 7.3 cm (3 inches) tall at the shoulder. The chihuahua, called Danka Kordak Slovakia, is 18.8 cm (7.4 inches) long and lives in Slovakia.

There are more than 400 breeds of dog and all are members of the same species. Any dog can breed with any other. No other creature in the world comes in such a wide range of shapes and sizes. No one knows why this is.

The unique variety amongst dogs owes a lot to human intervention, but the puzzle is that all dog breeds are originally descended from grey wolves.

Doberman pinschers were created from German pinschers, Rottweilers, Manchester terriers, and possibly pointers, in just thirty-five years, apparently flying in the face of the Darwinian evolution of species, a process thought to operate over thousands or even millions of years.

For some unknown reason, when dogs are cross-bred, instead of getting an average between the two types you quite often get something totally unexpected. This new 'breed' also retains the ability to interbreed.

The chihuahua is named after a state in Mexico, because it was believed (on the basis of Toltec and Aztec art) that the breed was indigenous there. However, there are no archaeological remains to support this belief; and it is now thought that the animal depicted is most probably a variety of rodent.

It is much more likely that the ancestors of the breed were brought by Spanish merchants from China, where the practice of dwarfing both plants and animals has had a long history.

Chihuahua cheese is popular in Mexico but it comes from the state, not from the dog.

HOW DO DOGS MATE?

Dogs mate back to back, not doggy style.

When you see a dog doing the mount-and-pump it's actually performing a dominance gesture. Ejaculation is very rare.

That is why your next-door neighbour's dog seems to choose children's legs to hump. It isn't primarily sexual: it's establishing its position in the pack and chooses the smallest first.

Dogs actually mate by going in from behind but then getting a leg over so that they end up rear-to-rear. Once this happens the tip of the male dog's penis (called the *bulbus glandis*) engorges with blood making withdrawal impossible.

This is called 'knotting' (as in the expression 'get knotted!'). It is designed to minimise semen leakage: a classic example of 'sperm competition', or keeping other dogs' genetic material out. There's a period of 'jostling' until ejaculation occurs and the penis eventually shrinks so the dogs can separate.

I wonder if other dogs think poodles are members of a weird religious cult.
RITA RUDNER

First-timers do sometimes react badly to finding themselves 'knotted'. In these cases the jostling and its accompanying yelps sound much more like fighting than romance.

HOW DID CATHERINE THE GREAT DIE?

Catherine the Great, Empress of all the Russias, died of a stroke, in bed, in 1796, aged sixty-seven.

It's true that when she collapsed from the stroke she was at her *toilette*, but she was cared for thereafter in bed, where she died.

She wasn't crushed by a well-hung stallion being lifted on to her, or through injuries sustained by crushing her chamber pot under her enormous *derrière*. Nor is there any evidence that she had an especial fondness for horses as a younger woman, except as creatures to ride on.

It isn't clear where these stories come from. It may be a spectacularly successful piece of black propaganda invented by her resentful son, Paul I, whose court was notoriously gossipy. Or it may be the dastardly French, who were at war with a coalition of nations including Russia in the years after the Revolution (the stories about Marie Antoinette were even worse).

Wherever it started it is certainly true that

181

Catherine's behaviour created an erotic *frisson*. She did take many lovers and it seems some of them were road-tested on her ladies-in-waiting. If they passed, they were given an honorary position and installed at Court.

One of her procurors was a former lover himself—Potemkin of *Battleship* fame, who died at the age of fifty-two 'in consequence of eating a whole goose while in a high state of fever'.

Whether her extra-marital relationships number just eleven (confirmed by her correspondence) or the 289 cited by scandalmongers, Catherine's more important legacy is in her political and cultural achievements.

She built more of St Petersburg than Peter the Great himself; sorted out the complexity of Russian law; commissioned magnificent gardens; filled Russian galleries with great European art; introduced smallpox inoculation and became a patron of writers and philosophers across Europe, including Diderot and Voltaire, who called her 'the Star of the North'.

Her genetic legacy was less impressive. Her son Czar Paul I (1754–1801) once court-martialled and executed a rat for knocking over his toy soldiers. Later, he had his horse court-martialled and sentenced to fifty lashes. In due course, he was murdered by his own nobles (without trial) and replaced by his son.

WHAT SURPRISED JOHN RUSKIN ON HIS WEDDING NIGHT?

It is generally believed that John Ruskin was shocked into impotence by the sight of his wife Effie's pubic hair on their wedding night.

The story was that, as the most influential art critic of his day, his knowledge of the naked female form derived entirely from the 'pubes-free' marble of classical sculpture and painting.

There is no evidence for this theory, which was first advanced in Mary Lutyens's biography of the Ruskins in 1965, and it is clear from a frank correspondence he had with his mother that he was not ignorant in the way suggested. The notion of extreme prudery amongst the Victorians is, at least to some degree, an invention of the mid-twentieth century.

What is true is that Ruskin did not consummate the marriage. This situation continued for six years until, on a painting expedition, Ruskin left Effie alone in a rustic cabin with his friend, the painter John Everett Millais (1829–96). Millais knew what to do, and Effie enjoyed it so much she filed for divorce. The marriage was annulled on the grounds of Ruskin's 'incurable impotency'.

Effie married Millais and had a large family with him. The whole business caused a scandal and meant that Effie was no longer asked to any party at which the Queen would be present.

Ruskin's underlying problem was that he had a penchant for young girls. In spite of this (or maybe because of it), Ruskin was a huge influence on

It is far more difficult to be simple than to be complicated.
JOHN RUSKIN

Victorian art and architecture, an early promoter of Turner and the Pre-Raphaelites, a founding father of the Trades Unions and the man behind the Arts and Crafts movement and the National Trust.

He wrote 250 books and taught art to Oscar Wilde. He paid the Friends of the Guild of St George to sweep the steps in front of the British Museum. He resigned as Slade Professor of Art when vivisection was allowed in the medical school, and in later life went mad, believing that his cook was really Queen Victoria. Gandhi cited him as the single greatest influence in his life.

Another possible example of pubic hair being blamed for dysfunction concerns the alleged affair of D.H. Lawrence and the painter Dorothy Brett in 1926. Lawrence apparently left the naked Brett in bed having made the excuse for his incapacity: 'your pubes are wrong'.

Most of Lawrence's biographers believe this was fantasy on Brett's part, not least because she first told the story months before her death in 1976.

HOW LONG DO YOUR FINGERNAILS AND HAIR GROW AFTER DEATH?

'For three days after death, hair and fingernails continue to grow but phone calls taper off' was one of the late, great Johnny Carson's best lines.

But hair and fingernails don't grow at all after death. This is a complete myth. When we die, our

184

bodies dehydrate and our skin tightens creating an illusion of hair and nail growth.

The idea owes a great deal to Erich Maria Remarque's classic novel *All Quiet on the Western Front*, in which the narrator, Paul Bäumer, reflects on the death of his friend Kemmerich: 'It strikes me that these nails will continue to grow like lean fantastic cellar-plants long after Kemmerich breathes no more. I see the picture before me. They twist themselves into corkscrews and grow and grow, and with them the hair on the decaying skull, just like grass in a good soil, just like grass . . .'

Despite this, there is plenty of action after death: your body will positively thrive with life. Bacteria, beetles, mites and worms will enjoy a feeding frenzy, contributing enormously to the decomposition process.

One of your body's most enthusiastic customers is the humpbacked *phorid* or 'coffin fly'. The fly, also known as the 'scuttle fly' because of its awkward flight, is able to live its entire life underground in a corpse.

Scuttle flies are particularly greedy when it comes to human flesh, and it's not uncommon for them to dig nearly a metre (3 feet) down through the soil to reach a buried coffin.

One type of phorid, from the genus *Apocephalus*, has recently been deployed in an attempt to control the rampant fire ant populations in the American south-east which were introduced via a Brazilian cargo ship in the 1930s. The flies lay their eggs in the head of the ant. The larvae feed on the contents of the fire ant's head and emerge several days later.

WHAT DID ATLAS CARRY ON HIS SHOULDERS?

Not the world but the heavens.

Atlas was condemned to support the sky by Zeus after the Titans revolted against the Olympians. However, he is often shown holding up something that looks like the globe, most famously on the cover of a collection of maps by the Flemish geographer Mercator.

Closer inspection reveals that this globe was, in fact, the heavens, not the Earth. Furthermore, Mercator had actually named his volume, not after the Titan, but the mythical philosopher King Atlas of Mauretania (after whom the mountains are named) who was supposed to have produced the first such 'celestial' (as opposed to 'terrestrial') globe.

The volume became known as *Mercator's Atlas* and the name was applied to any collection of maps thereafter.

Gerard Mercator, the son of a cobbler, was born Gerard Kremer, in 1512. His surname meant 'market' in Flemish, so he latinised this to Mercator, meaning 'marketeer'.

Mercator was the father of modern cartography and arguably the most influential Belgian of all time.

His famous projection of 1569—the first attempt to portray the world accurately with straight lines of latitude and longitude—remains the most persuasive vision of 'the world' for most people. More importantly it enabled accurate navigation for the first time, giving the Age of Discovery its scientific basis.

Because of its distortions, Mercator's projection is now rarely used in maps and atlases: in 1989 the leading US cartographic associations asked for it to be eliminated altogether.

Oddly, that hasn't stopped NASA using it to map Mars.

HOW HIGH IS CLOUD NINE?

According to the International Cloud Atlas scale, Cloud 0 is the highest type of cloud, known as cirrus, the wispy streaks that can be as high as 12,000 metres (nearly 40,000 feet).

Cloud Nine is the cumulonimbus, the massive, brooding thunder cloud. It's at the bottom of the scale because a single cloud can cover the whole range from as low as a few hundred feet to the very edge of the stratosphere (15,000 metres or nearly 50,00 feet).

As with the origins of most phrases, it's unlikely that 'cloud nine' can be tied to one specific source. Clouds seven, eight and thirty-nine have all been recorded, so it seems likely that people settled on nine because it's regarded as a lucky number ('dressed up to the nines' and 'the whole nine yards' have equally obscure origins). And the idea of being carried along on a big billowy cloud is undeniably attractive.

The International Cloud Atlas was published in 1896, as a result of the International Meteorological Conference establishing a Cloud Committee to agree an international system for the naming and identification of clouds.

The ten categories were themselves based on the

pioneering work of Luke Howard (1772–1864), an English chemist, who published his *Essay on the Modification of Clouds* in 1802.

Howard's work was influenced by his experience of freak weather conditions as a child, when volcanic eruptions in Japan and Iceland in 1783 created a 'Great Fogg' which covered much of Europe.

His work inspired the landscape paintings of John Constable, J. M. W. Turner and Caspar David Friedrich. Goethe wrote four poems in Howard's honour and considered this modest English Quaker to be the 'Godfather of Clouds'.

Clouds are collections of tiny water droplets or ice crystals held in suspension in the atmosphere. The droplets or crystals are formed by the condensation of water vapour around even smaller particles of things like smoke or salt. These are called condensation nuclei.

Cirrus clouds are the only clouds in the sky made entirely of ice. They are much more common in the atmosphere than was once thought and help to regulate the Earth's temperature. They are often triggered by the condensation trails of high-flying jets.

When air traffic was stopped after 11 September 2001, daily temperature variation across the USA grew by up to $3\,°C$ over the following forty-eight hours as the cirrus protection shrank: letting more heat out by night and more sunlight in by day.

WHAT MAKES CHAMPAGNE FIZZ?

It's not carbon dioxide, it's dirt.

In a perfectly smooth, clean glass, carbon dioxide molecules would evaporate invisibly, so for a long time it was assumed that it was slight imperfections in the glass which enabled the bubbles to form.

However, new photographic techniques have shown that these nicks and grooves are much too small for bubbles to latch on to: it's the microscopic particles of dust and bits of fluff in the glass that enable them to form.

Technically speaking, the dirt/dust/ lint in the glass act as condensation nuclei for the dissolved carbon dioxide.

My only regret in life is that I did not drink more champagne.
JOHN MAYNARD KEYNES

According to Moët et Chandon, there are 250 million bubbles in the average bottle of champagne.

Chekhov's last words were 'I haven't had champagne for a long time.'

German medical etiquette of the time demanded that when there was no hope, the doctor would offer the patient a glass of champagne.

WHAT SHAPE IS A RAINDROP?

Raindrops are spherical, not teardrop-shaped.

Ball-bearing and lead-shot makers exploit this property of falling liquids in their manufacturing process: molten lead is dropped through a sieve from a great height into a cooling liquid, and comes out spherical.

Shot-drop towers used to be built for the purpose—until the Festival of Britain in 1951 there was one next to Waterloo Bridge in London.

At just over 71 m (234 feet) Phoenix Shot Tower in Baltimore (still standing) was the tallest building in America until the Washington Monument surpassed it after the Civil War.

WHAT PRODUCES MOST OF THE EARTH'S OXYGEN?

Algae.

They release oxygen as a waste-product of photosynthesis. Their net oxygen output is higher than that produced by all the trees and other land-based plants put together.

Ancient algae are also the main constituent of oil and gas.

Blue-green algae or cyanobacteria (from Greek *kyanos*—'dark greeny blue') is Earth's earliest known life form, with fossils that date back 3.6 billion years.

While some algae are included with the plants in the Eukaryote domain (*eu*, 'true', and *karyon*, 'nut', referring to their cells having true nuclei, which bacteria don't), the cyanobacteria are now firmly in the Bacteria kingdom, with their own phylum.

One form of cyanobacteria, spirulina, yields twenty times more protein per acre than soya beans. It consists of 70 per cent protein (compared with beef's 22 per cent), 5 per cent fat, no cholesterol and an impressive array of vitamins and minerals. Hence the increasing popularity of the spirulina smoothie.

It also boosts the immune system, particularly the production of protein interferons, the body's front-line defence against viruses and tumour cells.

The nutritional and health benefits of spirulina were recognised centuries ago by the Aztecs, sub-Saharan Africans and flamingos.

Its significance for the future may be that algae can be grown on land that isn't fertile, using (and recycling) brackish water. It's a crop that doesn't cause soil erosion, requires no fertilisers or pesticides and refreshes the atmosphere more than anything else that grows.

WHAT WERE FIRST WORLD WAR GERMAN UNIFORMS MADE FROM?

Nettles.

During the First World War, both Germany and Austria ran short on supplies of cotton.

In search of a suitable replacement, scientists chanced upon an ingenious solution: mixing very small quantities of cotton with nettles—specifically, the hardy fibres of the stinging nettle (*Urtica dioica*).

Without any form of systematic production, the Germans cultivated 1.3 million kg of this material in 1915, and a further 2.7 million kg the following year.

After a brief struggle, the British captured two German overalls in 1917, and their construction was analysed with some surprise.

Nettles have many advantages over cotton for agriculture—cotton needs a lot of watering, it only grows in a warm climate, and requires a lot of pesticide treatment if it is to be grown economically.

There's no danger of being stung by a 'full nettle jacket' either, as the stinging hairs—little hypodermic syringes made of silica and filled with poison—are not used in production. The long fibres in the stems are all that are useful.

The Germans were by no means the first to stumble across this plant's many uses. Archaeological remains from around Europe reveal that it's been used for tens of thousands of years for fishing nets, twine and cloth.

The Bottle Inn, a pub in Marshwood, Dorset, England, holds an annual World Stinging Nettle Eating Championship. Rules are strict: no gloves, no mouth-numbing drugs (other than beer) and no regurgitation.

The trick appears to be to fold the top of the nettle leaf towards you and push it past your lips before swigging it down with ale. A dry mouth, they say, is a sore mouth. The winner is the one who has the longest set of bare stalks at the end of an hour.

The current record is 14.6 m (48 feet) for men, and about 8 m (26 feet) for women.

WHO DISCOVERED PENICILLIN?

Sir Alexander Fleming is a long way down the list.

Bedouin tribesmen in North Africa have made a healing ointment from the mould on donkey harnesses for over a thousand years.

In 1897, a young French army doctor called Ernest Duchesne rediscovered this by observing how Arab stable boys used the mould from damp saddles to treat saddle sores.

He conducted thorough research identifying the mould as *Penicillium glaucum,* used it to cure typhoid in guinea pigs and noted its destructive effect on *E. coli* bacteria. It was the first clinically tested use of what came to be called penicillin.

He sent in the research as his doctoral thesis, urging further study, but the Institut Pasteur didn't even acknowledge receipt of his work, perhaps because he was only twenty-three and a completely unknown student.

Army duties intervened and he died in obscurity in 1912 of tuberculosis—a disease his own discovery would later help to cure.

Duchesne was posthumously honoured in 1949, five years after Sir Alexander Fleming had received his Nobel Prize for his re-rediscovery of the antibiotic effect of penicillin.

One sometimes finds what one is not looking for.
ALEXANDER FLEMING

Fleming coined the word 'penicillin' in 1929. He accidentally noticed the antibiotic properties of a mould which he identified as *Penicillium rubrum*. In fact, he got the species wrong. It was correctly identified many years later by Charles Thom as *Penicillium notatum*.

The mould was originally named *Penicillium* because, under a microscope, its spore-bearing arms were thought to look like tiny paintbrushes. The Latin for a writer's paintbrush is *penicillum*, the same word from which 'pencil' comes. In fact, what the mould cells of *Penicillium notatum* much more closely and spookily resemble is the hand-bones of a human skeleton. There is a picture of it here:

http://botit.botany.wisc.edu/Toms_fungi/nov2003.html

Stilton, Roquefort, Danish Blue, Gorgonzola, Camembert, Limburger and Brie all contain penicillin.

WHAT CAUSES STOMACH ULCERS?

It's not stress or spicy food.

Contrary to decades of medical advice to the contrary, it turns out that stomach and intestinal ulcers are not caused by stress or lifestyle but by bacteria.

Ulcers are still relatively common, afflicting one in ten people. They are painful and potentially lethal. Napoleon and James Joyce both died from complications connected with stomach ulcers.

In the early 1980s, two Australian pathologists, Barry Marshall and Robin Warren, noticed that a previously unidentified bacterium colonised the bottom part of the stomachs of people who suffered from gastritis or ulcers. They cultivated it, gave it a name (*Helicobacter pylori*), and began to run trials. They found that when the bacteria were eliminated, the ulcers healed.

Even today, most people still think that ulcers are caused by stress. The medical explanation was that stress diverted blood from the stomach, which reduced the production of its protective mucus lining. This gradually left the tissue beneath vulnerable to stomach acid and the result was an ulcer.

What Marshall and Warren were proposing—that a common physiological condition, akin to a blister or a bruise, might actually be an infectious disease—was unprecedented in modern medicine.

Marshall decided to become his own experiment. He drank a Petri dish full of the bacteria, and soon came down with a severe case of gastritis. He tested himself for the bacteria—his stomach was teeming with them—and then cured himself with a course of antibiotics. The medical establishment had been proved wrong.

In 2005, Marshall and Warren were rewarded for their tenacity and vision, winning the Nobel Prize for Medicine.

Helicobacter pylori is present in half the human population, and in almost everyone in developing countries. It is usually contracted in early childhood and can stay in the stomach for life. It only leads to ulcers in 10 to 15 per cent of those infected.

We still don't know why this should be, but we do know how to treat it.

WHAT ARE GUINEA PIGS USED FOR?

Lunch.

Guinea pigs, or cavies, are almost never used for vivisection these days, but Peruvians consume an estimated 65 million of them each year. They are also eaten in Colombia, Bolivia and Ecuador. The best bits are the cheeks, apparently.

Ninety-nine per cent of laboratory animals are mice and rats, and more rabbits and chickens are used as 'guinea pigs' than guinea pigs are.

Rats and mice are easier to manipulate genetically and can be made to model a greater range of human conditions than guinea pigs, which were much more popular victims of medical research in the nineteenth century. In 1890, the antitoxin for diphtheria was discovered using guinea pigs and saved the lives of millions of children.

One area where they are still used today is in the study of anaphylactic shock. They are also useful in nutritional research because guinea pigs are the only mammals (apart from primates) that cannot synthesise their own vitamin C and have to absorb it through their food.

Ordinary guinea pigs weigh on average 250 g (about half a pound) to 700 g (around a pound and a half), but researchers at La Molina National University in Peru have developed guinea pigs that weigh a kilogram (or over 2 lb), which they hope will catch on in the export market. The meat is low in fat and cholesterol and tastes like rabbit.

In Peru, the animals are kept in the kitchen because of the ancient Andean belief that they need smoke, and folk doctors in the Andes use guinea pigs to detect illness in people—they believe that when the rodent is pressed against a sick person, it will squeak when near the source of disease. In the cathedral of the city of Cuzco, Peru, there's a painting of the Last Supper in which Jesus and the disciples are shown about to eat roast guinea pig.

In 2003, archaeologists in Venezuela discovered the fossilised remains of a huge guinea pig-like creature that lived eight million years ago. *Phoberomys pattersoni* was the size of a cow and weighed 1,400 times more than the average pet guinea pig.

Nobody really knows where the expression 'guinea pig' comes from but the most likely suggestion is that they reached Europe as part of the triangle of slave-trade routes that linked South America to the Guinea coast of West Africa.

WHAT WAS THE FIRST ANIMAL IN SPACE?

The fruit fly.

The tiny astronauts were loaded on to an American V2 rocket along with some corn seeds, and blasted into space in July 1946. They were used to test the effects of exposure to radiation at high altitudes.

Fruit flies are a lab favourite. Three-quarters of known human disease genes have a match in the genetic code of fruit flies They also go to sleep every night, react in a similar way to general anaesthetics and, best of all, reproduce very quickly. You can have a whole new generation in a fortnight.

Space is defined as starting at an altitude of 100 km (62 miles). After fruit flies, we sent first moss, then monkeys.

The first monkey in space was Albert II in 1949, reaching 134 km (83 miles). His predecessor, Albert I, had suffocated to death a year earlier, before reaching the 100 km barrier. Unfortunately, Albert II also died, when the parachute on his capsule failed on landing.

It took until 1951 for a monkey to return safely from space, when Albert VI and his eleven mice companions managed it (although he died two hours later).

197

Generally, pioneering space monkeys were not distinguished by their longevity, with the honourable exception of Baker, the squirrel monkey, who survived his 1959 mission by twenty-five years.

The Russians preferred dogs. The first animal in orbit was Laika on Sputnik 2 (1957), who died of heat stress during the flight. At least ten more dogs were launched into space before the first man, Yuri Gagarin, made it up there in 1961. Six of the dogs survived.

The Russians also sent the first animal into deep space in 1968. It was a Horsefield's tortoise and it became the first living creature to orbit the moon (as well as the world's fastest tortoise).

Space isn't remote at all. It's only an hour's drive away if your car could go straight upwards.
FRED HOYLE

Other animals in space have included chimps (who all survived), guinea pigs, frogs, rats, cats, wasps, beetles, spiders and a very hardy fish called the mummichog. The first Japanese animals in space were ten newts in 1985.

The only survivors of the Columbia space-shuttle disaster in 2003 were some nematode worms from the shuttle's lab found among the debris.

WHICH HAS THE MOST NECK BONES, A MOUSE OR A GIRAFFE?

They both have seven neck vertebrae, as do all mammals except for manatees and sloths.

Because two-toed sloths have only six neck vertebrae, they find it hard to turn their heads.

Birds, who need to turn their heads a lot to preen, have many more neck vertebrae than mammals. Owls have fourteen; ducks, sixteen; but the record-holder is the mute swan with twenty-five.

Owls can't turn their head through 360°, as some people claim, but they do manage 270°. This is made possible by the extra vertebrae and specialised muscles that allow the bones to move independently of one another.

It compensates for the fact that owls can't move their eyes. If they want to change their view, they have to swivel their head.

An owl's eyes are forward-facing to increase their binocular vision, which is the ability to see things in three dimensions. This is essential for hunting at night. Their eyes are also very large to capture as much light as possible. If we had eyes on the same scale, they'd be the size of grapefruits.

Owls' eyes are tubular rather than spherical to create an even larger retina. A tawny owl's eyes are one hundred times more sensitive to light than ours. They can still see a mouse on the ground if the light level is reduced to a single candle 500 metres (about 547 yards) away.

HOW LONG HAVE THE CELTS LIVED IN BRITAIN?

Since 21 June 1792.

It was then that a group of London 'bards' staged an entirely invented ceremony on Primrose Hill in London, involving a stone circle made from pebbles, and claimed they were reviving a ritual that stretched back to the ancient Celtic nation and its Druids.

Prior to this, there is no record of the word 'Celt' having been used to describe the pre-Roman inhabitants of Britain or Ireland and it was certainly never a term they used to describe themselves.

The word 'Celt' was coined by the Greek historian Herodotus in 450 BC when he described the peoples of the headwaters of the Danube north of the Alps.

The Roman name for such people was *Galli* ('chicken people') and they called the inhabitants of the British Isles *Britanni*, never Celts.

The use of the term 'Celt' in English dates from the seventeenth century.

A Welsh linguist living in Oxford called Edward Lluyd noted the similarities between the languages spoken in Ireland, Scotland, Wales, Cornwall and Brittany. He called these languages 'Celtic' and the name stuck.

The word 'Celtic' has also been used to describe the curly-wurly style of design found in Irish gift-shops. There is no evidence to suggest that this was produced by an ethnically homogeneous group of people.

Most historians believe the language and culture we call 'Celtic' spread by contact not invasion. People 'became' Celtic by adopting the architecture, fashions and ways of speaking because they were useful or attractive, not because they belonged to the same ethnic group.

The romantic notion of a Celtic Empire of horse-loving master craftsmen, wise old Druids, harp-strumming poets, and fierce bearded warriors is the product of the Celtic Revival that started in the late eighteenth century.

It has more to do with modern Irish, Welsh and Scottish nationalism than with any historical reality.

WHO WAS THE FIRST MAN TO CIRCUMNAVIGATE THE GLOBE?

Henry the Black.

An unfamiliar name to almost everyone, Enrique de Malaca was Magellan's slave and interpreter.

Ferdinand Magellan himself never completed his circumnavigation. He was killed in the Philippines in 1521, when he was only halfway round.

Magellan first visited the Far East in 1511, arriving from Portugal across the Indian Ocean. He found Henry the Black in a slave market in Malaysia in 1511 and took him back to Lisbon the way he had come.

Henry accompanied Magellan on all his subsequent voyages, including the round the world attempt which set off in 1519. This went in the other direction, across the Atlantic and the Pacific oceans, so when it arrived in the Far East in 1521, Henry became the first man to have been right round the world.

No one knows where Henry the Black was born—he was probably captured and sold into slavery by Sumatran pirates as a child—but when he arrived in the Philippines, he found the locals spoke his native language.

After Magellan's death, the expedition continued on its way, successfully completing the circumnavigation under Juan Sebastián Elcano, the Basque second-in-command.

Henry the Black was not with them. Elcano had refused to honour the promise made in Magellan's will to release Henry from slavery, so he escaped and was never seen again.

Juan Sebastián Elcano gets the credit for being the first man to travel round the world in a single trip.

He returned to Seville in September 1522. Five ships had set sail four years earlier but only the *Victoria* made it back. It was full of spices, but just eighteen of the original crew of 264 had survived: scurvy, malnutrition and skirmishes with indigenous peoples had accounted for the rest.

The Spanish king awarded Elcano a coat of arms depicting the globe and carrying the motto 'You first circumnavigated me'.

Henry the Black is a national hero in several South-East Asian nations.

WHO WAS THE FIRST TO CLAIM THAT THE EARTH GOES ROUND THE SUN?

Aristarchus of Samos, born 310 BC, a whole 1,800 years before Copernicus.

Not only did Aristarchus suggest the Earth and planets travelled round the Sun, he also calculated the relative sizes and distances of the Earth, Moon and Sun and worked out that the heavens were not a celestial sphere, but a universe of almost infinite size. But no one paid much attention.

Aristarchus was most famous in his lifetime as a mathematician not an astronomer. We don't know much about him, except that he studied at the Lyceum at Alexandria and is later mentioned by the Roman architect Vitruvius as a man who was 'knowledgeable across all branches of science'. He also invented a hemispherical sundial.

Only one of his works has survived, *On the Sizes and Distances of the Sun and Moon*. Unfortunately, it doesn't mention his sun-centred theory. The reason we know about it at all is due to a single remark in one of Archimedes' texts, which mentions Aristarchus' theories only to disagree with them.

Copernicus was certainly aware of Aristarchus because he credits him in the manuscript of his epoch-making *On the Revolutions of the Heavenly Spheres*. However, when the book was printed in 1514, all mentions of the visionary Greek had been removed, presumably by the publisher, nervous of it undermining the book's claims for originality.

WHO INVENTED THE THEORY OF RELATIVITY?

It wasn't Einstein. The theory of relativity was first stated by Galileo Galilei in his *Dialogue concerning the World's Two Chief Systems* in 1632.

To understand relativity we need to understand the theory that it replaced. This was the theory of 'absolute rest' postulated by Aristotle in the fourth century BC which stated that rest was the natural state of any object and that an object would return to this state if left to its own devices.

The theory of relativity says that the motion of all objects is relative to the motion of each other, and that to define one as being 'at rest' is simply a matter of convention. It follows from this that the speed of an object cannot be stated absolutely—only as 'relative' to something else.

Galileo, the Italian astronomer and philosopher,

203

was also one of the founders of modern physics. He is most famous for his support of the 'Copernican' (or Aristarchan) theory, that the Earth went round the Sun.

The Catholic Church rounded smartly on him, but Galileo did not rot in a rat-infested cell for his principles. He began his sentence in the luxurious home of the Archbishop of Siena, before being taken back to a comfortable house arrest in his villa near Florence. It wasn't until 1992 that the Catholic Church finally admitted that Galileo's views on the solar system were correct.

While Galileo may have been right about this, he was perfectly capable of making mistakes: his favourite argument for a moving Earth was that this movement caused the tides. He observed that the Mediterranean is more tidal than the Red Sea, and attributed this to the water being sloshed about by the Earth's spin—which he said acted more strongly on the Mediterranean because it is aligned East-West.

This argument was refuted by the eyewitness testimony of seafarers, who pointed out that there were two tides a day, not one as Galileo had assumed. Galileo refused to believe them.

Albert Einstein realised that Galileo had also made a mistake in his theory of relativity, or rather that the theory broke down in special circumstances.

Einstein's 1905 work, *On the Electrodynamics of Moving Bodies*, was the first to talk about the Special Theory of Relativity, which describes the strange properties of particles moving at close to the speed of light in a vacuum.

The General Theory of Relativity, which applied the special theory to large-scale phenomena like gravity, was published ten years later in 1915.

WHAT SHAPE DID COLUMBUS THINK THE EARTH WAS?

a) Flat
b) Round
c) Pear-shaped
d) An oblate spheroid

Columbus himself never said the world was round—he thought it was pear-shaped and about a quarter of its actual size.

Despite his later reputation, his voyage of 1492 wasn't intended to discover a new continent but to prove that Asia was much closer than anyone imagined. He was wrong.

Columbus never actually set foot on mainland America—the closest he came was the Bahamas (probably the small island of Plana Cays)—but made his crew swear an oath that, if asked, they would say they'd reached India. He died in Valladolid in 1506 and remained convinced to the end that he'd reached the coast of Asia.

There is a remarkable degree of uncertainty about Columbus. Most of the evidence points to him being the son of a Genoese weaver called Domenico Columbo, but there are enough inconsistencies for him to be claimed as Sephardic Jewish, Spanish, Corsican, Portuguese, Catalan or even Greek.

He spoke the Genovese dialect (not Italian) as his first tongue and learnt to read and write in Spanish (with a marked Portuguese accent) and Latin. He even wrote a secret diary in Greek.

We don't know what he looked like, as no

The fact that some geniuses were laughed at does not imply that all who are laughed at are geniuses. They laughed at Columbus, they laughed at Fulton, they laughed at the Wright Brothers. But they also laughed at Bozo the Clown.
CARL SAGAN

authentic portrait survives, but his son claimed he was blond until the age of thirty, whereupon his hair turned completely white.

We don't even know where he is buried. We do know his corpse had its flesh removed, as was the style for the great and the good in the sixteenth century, and that his bones were interred first in Valladolid, then in the Carthusian monastery in Seville, then in Santa Domingo, Cuba, then Havana, then, and apparently finally, in Seville Cathedral in 1898.

However, a casket with his name on remains in Santa Domingo and now Genoa and Pavia have also made competing claims to hold bits of him. DNA tests are under way, but it seems likely that the final resting place of Columbus—or Columbo, or Colón (as he preferred)—will remain as contentious as the rest of his life and achievements.

WHAT SHAPE DID MEDIEVAL PEOPLE THINK THE EARTH WAS?

Not what you think.

Since around the fourth century BC, almost no one, anywhere, has believed that the Earth is flat. However, if you did want to show the Earth as a flat disc, you'd end up with something very similar to the United Nations flag.

Belief in a flat Earth may not even have actually originated until the nineteenth century. The guilty text was Washington Irving's semi-fictional *The Life and Voyages of Christopher Columbus* (1828) which, incorrectly, suggests that Columbus's voyage was made to prove the world was round.

The idea of a flat Earth was first seriously put forward in 1838 by the eccentric Englishman Samuel Birley Rowbotham who published a sixteen-page paper entitled: 'Zetetic Astronomy: A Description of Several Experiments which Prove that the Surface of the Sea Is a Perfect Plane and that the Earth Is Not a Globe' ('Zetetic' derives from the Greek *zetein*, meaning 'to search, or inquire').

More than a century later, a member of the Royal Astronomical Society and devout Christian called Samuel Shenton re-branded the Universal Zetetic Society as the International Flat Earth Society.

The NASA space programme of the 1960s, culminating in the lunar landings, should have buried the issue. But Shenton was undeterred. Looking at photographs of a spherical earth taken from space, he commented: 'It's easy to see how a photograph like that could fool the untrained eye.' The Apollo landings were, apparently, a Hollywood hoax, scripted by Arthur C. Clarke. Membership shot up.

Shenton died in 1971 but not before choosing his successor as President of the Society. The odd but charismatic Charles K. Johnson took over and made the Society a rallying point for a heroic, homespun 'anti-Big Science' movement. By the early 1990s, membership had surged to over 3,500.

Johnson, who lived and worked in the vast flatness of the Mojave desert, proposed a world in which we live on a disc, with the North Pole at its centre, surrounded by a 150-foot-high perimeter wall of ice. The Sun and Moon are both 32 miles in diameter, and the stars are 'about as far away as San Francisco is from Boston'.

Johnson's desert hideaway burnt down in 1995, destroying all the Society's archives and membership lists. Johnson died in 2001, by which time the Society had shrunk to a few hundred members. It exists today solely as a web forum, www.theflatearthsociety.org, with around 800 registered users.

WHO FIRST DISCOVERED THAT THE WORLD WAS ROUND?

Not who, what. Bees worked it out first.

Honeybees have evolved a complex language to tell each other where the best nectar is, using the sun as a reference point. Amazingly, they can also do this on overcast days and at night, by calculating the position of the sun *on the other side of the world*. This means they can actually learn and store information, despite having a brain 1.5 million times smaller than our own.

A bee's brain has about 950,000 neurons. A human brain has between 100 and 200 billion.

Honeybees have an in-built 'map' of the sun's movements across the sky over twenty-four hours and can modify this map to fit local conditions very quickly—all decisions about where to fly are made within five seconds.

The honeybee is also more sensitive to the Earth's magnetic field than any other creature. They use this for navigation and for making the honeycomb panels of their hives. If a strong magnet is put next to a hive under construction, a strange cylindrical comb results, unlike anything found in nature.

The temperature of a beehive is the same as that of a human body.

Bees evolved about 150 million years ago in the Cretaceous period, roughly at the same time as flowering plants. The honeybee family, *Apis*, didn't appear until 25 million years ago. They are really a form of vegetarian wasp.

Bees smell with their antennae. Queen honeybees give off a chemical called 'queen-substance' which prevents worker bees developing ovaries.

It takes the entire lifetimes of twelve bees to make enough honey to fill a teaspoon. Bees will travel as much as 12 km (7.5 miles) per trip, several times a day. A single bee would have to travel about 75,000 km (46,600 miles) to make a pound of honey (or less than half a kilo), which is almost twice round the world.

WHY DO BEES BUZZ?

To communicate.

Bees use their buzzing much as they use their movements, or 'dancing': to pass on information. Ten distinct sounds have been identified and some have been linked to specific activities.

The most obvious of these uses is 'fanning' to cool the hive. It is loud and steady at about 250 beats per second, and is amplified by the hive itself. Bees also buzz more loudly to signal danger (anyone who has approached a hive will have noticed the change in tone) followed by a sequence of 500 beats per second pulses to sound the 'all clear' and calm the hive.

The queen bee has a particularly rich range of sounds. When a new queen hatches she makes a high-pitched chirrup called 'piping' or 'tooting'. Her sisters (still curled up inside their cells) answer with a croak-like call called 'quarking'. This is a big mistake: there can only be one queen. Using the 'quarks' as a guide, the hatched queen picks each off in turn, tearing open their cells and either stinging them to death or ripping their heads off.

Bees use their legs to hear: sound 'messages' in the hive are communicated through the intensity of the vibration. However, recent research into bees' antennae suggest that as well as the chemical receptors they use to 'smell', the antennae are covered in eardrum-like plates, which might be 'ears'.

This would explain why other workers touch the dancing bee's thorax with their antennae rather than the 'waggling' abdomen during the 'waggle dance'—

they are hearing the directions to the nectar rather than seeing them. After all, it's dark in a hive.

How bees buzz is more controversial. Until recently, the main theory was that they used the fourteen breathing holes along their sides (called 'spiracles') rather as a trumpeter controls the sound of his instrument with his lips.

Entomologists at the University of California have ruled out this theory by carefully blocking the spiracles. The bees still buzzed.

The latest hypothesis is that buzzing is partly caused by the vibration of the wings, with some amplification from the thorax. Clipping a bee's wings doesn't stop the buzzing, though it does change its timbre and intensity.

WHAT HAS THE LARGEST BRAIN IN COMPARISON TO ITS SIZE?

a) Elephants
b) Dolphins
c) Ants
d) Humans

The ant.

An ant's brain is about 6 per cent of its total body weight—if we were to apply the same percentage to humans, our heads would have to be nearly three times as large, making us all look rather like the Mekon or Morrissey.

An average human brain weighs 1.6 kg (3.5 lb), which is a little over 2 per cent of body weight. An

211

ant's brain weighs approximately 0.3 mg.

Although an ant's brain has only a fraction of the neurons of a human brain, a colony of ants is a super-organism. An average-sized nest of 40,000 ants has about the same number of brain cells as a person.

Ants have been around for 130 million years and there are about 10,000 trillion of them at large as we speak. The total mass of ants on the planet is slightly heavier than the total mass of human beings.

There are about 8,000 known species of ant. Ants account for about 1 per cent of all the insects on earth. The total number of insects in the world has been calculated at one quintillion (or 1,000,000,000,000,000,000.

Ants sleep for only a few minutes a day and can survive for nineteen days under water. A wood ant can manage for twenty-four days without its head. A single ant cannot live alone outside the colony, head on or not.

Ants are so much like human beings as to be an embarrassment. They farm fungi, raise aphids as livestock, launch armies into war, use chemical sprays to alarm and confuse enemies, capture slaves, engage in child labour, exchange information ceaselessly. They do everything but watch television.
LEWIS THOMAS

Ants appear to have photographic memories to help them navigate. They seem to take a series of snapshots of landmarks. Scientists do not understand how ants' tiny brains can store so much information.

Ants are not stronger than people. Though ants can lift many times their own weight, this is only because they are small. The smaller an animal is, the stronger its

212

muscles are in relation to its body mass. If people were the same size as ants, they would be equally strong.

HOW MUCH OF OUR BRAINS DO WE USE?

One hundred per cent.

Or 3 per cent.

It's commonly said we only use 10 per cent of our brain. This usually leads to discussions of what we might do if only we could harness the other 90 per cent.

In fact, all of the human brain is used at one time or another. On the other hand, a recent paper by Peter Lennie of the New York University Center for Neural Science indicates that the brain should ideally have no more than 3 per cent of neurons firing at any one time, otherwise the energy needed to 'reset' each neuron after it fires becomes too much for the brain to handle.

The central nervous system consists of the brain and the spinal cord and is made of two kinds of cells: neurons and glia.

Neurons are the basic information processors, receiving input and sending output between each other. Input arrives through the neuron's branch-like dendrites; output leaves through the cable-like axons.

Each neuron may have as many as 10,000 dendrites but only has one axon. The axon may be thousands of times longer than the tiny cell body of the neuron itself. The largest axon in a giraffe is 4.5 metres (15 feet) long.

Synapses are the junctions between axons and dendrites, where electrical impulses are turned into

213

chemical signals. The synapses are like switches, linking neurons to one another and making the brain into a network.

Glia cells provide the structural framework of the brain, they manage the neurons and provide a housekeeping function, removing debris after neurons die. There are fifty times more glia than neurons in the brain.

There are nearly five million km (about three million miles) of axons, one quadrillion (1,000,000,000,000,000) synapses, and up to 200 billion neurons in a single human brain. If the neurons were spread out side by side they would cover 25,000 square metres (nearly 30,000 square yards): the size of four football fields.

The number of ways information is exchangeable in the brain is greater than the number of atoms in the universe. With such astonishing potential, whatever percentage of our brains we use, we could all, clearly, do a little better.

WHAT COLOUR IS YOUR BRAIN?

So long as you're alive, it's pink. The colour comes from the blood vessels. Without fresh oxygenated blood (as when it's removed from the body) the human brain appears grey.

To confuse things, about 40 per cent of the living brain is made of so-called 'grey matter' and 60 per cent of 'white matter'. These terms are not accurate descriptions of the colours you see, but thinly sliced, and in section, they are clearly two different kinds of brain tissue.

Using brain scans, we have begun to understand what functions they each perform. Grey matter contains the cells where the actual 'processing' of information is done. It consumes about 94 per cent of the oxygen used by the brain.

The white matter is a fatty protein called *myelin* which sheaths and insulates the dendrites and axons that extend out from the cells. It is the brain's communication network, linking different parts of the grey matter together and linking the grey matter to the rest of the body.

A good analogy is the computer. The grey matter is a processor, the white matter is the wiring. What we call intelligence requires both to work together at high speed.

Now it gets even more interesting. Recent studies at the Universities of California and New Mexico scanned the brains of men and women with identical IQs. The results were surprising: the men had six and a half times more grey matter than women, and women had nearly ten times more white matter than men.

The women's white matter was found in a high concentration in the frontal lobes, whereas the men had none. This is significant, as the frontal lobes are believed to play a key role in emotional control, personality and judgement.

So, all the various 'Mars and Venus' theories of gender difference might find soon find a physiological justification. Men's and women's brains do seem to be differently wired and configured. The output (intelligence) is the same, but the way it is produced is very different.

WHAT EFFECT DOES ALCOHOL HAVE ON BRAIN CELLS?

Good news. Alcohol doesn't 'kill' brain cells. It just makes new cells grow less quickly.

The idea that alcohol destroys brain cells dates back at least as far as the temperance campaigners of the early nineteenth century, who wanted all alcoholic drinks banned. It has no basis in scientific fact.

Samples from alcoholics and non-alcoholics show no significant difference in either the overall number or the density of neurons between the two groups. Many other studies have shown that moderate drinking can in fact help cognition. A study in Sweden showed that *more* brain cells are grown in mice that are given alcohol.

Alcohol abuse does causes serious damage, not least to the brain, but there is no evidence that these problems are to do with the death of cells—it's more likely that alcohol interferes with the working processes of the brain.

A hangover comes from the brain shrinking due to dehydration, causing the brain to tug on its covering membrane. It's the membrane which is sore. The brain itself feels nothing, even if you stick a knife in it.

The philtrum is the vertical groove on your upper lip that nobody knows the word for. It allows you to drink beer from the bottle by letting the air in.

If you were to open a beer can in zero gravity all

the beer would come out at once and float around in spherical droplets.

What is said when drunk has been thought out beforehand.
FLEMISH PROVERB

Astronomers have recently discovered a massive amount of alcohol in our region of the Milky Way. The giant cloud of methanol measures 463 billion km (288 billion miles) across. Although the alcohol we like to drink is grain alcohol (otherwise known as ethyl alcohol or ethanol) and methanol would poison us, the discovery goes some way to supporting the theory that the universe is here so that we can drink it.

WHAT DO DOLPHINS DRINK?

They don't drink at all.

Dolphins are like animals in a desert, without any access to fresh water. They get liquid from their food (which is mainly fish and squid) and by burning their body fat, which releases water.

Dolphins are whales—the killer whale is the largest member of the dolphin family. Their name is a reversal of the original Spanish, *asesina-ballenas*, meaning 'whale killer'. They were so called because packs of them sometimes hunt and kill much larger whales.

Pliny the Elder didn't help their reputation. According to him, an orca 'cannot be properly depicted or described except as an enormous mass of flesh armed with savage teeth'.

Dolphins have up to 260 teeth, more than any other

mammal. Despite this, they swallow fish whole. Their teeth are used solely to grasp prey.

Dolphins sleep by shutting down one half of their brain and the opposite eye at a time. The other half of the brain stays awake, while the other eye watches out for predators and obstacles, and remembers to go to the surface to breathe. Two hours later, the sides flip. This procedure is called 'logging'.

Dolphins have been working for the US Navy since the Vietnam War, where they saw extensive service. The US Navy currently employs about a hundred dolphins and thirty other assorted sea mammals. Six sea lions have recently been posted to join the Task Force in Iraq.

After Hurricane Katrina, a story circulated that thirty-six US Navy-trained attack dolphins had escaped and were roaming the sea armed with toxic dart guns. The story seems to have been a hoax; apart from anything else, 'military' dolphins aren't trained for attack, only for finding things.

WHAT WAS JAMES BOND'S FAVOURITE DRINK?

Not the vodka martini.

A painstaking study at www.atomicmartinis.com of Fleming's complete oeuvre has shown that James Bond consumed a drink, on average, every seven pages.

Of the 317 drinks consumed in total, his preferred tipple was whisky by a long margin—he drinks 101 in all, among them fifty-eight bourbons and thirty-eight Scotches. He's pretty fond of champagne (thirty glasses) and in one book, *You Only Live Twice* (1964), which is mostly set in Japan, Bond tries sake. He likes it: he has thirty-five of them.

Bond only opts for his supposed favourite, vodka martini, nineteen times, and he drinks almost as many gin martinis (sixteen—though most of these are bought for him by other people).

The famous 'shaken, not stirred' line appears for the first time in *Diamonds are Forever* (1956) but isn't used by Bond himself until *Dr No* (1959). Sean Connery was the first screen Bond to utter 'shaken, not shtirred', in *Goldfinger* (1964), and it occurs in most of the films thereafter. In 2005, the American Film Institute voted it the 90th greatest movie quote of all time.

James Bond's personal martini recipe, taken from the first book, *Casino Royale* (1953), is: 'Three measures of Gordon's, one of vodka, half a measure of Kina Lillet. Shake it very well until it's ice-cold, then add a large thin slice of lemon-peel.'

This is the only time he drinks a gin and vodka mix. He calls it the Vesper, after Vesper Lynd, the double agent and love interest in the novel. She is also the girl who drinks most in all the novels and stories.

Why does Bond insist on 'shaken' martinis? Strictly speaking, a shaken gin martini is called a Bradford. Purists frown on them because the intake of air caused by the shaking oxidises—or 'bruises'— the aromatic flavourings in the gin. But there's no such problem with vodka, and the action of shaking makes the drink colder and sharper.

Ian Fleming himself preferred his martinis shaken, and made with gin. On his doctor's orders he switched from drinking gin to bourbon later in life, which may explain his hero's predilection. Fleming and Bond were both men who knew what they liked.

WHAT SHOULDN'T YOU DRINK IF YOU'RE DEHYDRATED?

Alcohol is fine. So are tea and coffee.

Virtually any fluid will help to hydrate you, although you should steer clear of seawater.

There's no scientific basis for the curious idea that fluids other than water cause dehydration. As a diuretic (something that makes you pass water), caffeine does cause a loss of water, but only a fraction of what you're adding by drinking the coffee. Tea, coffee, squash and milk for children are all equally good at replacing fluids.

Ron Maughan, Professor of Human Physiology at the University of Aberdeen Medical School, has looked at the effects of alcohol, considered to be another diuretic, and found that, in moderation, it too has little impact on the average person's state of fluid balance.

His results, published in the *Journal of Applied Physiology*, showed that alcoholic drinks with an alcohol content of less than 4 per cent, such as light beer and lager, can be used to stave off dehydration.

Seawater, on the other hand, is an emetic, so, if you drink it, you'll throw up. If you do manage to keep any of it down, then all the water in your body's cells will move towards the highly concentrated salty fluid, by osmosis, in an attempt to dilute it.

This will leave your cells dehydrated, and in

severe cases can lead to spasms, the breakdown of brain functions, and liver and kidney failure.

WHAT CONTAINS THE MOST CAFFEINE: A CUP OF TEA OR A CUP OF COFFEE?

A cup of coffee.

Dry tea-leaves contain a higher proportion of caffeine by weight than coffee beans. But an average *cup* of coffee contains about three times as much caffeine as an average cup of tea, because more beans are needed to make it.

If this is coffee, please bring me some tea; if this is tea, please bring me some coffee.
ABRAHAM LINCOLN

The amount of caffeine in coffee and tea depends on several factors. The higher the temperature of the water, the greater the caffeine extracted from beans or leaves. Espresso, which is made with pressurised steam, contains more caffeine, drop for drop, than brewed coffee. The amount of time that water is in contact with coffee beans or tea-leaves affects the caffeine content. Longer contact equals higher levels of caffeine.

Also important are the variety of coffee or tea, where it is grown, and the roast of the coffee and cut of the tea-leaf.

The darker the roast of coffee, the lower the caffeine content. With tea, the tips of the plant contain a higher concentration than the larger leaves.

Paradoxically, an average 30 ml (1 fl. oz) espresso contains about the same amount of caffeine as a 150 ml (5 fl. oz) cup of PG Tips. So a single-shot cappuccino or latte won't give you much more of a caffeine hit than a cuppa. A cup of instant coffee, on the other hand, contains only half the caffeine of a filter coffee.

WHAT KIND OF FRUIT ARE JAFFA CAKES MADE FROM?

Apricots.

The 'orange jam' at the heart of Britain's eighth most popular biscuit is actually apricot pulp, sugar, and a squirt of tangerine oil. This assertion appeared in the *Daily Telegraph* in September 2002.

(If it's not true perhaps someone from McVitie's would like to get in touch with us and correct this heinous slur. We note in passing that even the company's advertising refers to it as the 'smashing *orangey* bit' (our italics), which doesn't strictly imply the presence of actual oranges.)

It would take a 70-kg (11-stone) man a 90-minute football match to work off the 809 calories gained by a packet of Jaffa Cakes. Over 750 million Jaffa Cakes are eaten every year, generating sales of £25 million. If placed end to end, they would stretch from London to Australia and back again.

In 1991 McVitie's won a landmark case (United Biscuits (UK) Ltd v The Commissioners of Customs and Excise) to prove that Jaffa Cakes are, in fact, cakes not biscuits.

This was to avoid paying VAT—cakes and biscuits are zero-rated by the UK Customs and Excise, except for chocolate-coated biscuits, which are taxable as luxury items. McVitie's had to show that Jaffa Cakes were chocolate cakes, rather than chocolate biscuits.

The evidence turned on what happens when they go stale: like cakes, Jaffa Cakes grow harder, while biscuits become soft.

McVitie's is the third largest biscuit company in the world and is owned by United Biscuits. United Biscuits is owned, in turn, by Nabisco. Nabisco is owned by Kraft Foods Inc., the second largest food corporation in the world after Nestlé. Kraft has 98,000 employees and turned over $32 billion in 2004.

Kraft itself is 85 per cent owned by the Altria Group, formerly Philip Morris, the world's largest tobacco company.

WHAT DO DIGESTIVE BISCUITS DO?

Not a lot.

Digestive biscuits were invented by McVitie's in Edinburgh by a young employee, Alexander Grant, in 1892.

They were advertised as 'aiding digestion' (a euphemism for reducing wind) because of the high content of baking soda and coarse brown flour. This has never been scientifically proven and it is consequently illegal to sell them under that name in the USA. The US equivalent is the graham cracker.

McVitie's Original Digestive is still the ninth-biggest biscuit brand in Britain, with annual sales of £20m.

McVitie's best-selling biscuit and the second

biggest biscuit brand in Britain is the chocolate digestive launched in 1925. KitKat remains the biggest UK brand in the sector.

The annual sales of chocolate digestives are over £35m—that's 71 million packets, or 52 biscuits per second. Despite recent controversial mint, orange and caramel versions, it remains the chocolate biscuit of first resort. The American travel writer Bill Bryson has called it a 'British masterpiece'.

Biscuits are one of the oldest-known foods. Six-thousand-year-old biscuits have been found in Switzerland. They were eaten in ancient Egypt and were being baked in ancient Rome in the second century AD.

Biscuit means 'twice-cooked' in French, but the English came directly from the Latin *biscoctum panem*—'twice cooked bread'—and was, until the mid-eighteenth century, correctly spelt 'bisket'.

The adoption of the French spelling 'biscuit' (without the French pronunciation) was not only pretentious and pointless, but wrong as well. In French, *un biscuit* is not a biscuit but a cake—a sponge-cake to be precise. A biscuit in the English sense is *un biscuit sec*.

In North America 'biscuits' are more like scones. What Britons call biscuits, Americans call either cookies or crackers. The American English word cookie comes from the Dutch *koekje*, which means 'cake'.

Biscuits were cooked more than once to make them last longer than bread, but most biscuits are no longer cooked twice. In fact, most biscuits have never been cooked twice. According to Dr Johnson's *Dictionary*, biscuits designed for long sea voyages were usually cooked four times.

224

HOW WAS TEFLON DISCOVERED?

Despite persistent claims to the contrary, Teflon was not discovered as a by-product of the space programme.

Teflon is the trade name of polytetrafluoroethylene (PTFE), or fluoropolymer resin, discovered serendipitously by Roy Plunkett in 1938 and first sold commercially in 1946.

While experimenting with chlorofluorocarbons (CFCs) used in refrigeration, Plunkett found that a sample had frozen overnight into a whitish, waxy solid with unusual properties: it was extremely slippery as well as inert to virtually all chemicals, including highly corrosive acids.

His employers, DuPont, soon found a range of uses for the new material, initially in the Manhattan Project (the codename for the development of nuclear weapons in 1942–6) and subsequently in cookware.

No one has been able to find a precise source for the 'space programme' myth, except that the Apollo missions all depended on Teflon for cable insulation.

Other myths about Teflon include the belief that Teflon-coated bullets are better at piercing body armour than other kinds; actually the Teflon coating is there to reduce the amount of wear on the inside of the rifle barrel, and has no bearing on the effectiveness of the bullet.

Teflon does, however, have the lowest friction rating of any known solid material, which is why it works so well as a non-stick surface for frying pans.

If it's so slippery, how do they get it to stick to the pan? The process involves sandblasting to create tiny scratches on the pan's surface, then spraying on a thin coat of liquid Teflon which flows into the scratches. This is baked at high heat, causing the Teflon to harden and get a reasonably secure mechanical grip. It's then coated with a sealant and baked again.

WHICH ORGANISATION INVENTED QUAKER OATS?

Not the Quakers.

The Quaker Oats Company, started in Pennsylvania in 1901, was named after the Quakers because there were a lot of them in Pennsylvania and they had a reputation for honesty.

However, Quaker Oats, now part of the huge PepsiCo corporation, has no affiliation at all with the Quakers (or Religious Society of Friends) and, unlike the chocolate companies Cadbury's, Fry's and Rowntree, was not founded by Quakers, or established on Quaker principles.

This has caused some distress among The Society of Friends.

In the 1950s, researchers from Quaker Oats, Harvard University and the Massachusetts Institute of Technology conducted experiments to try to understand how nutrients from cereals travelled through the body.

Parents of educationally subnormal children at the Walter E. Fernald State School (formerly known as the Massachusetts School for Idiotic Children) were asked to let their children become members of a special Science Club. As part of the club, the children were put on a diet high in nutrients and taken to baseball games.

What was not made clear, however, was that the food the children were given was laced with iron and radioactive calcium so its path could be traced in the body. The parents sued the Quaker Oats company, who agreed to pay out $1.85 million to more than 100 participants in 1997.

The cheery character on the front of the box is sometimes said to be William Penn, the founder of Pennsylvania in 1682, and an influential Quaker. The Quaker Oats company, perhaps wishing to improve relations with the Society, has emphatically denied this.

It was painted by Haddon Sundblom in 1957, the artist who also created Coca Cola's iconic Santa Claus images in the 1930s. Sundblom's last commission was a Christmas cover for *Playboy* in the early 1970s.

It is often alleged that The Society of Friends got the nickname 'Quakers' following the trial for blasphemy in 1650 of George Fox, the founder of the movement, who suggested during sentencing that the judge should 'tremble at the word of the Lord'. However, the sect already had the reputation for 'trembling' in religious ecstasy and this seems a more likely source.

WHAT SHOULDN'T YOU DO TWENTY MINUTES AFTER EATING?

Swim, is the answer your parents would have given, but there's no evidence that normal swimming after

The chief danger in life is that you may take too many precautions.
ALFRED ADLER

normal eating is risky.

Swimming pools are not particularly dangerous places—according to government statistics you are much more likely to injure yourself taking off a pair of tights, chopping vegetables, walking the dog or pruning the hedge.

And keep well clear of cotton buds, cardboard boxes, vegetables, aromatherapy kits and loofahs. All of these things are becoming more dangerous.

The idea behind the popular injunction against swimming after eating—frequently posted at pools to this day—is that blood will be diverted from other muscles to the stomach, to assist in digesting food, leaving your limbs with insufficient blood, thus leading to paralysing cramps. (In less sophisticated versions, the weight of the food in your gut sinks you.)

Even if you overeat before swimming, the most likely result is a stitch in the side, or a touch of nausea. There is nothing intrinsically dangerous about the combination of food and water.

A greater risk is dehydration from not drinking, or weakness caused by fasting.

On the other hand, the Royal Society for the Prevention of Accidents (RoSPA) advocates 'common sense', arguing that there's at least a theoretical risk of regurgitation, which might be more dangerous in water than on land.

The 2002 RoSPA report revealed the following causes of accidents for one year in the UK:

Trainers	71,309
Tights	12,003

Cardboard boxes	10,492
Indoor swimming pool	8,795
Cotton buds	8,751
Trousers	8,455
Twigs	8,193
Aromatherapy	1,301
Loofahs and sponges	942

HOW DOES TELEVISION DAMAGE YOUR HEALTH?

Not by sitting too close to one.

Until the late 1960s, cathode-ray-tube television sets emitted extremely low levels of ultraviolet radiation and viewers were advised to sit no nearer than six feet from them.

Children were at greatest risk. Their eyes are so good at accommodating changes in distance that they were able to sit and watch at a much closer range than most adults.

Almost forty years ago, the Radiation Control for Health & Safety Act compelled all manufacturers to use leaded glass for their cathode-ray tubes, rendering television sets perfectly safe.

The real damage caused by television is the lazy lifestyle it creates. Obesity rates among children in the UK have tripled in the last twenty years, and this has been linked to television. The average UK child aged between three and nine years old spends fourteen hours a week watching television and just over an hour playing sport or doing outdoor activities.

A 2004 study in the journal *Pediatrics* concluded that children who watched two to three hours' television a day had a 30 per cent higher chance of developing attention deficit disorder (ADD).

In 2005, the research company Nielsen revealed that the average US home tuned in to eight hours of television per day. This is 12.5 per cent higher than ten years ago, and the highest level since television viewing figures were first measured in the 1950s.

The American Academy of Pediatrics estimates that by the time they reach the age of seventy, Americans will have spent an average of eight whole years watching television.

HOW MUCH SLEEP SHOULD YOU HAVE EVERY NIGHT?

It is, apparently, dangerous to have eight hours' sleep a night.

Adults who sleep eight hours a night or more die younger than those who sleep only six to seven hours a night.

A six-year study involving 1.1 million people published by Professor Daniel Kripke at the University of California in 2004 showed that a significantly larger number of people who slept eight or more hours (or less than four hours) a night died during the six-year study.

The average Briton gets between six and seven hours' sleep a night, which is one and a half hours less every night than our grandparents did. In 1900, a normal night's sleep was nine hours.

There is evidence to suggest that sleep deprivation

leads to short-term loss of IQ, memory and the ability to reason.

Leonardo da Vinci spent almost half his life asleep. Like Einstein, he took short naps during the day, in his case fifteen minutes every four hours. The great lexicographer Dr Johnson rarely got up before noon. The French philosopher Pascal also spent much of his day dozing in bed.

On the other hand, the famously long-lived elephant sleeps for only two hours a day. Koalas sleep for twenty-two hours a day but only live ten years. Ants, as noted earlier, sleep for only a few minutes a day.

The average person takes seven minutes to fall asleep. Normal healthy sleepers wake up between fifteen and thirty-five times every night.

There are currently eighty-four recognised sleep disorders, including insomnia, excessive snoring, narcolepsy (falling asleep during the day), apnoea (ceasing to breathe while asleep) and restless leg syndrome. The UK has twenty-five sleep clinics, all of which are 'overwhelmed' with patients.

Twenty per cent of all UK motorway accidents are caused by drivers falling asleep. The best way to stop this happening is to trap a lock of your hair in the sun-roof.

The second-best way is to eat an apple. This stimulates digestion and provides slow-release energy, which is more effective than the short-term hit of coffee.

WHAT WILL BE THE BIGGEST KILLER IN THE WORLD BY 2030?

a) Tuberculosis
b) AIDS
c) Malaria
d) Tobacco
e) Murder

According to the World Health Organisation, tobacco is currently the second major cause of death in the world. It is responsible for the death of one in ten adults worldwide, about five million deaths each year, while cancer is currently killing seven million people a year.

If figures continue to rise at current levels, tobacco—and a range of smoking-related diseases—will become the world's biggest killer by 2030, killing ten million people a year.

Around 1.3 billion people are regular smokers. Half of them—that is 650 million people—will eventually be killed by tobacco.

Developing countries will suffer the most. Eighty-four per cent of smokers currently reside in middle-to low-income countries, where smoking has been steadily on the increase since 1970.

In contrast, smoking levels among men from the United States declined from 55 per cent in the 1950s to 28 per cent in the 1990s. In the Middle East—where half the adult males smoke—tobacco consumption increased 24 per cent between 1990 and 1997.

The economic consequences of smoking in the

developing world are just as disastrous as the implications for health. In places like Niger, Vietnam and Bangladesh, impoverished households are spending one third more on tobacco products than on food.

It was not until the late 1940s that modern science linked disease to tobacco and, in the UK, it wasn't until the Royal College of Physicians report in 1964 that the government fully accepted the link between smoking and cancer. It was another seven years before warnings appeared on cigarette packets.

Despite thirty years of mounting evidence, one in four UK adults (13 million people) continue to smoke regularly (although 70 per cent of those are trying to give up).

In 2004, the Himalayan Kingdom of Bhutan not only banned smoking in public, but also banned tobacco sales, the first country ever to do so.

WHAT ILLNESS DO BRITISH DOCTORS TREAT MOST OFTEN?

a) The common cold
b) Ear infections
c) Depression
d) Sleep disorders

Depression is the commonest illness treated by doctors in Britain and the fourth commonest illness in the world after pneumonia/bronchitis, diarrhoea and HIV/AIDS (WHO 1999).

It is estimated that up to 10 per cent of women and 3 to 5 per cent of men worldwide suffer from clinical (i.e. severe) depression in any given year.

Approximately 3.2 million people in Britain (7 per cent) are clinically depressed and it's getting worse. Between 1990 and 2000, the number of prescriptions written for depression every year in the UK rose by more than ten million.

It is estimated that depression costs the UK economy £8 billion a year through time off work, treatment costs, suicides and reduced productivity—equivalent to £160 a year for every man, woman and child.

This is not just a function of innate British miserabilism or climate: 25 million Americans (9 per cent) are clinically depressed at any one time. In Australia, children as young as five are currently being treated for depression.

In Bangladesh, by far the commonest illness is diarrhoea, followed by intestinal worm infections. But depression is widespread (particularly among women), running at about 3 per cent.

In Africa, depression is the eleventh most common illness, HIV and malaria being first and second. In most developing countries, cultural suspicion of mental illness means diagnosis is difficult and symptoms are more likely to manifest themselves physically than in the West.

IS THE ANSWER TO DEPRESSION JUST TO 'WALK IT OFF'?

Yes. It's at least as effective as drugs.

Recent research involving subjects aged twenty-four to forty-five found that half an hour's exercise three to five times a week has the same (or better) effect on depression than drugs, regularly reducing symptoms by nearly 50 per cent.

I got the blues thinking of the future, so I left off and made some marmalade. It's amazing how it cheers one up to shred oranges and scrub the floor.
D. H. LAWRENCE

According to *Science News*, placebos are more effective at curing depression than either drugs or herbal remedies. In a series of trials carried out between 1979 and 1996, Seattle psychiatrist Dr Arif Khan found that St John's Wort completely cured 24 per cent of cases, the anti-depressant drug Zoloft cured 25 per cent of cases, but the sugar-pill placebos effected a complete cure in 32 per cent of patients.

In a more recent study comparing the anti-depressants Prozac and Efexor with placebos, the drugs won with a 52 per cent cure rate, but the placebos still scored impressively with 38 per cent. But as soon as the deception was revealed, the patients' condition worsened rapidly.

Many commentators believe that the context of the treatment—a clinical trial with lots of professional attention being paid to the participants—was an important factor. The conclusion seems to be that a combination of drugs and personal care produces the quickest and longest-lasting cure.

Meditation also seems to work. In a research project involving Tibetan monks recommended by the Dalai Lama, Richard Davidson, Professor of Neuroscience at the University of Wisconsin-Madison, asked the monks to meditate on 'unconditional loving-kindness and compassion'.

The result was an extraordinary pattern of gamma

brainwaves, usually very difficult to detect. The implication seems to be that, if trained to do so, the brain can produce its own dopamine—the chemical whose lack causes depression.

Using drugs leads your brain stop producing its own dopamine almost completely.

By training yourself to 'be positive' you can make yourself cheerful again. This may also be why placebos work: belief is a powerful thing.

WHICH COUNTRY HAS THE WORLD'S HIGHEST SUICIDE RATE?

Lithuania, which in 2003 boasted an astonishing forty-two suicides per 100,000 of population. This is over 1,500 people: more than are killed by traffic accidents and twice as many as a decade ago.

To put it in an international context Lithuanian suicides outstrip the British figure by six to one, the USA's by five to one, and are almost three times the world average. Nobody knows why, but it is interesting that seven of the top ten suicide nations are Baltic states or other former members of the Soviet Union. Perhaps it's because Lithuania also has the world's highest density of neurologists.

Across the world, including the Baltic, the people most likely to commit suicide are men (young and old) living in rural areas. This makes sense: anyone who's spent time on a struggling farm knows that alcohol, isolation, debt, the weather and the inability to ask for help (known by psychologists as 'helpless male' syndrome), combined with proximity to firearms and dangerous chemicals, make a lethal combination.

The exceptions are China and southern India where young women in rural areas are most at risk. The respective rates are 30 and 148 per 100,000. In China this is thought to be because young brides are often left isolated by their new husbands, who immediately leave to work in the city. In India, self-immolation accounts for a third of all suicides by teenage girls.

Suicide, generally, is on the rise—accounting for a million deaths a year, or one every forty seconds. That's half of all violent deaths: more people now kill themselves than die in wars.

On the other hand, Sweden, for a long time plagued with the 'so boring, everyone kills themselves' tag, is no longer even in the top twenty.

The precise historical basis of the 'Swedish suicide' myth is lost in the fog of post-war reconstruction, but many Swedes blame Dwight D. Eisenhower, President of the USA 1953–61, who used their (at that time) high suicide rate to undermine the cheerful, dangerously anti-capitalist egalitarianism of Swedish social democracy.

WAS HITLER A VEGETARIAN?

No.

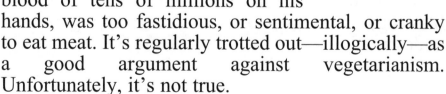

It's a good story. The twentieth century's worst dictator, with the blood of tens of millions on his hands, was too fastidious, or sentimental, or cranky to eat meat. It's regularly trotted out—illogically—as a good argument against vegetarianism. Unfortunately, it's not true.

Various biographers, including those who knew

the dictator intimately, record his passion for Bavarian sausages, game pie and (according to his chef) stuffed pigeon.

He was, however, plagued by chronic flatulence, for which his doctors regularly recommended a vegetarian diet (a remedy which will surprise many vegetarians). He also received regular injections of a high-protein serum derived from pulverised bull's testicles. That's a long way from a mushroom timbale or lentil bake.

There is no evidence in his speeches or writings that he was ideologically sympathetic to vegetarianism, and not one of his lieutenants was a veggie. In fact, he was far more likely to have criminalised vegetarians along with Esperanto speakers, conscientious objectors and other detested 'internationalists'.

Nor was he an atheist. Here he is in full, unambiguous flow in *Mein Kampf* (1925): 'I am convinced that I am acting as the agent of our Creator. By fighting off the Jews, I am doing the Lord's work.' He was to use the same form of words in a Reichstag speech in 1938.

Three years later he told General Gerhart Engel: 'I am now, as before, a Catholic and will always remain so.'

Far from being a 'godless' state, Nazi Germany enthusiastically worked with the Catholic Church. Infantry soldiers each wore a belt with *Gott mit uns* (God is with us) inscribed on the buckle, and blessings of troops and equipment were regular and widespread.

WHICH NATION INVENTED THE CONCENTRATION CAMP?

If you still think it's Germany, you must have been living in a cave.

The usual answer is Britain, because of their use of internment camps for families in the Second Boer War of 1899–1902.

In actuality, the concept is Spanish. In their struggle to retain Cuba in 1895, they first came up with the idea of 'concentrating' civilians in one place to make them easier to control. That struggle ended in defeat for Spain, and their troops began to withdraw from the island in 1898. The USA stepped into the vacuum, exerting a military influence on the island until Castro's revolution of 1959.

The British translated the Spanish term, *reconcentratión*, when faced with a similar situation in South Africa. The camps had been made necessary by the British policy of burning down Boer farms. This created a large number of refugees. The British decided to round up all the women and children left behind by the Boer troops, to stop them resupplying the enemy.

In total, there were forty-five tented camps for Boer women and children and sixty-four for black African farm labourers and their families.

Despite the humane intentions, conditions in the camps quickly degenerated. There was very little food, and disease spread rapidly. By 1902, 28,000 Boers (including 22,000 children) and 20,000 Africans had died in the camps—twice as many as the soldiers killed in the fighting.

Shortly after this, the Germans also established their first concentration camps in their attempts to colonise South-West Africa (now Namibia).

Men, women and children of the Herero and Namaqua peoples were arrested and imprisoned and forced to work in camps. Between 1904 and 1907, 100,000 Africans—80 per cent of the Herero and 50 per cent of the Namaqua—died through violence or starvation.

The UN now considers this the first genocide of the twentieth century.

WHICH AEROPLANE WON THE BATTLE OF BRITAIN?

The Hawker Hurricane.

The Spitfire was a more advanced design, faster, lighter to handle and capable of operating at altitudes of up to 30,000 feet. But the records clearly show that the heavy fighting in the Battle of Britain was done by the Hawker Hurricane.

There were more of them, for a start. In 1940, Hurricane squadrons outnumbered Spitfire squadrons by three to two; 1,715 Hurricanes were used in the battle, more than all the other RAF aircraft put together.

And they downed more planes. In Francis K. Mason's exhaustive account, *Battle over Britain* (1969), he shows that of 11,400 reported engagements, Hurricanes accounted for 55 per cent of all kills, to the Spitfires' 33 per cent.

In general, the Hurricanes specialised in attacking bombers, while the Spitfires took the fighters.

However, the highest-scoring RAF pilot in the battle, Sergeant Josef František (a Czech), only flew Hurricanes and still managed to down nine Me 109s—the fastest and best-equipped German fighter—among his total of seventeen enemy aircraft.

The first Hawker Hurricane flew in 1935 and was basically a single-winged Hawker Fury, one of the most reliable of the biplanes designed for Hawker between the wars by Sydney Camm. Hurricanes were built from 1937 to 1944 on a steel frame with a linen fabric covering. The Spitfire was all metal.

The Hurricane was cheap to make and easy to repair. Its fabric skin meant bullets could pass right through, and on more than one occasion Hurricanes returned safely with large pieces of wing missing.

Hurricanes could be turned around more quickly for battle, absorbed the shudder of eight guns rather better than Spitfires and, because the cockpits were larger, fighter pilots could wrap up warmer. There was no cockpit heating in either plane.

Spitfires scored their first kills for the RAF in September 1939 when they inadvertently shot down some of their own Hurricanes.

The RAF lost 1,173 planes and 510 pilots and gunners in the Battle of Britain, including 538 Hurricanes and 342 Spitfires. The Luftwaffe lost 1,733 planes, and 3,368 airmen were killed or captured.

WHEN DID THE LAST SURVIVOR OF THE CRIMEAN WAR DIE?

2004.

The last veteran of the Crimean War, which ended in 1856, was Timothy, a Mediterranean spur-thighed tortoise. He was thought to be approximately 160 years old at the time of his death, and the UK's oldest known resident.

Timothy was found aboard a Portuguese privateer in 1854 by Captain John Courtenay Everard of the Royal Navy and served as a mascot on a series of Navy vessels until 1892, including service as ship's mascot of HMS *Queen* during the first bombardment of Sebastopol in the Crimean War.

You can't trample infidels when you're a tortoise... all you could do is give them a meaningful look.
TERRY PRATCHETT

He then retired to Powderham Castle, where he was taken in by Everard's relative, the tenth Earl of Devon.

Timothy had the Devon's family motto—'Where have I fallen? What have I done?'—inscribed on his underside.

During the Second World War, he left the shade of his favourite wisteria and dug his own air-raid shelter under the terrace steps. Lady Gabrielle Courtenay, aunt to the current Earl and Timothy's keeper, claimed this was because the vibration from bombs falling on nearby Exeter had disturbed him. She also believed he could recognise people's voices, and always came when called.

After the war, he returned to the same rose-bed to hibernate every year, wearing a large tag marked 'My name is Timothy—I am very old. Please do not pick me up.'

According to Rory Knight-Bruce, Timothy's biographer, the few who were allowed to carry him 'would have held a doughty veteran with a gimlet eye whose density of weight was about that of a medium-sized Le Creuset pot.'

In 1926, the Devons decided that Timothy should mate. It was then discovered that Timothy was actually female. Given her age, they decided against changing his/her name, and although they did introduce a potential mate called Toby, she died without an heir.

Timothy was buried in the family burial plot in the castle grounds.

HOW MANY DOG YEARS EQUAL ONE HUMAN YEAR?

It's not seven.

No reliable authority can be found to help us make simple cross-species age comparisons.

Some twelve-year-old cats and dogs have a much higher level of physical capability than even the most sprightly eighty-four-year-old human and there does seem to be significant variation between different breeds.

The best that can be done is to apply a widely accepted approximate formula which suggests that kittens and puppies mature much faster than babies, with the rate of ageing slowing down significantly after two years.

243

Therefore, a one-year-old cat might be roughly sixteen in human years, while a four-year-old could be compared to a man or woman of thirty-two, an eight-year-old to a sixty-four-year-old and so on.

HOW LONG IS A DAY?

That depends.

A day is a single rotation of the Earth about its axis. It is never exactly twenty-four hours long.

Astonishingly, it can be as much as fifty whole seconds longer or shorter. This is because the speed of the Earth's rotation is continually changing as a result of friction caused by tides, weather patterns and geological events.

Over a year, an average day is a fraction of a second shorter than twenty-four hours.

Once atomic clocks had recorded these discrepancies, the decision was made to redefine the second, hitherto a set fraction of the 'solar' day—i.e. an eighty-six-thousand-and-four-hundredth of a day.

The new second was launched in 1967 and defined as: 'the duration of 9,192, 631,770 periods of the radiation corresponding to the transition between the two hyperfine levels of the ground state of the caesium-133 atom.' Accurate, but not easy to say when tired at the end of a long day.

This new definition of a second means that the solar day is gradually drifting away from the atomic day. As a result, scientists have introduced a 'leap second' into the atomic year, to bring it into line with the solar year.

The last 'leap second' added (the seventh since

244

Co-ordinated Universal Time (UTC) was established in 1972) was on 31 December 2005, on the instruction of the International Earth Rotation Service based at the Paris Observatory.

That's good news for astronomers and those of us who want our watches to correspond to the movement of the Earth around the Sun, but bad news for computer software and all technology based on satellites.

The idea was vigorously opposed by the International Telecommunication Union who made a formal proposal to abandon the leap second by December 2007.

One compromise might be to wait until the discrepancy between UTC and GMT reaches an hour (in about 400 years time) and adjust it then. In the meantime, the debate about what constitutes the 'real' time continues.

WHAT'S THE LONGEST ANIMAL?

Not the blue whale. Sorry.

Or the lion's mane jellyfish.

The bootlace worm, *Lineus longissimus*, reaches lengths of sixty metres (that's just under 200 feet), almost twice as long as a blue whale and a third longer than the longest lion's mane jellyfish, the previous record holder.

You could drape a bootlace worm from one end of an Olympic swimming pool to the other and still have some spare.

Bootlace worms, also known as ribbon worms, belong to the Nemertea worm family (Nemertea

Man cannot make a worm, yet he will make gods by the dozen.
MICHEL DE MONTAIGNE

comes from the Greek *Nemertes*, a sea-nymph). There are more than a thousand species, most of them aquatic. They are long and thin: even the longest may be only a few millimetres in diameter.

Many sources claim the bootlace worm only reaches 30 metres (nearly 100 feet) in length, which is not quite as long as the lion's mane jellyfish. But the latest information reveals that their capacity to stretch is extraordinary. Several have been found that are over 50 metres (165 feet) when fully extended.

Fossil evidence shows they have been around for at least 500 million years.

Bootlace worms have no hearts—their blood is pumped by their muscles—and they are the simplest organisms to have a separate mouth and anus.

They are voracious carnivores, shooting out a long thin tube which is sticky or armed with poisonous hooks, to skewer and stun small crustaceans. This can be three times as long as the worm's own body.

Most ribbon worms lurk in the murk of the ocean bottom but some are incredibly brightly coloured.

Nemerteans can regenerate if damaged. But some bootlace species actually reproduce by fragmenting into small pieces, each of which becomes a new worm.

WHAT'S THE LOUDEST THING IN THE OCEAN?

Shrimps.

Though the blue whale produces the loudest noise of any individual animal in the sea or on land, the loudest natural noise of all is made by shrimps.

The sound of the 'shrimp layer' is the only natural noise that can 'white out' a submarine's sonar, deafening the operators through their headphones.

Below the layer they can hear nothing above it and vice versa. Hearing from below can only be accomplished by raising a mast up through it.

The noise of the collected shrimps amounts to an ear-splitting 246 decibels, which even adjusting for the fact that sound travels five times faster in water, equates to about 160 decibels in air: considerably louder than a jet taking off (140 dB) or the human threshold of pain. Some observers have compared it to everyone in the world frying bacon at the same time.

The noise is caused by trillions of shrimps snapping their single oversized claw all at once. Snapping shrimps, members of the various *Alpheus* and *Synalpheus* species, are found in shallow tropical and subtropical waters.

But it's even more interesting than it sounds. Video shot at 40,000 frames per second shows clearly that the noise occurs 700 microseconds after the claw has snapped shut. The noise comes from burst bubbles—not the shutting of the claw itself—an effect known as 'cavitation'.

It works like this. A small bump on one side of the claw fits neatly into a groove on the other side. The claw is shut so rapidly that a jet of water travelling at 100 kilometres (62 miles) per hour squirts out, fast enough to create expanding bubbles of water vapour. When the water slows down and normal pressure is restored the bubbles collapse creating intense heat (as high as 20,000 °C), a loud pop and light—this last being a very rare phenomenon called sonoluminescence, where sound generates light.

Shrimps use this noise to stun prey, communicate and find mates. As well as ruining sonar, the sharp, hot intense noise makes dents in ships' propellers.

WHY ARE FLAMINGOS PINK?

Because they eat a lot of blue-green algae.

Flamingos do eat shrimps, but the colour of the birds comes from the algae. Despite their name, blue-green algae can be red, violet, brown, yellow or even orange.

Flamingos are named for their bright colour. Like *flamenco*, the word comes from the Latin for 'flame'. The red and white flag of Peru was inspired by them.

There are four species of flamingo. They are at least ten million years old and once ranged over Europe, America and Australia. Now they live in isolated pockets of Africa, India, South America and southern Europe.

All species are monogamous. They lay only one egg a year which is balanced on a mound of soil. Both parents take turns to incubate it and both produce bright red, highly nutritious 'milk' from their throats, which the chicks feed on for their first two months. Flamingos are one of only two kinds of bird to produce milk: the other is pigeons. In captivity, flamingos that are not parents will spontaneously produce milk if they hear the cries of chicks.

After leaving the nest, flamingos live in vast crèches. Though these may contain more than 30,000 birds, the young flamingo is fed only by its parents, who recognise it by its cry. A family of flamingos is called a 'pat'.

Flamingos eat with their heads upside down. Unlike other birds, they filter their food in the same way as whales and oysters. Their beaks are lined with rows of plates that sift items from the water. The lesser flamingo (*Phoeniconaias minor*) has such a dense filter it can strain single-celled plants less than $0.05\,\text{mm}$ ($\frac{2}{100}$ inch) in diameter. The flamingo's tongue acts as a pump, pushing water through its beak four times a second.

Pliny the Elder recommended eating flamingo tongue as a tasty delicacy.

Flamingos sleep on one leg, with one half of their body at a time—like dolphins—while the other remains alert for predators.

Flamingos can live for fifty years. They inhabit inhospitable lakes that have high levels of salt and soda, where the water is undrinkable by other animals and nothing grows. Their main predators are zookeepers.

WHAT COLOUR IS A PANTHER?

There is no such thing as 'a' panther.

The word probably comes from the Sanskrit for whitish-yellow, *pandarah*, which was originally applied to the tiger.

The Greeks borrowed the word and adapted it as *panthera*, meaning 'all beasts'. They used it to describe mythological as well as real animals.

In medieval heraldry, the panther was portrayed as a gentle, multicoloured beast that had a very sweet smell.

Scientifically speaking, all four of the largest species of big cat are panthers.

The lion is *Panthera leo*; the tiger, *Panthera tigris*, the leopard, *Panthera pardus* and the jaguar *Panthera onca*. They are the only cats that can roar.

The animals that most people think of as panthers are, in fact, either black leopards (in Africa or Asia), or black jaguars (in South America).

Neither animal is completely black. Close examination shows that their spots are still faintly visible on their skin. They carry a genetic mutation that means the black pigment in their fur dominates the orange.

Rare 'white panthers' are in fact albino leopards or jaguars.

In the USA, when people say 'panther' they mean a black puma. Despite many unproven reports and supposed sightings, no one has ever found one.

WHAT MAKES AN ANIMAL SEE RED?

The myth that bulls are infuriated by the colour red has been around since at least 1580, when the best-selling writer of the time, John Lyly, noted that: 'He that commeth before an Elephant will not wear bright colors, nor he that commeth to a Bul, red.'

The fact is that, like rats, hippos, owls and aardvarks, bulls are colour-blind. It is the movements of the bullfighter's cape that cause the bull to charge; the colour is merely for the benefit of the crowd.

Dogs can distinguish between blue and yellow, but can't tell green from red. At traffic lights, guide dogs decide whether it is safe to cross by listening to the traffic. Hence the peeping sounds on modern pedestrian crossings.

The creatures that have really strong views on red are chickens.

Poultry farmers know only too well the practical problems of a chicken 'seeing red'. When one of them bleeds, the others peck at it obsessively.

This cannibalistic behaviour, if unchecked, can lead to a killing spree and a rapid reduction in the farmer's flock.

The traditional solution is to trim the chickens' beaks with a hot knife so they are blunt and cause less damage. However, in 1989 a company called Animalens launched red-tinted contact lenses for egg-laying chickens. The early results were promising—because everything looked red, the chickens fought less and needed less feed because they weren't so active, but still laid the same number of eggs.

The egg industry operates on a tiny profit margin of about 1.6 per cent. There are 250 million egg-layers in the USA, 150 million of them on just fifty farms. Red contact lenses for chickens promised a tripling in profits.

Unfortunately, fitting the lenses was fiddly and labour-intensive. Deprived of oxygen, the chickens' eyes degenerated rapidly, causing pain and distress. Falling foul of the animal rights lobby, Animalens withdrew the product.

WHAT COLOUR WERE THE ORIGINAL OOMPA-LOOMPAS?

a) Black
b) Gold
c) Multi-coloured
d) Orange

In the first edition of Roald Dahl's classic 1964 children's novel *Charlie and the Chocolate Factory*, the tireless, loyal Oompa-Loompas were black, not orange.

Dahl described them as a tribe of 3,000 black pygmies imported by Mr Wonka from 'the very deepest and darkest part of the African jungle where no white man had been before', to replace the sacked white workers in his factory. They lived on chocolate, whereas before they had only eaten 'beetles, eucalyptus leaves, caterpillars and the bark of the bong-bong tree.'

Although it was well received at the time, Dahl's description of the Oompa-Loompas, with its overtones of slavery, veered dangerously close to racism and, by the early 1970s, his US publishers Knopf insisted on changes. In 1972, a revised edition of *Charlie and the Chocolate Factory* appeared. Out went the black pygmies, in came Oompa-Loompas looking like small hippies with long 'golden-brown hair' and 'rosy-white skin'.

Later, Dahl's illustrator Quentin Blake depicted them as multicoloured futuristic punks with Mohawk hairdos. The two Hollywood films in 1971 and 2005 made the Oompa-Loompas look like orange elves.

Dahl hated the 1971 film, not least because the (uncredited) screenwriter David Seltzer (later to write *The Omen*) had Wonka spouting poetic quotations that weren't in the book.

The film's title was changed to *Willy Wonka & the Chocolate Factory* allegedly because 'Charlie' had become US street slang for an African American.

WHAT COLOUR WERE ROBIN HOOD'S TIGHTS?

Red.

The earliest Robin Hood stories were ballads dating from the fifteenth century.

In the longest and most important of these, *A Gest of Robyn Hode*, Robin and his 'mery men' wear 'a good mantell of scarlet and raye', a kind of striped bright red wrap.

In other ballads, Robin wears red or scarlet while his men wear green. This reflects his status as leader—'scarlet' was the most expensive cloth in medieval England, dyed using kermes, the dried bodies of the female shield louse (*Kermes ilicis*).

This also explains the name Robin—associated with the robin redbreast—and that of one of his closest associates: Will Scarlet.

It is only in later versions that 'Lincoln Green' becomes the colour for the outlaws' gear but even this may not have been green.

Lincoln was the capital of the medieval English dyeing industry. 'Lincoln Green' was green (blue dye made from woad was over-dyed with yellow) but 'Lincoln Grain' was scarlet, dyed with kermes, known as 'graine'.

The early Robin Hood stories are obsessed by clothing. As well as Robin being named after his headgear, mantles, kirtles, coats, breeches, shirts and six different colours of cloth are mentioned in the *Gest*, and at one point Robin plays at being a draper, selling the King 123 feet of green cloth.

This has prompted the idea that the ballads may have been written for the Livery Guilds, companies of merchants involved in manufacturing. Many of them were founded at the time the *Gest* was written (*c*.1460); their preferred style of uniform was a coloured hood.

At least one historian has suggested that the real point of the Robin Hood stories is not the traditional 'forest versus town' or 'rich versus poor' battle, but the victory of the merchant adventurer over the failing, corrupt nobility.

Robin Hood, dressed in expensive red cloth, was really the champion of the emerging middle classes rather than the poor.

WHAT COLOUR ARE CARROTS?

Carrots didn't reveal their inner orangeness for almost 5,000 years.

The earliest evidence of carrots being used by humans dates from 3,000 BC in Afghanistan. These original carrots were purple on the outside and yellow on the inside.

The ancient Greeks and Romans cultivated the vegetable, but mostly for medicinal purposes: the carrot was considered a powerful aphrodisiac.

You ask 'What is life?' That is the same as asking, 'What is a carrot?' A carrot is a carrot and we know nothing more.

ANTON CHEKHOV

Galen, the famous second-century Roman physician, on the other hand, recommended carrots for expelling wind. He was the first to identify them as separate from their close relative the parsnip.

As Arab traders spread carrot seed through Asia, Africa and Arabia carrots blossomed into different shades of purple, white, yellow, red, green and even black.

The very first orange carrot was grown in sixteenth-century Holland, patriotically bred to match the colour of the Dutch Royal House of Orange.

By the seventeenth century, the Dutch were the main European producers of carrots and all modern varieties are descended from their four orange ones: Early Half Long, Late Half Long, Scarlet and Long Orange.

There is currently a vogue for non-orange carrots: white, yellow, dark red and purple varieties are available in the shops. In 1997, Iceland developed a chocolate-flavoured carrot as part of their child-focused Wacky Veg range. It was withdrawn after eight months.

According to the United Nations in 1903 there were 287 varieties of carrot but these now number just twenty-one, a fall of 93 per cent.

Some breeds of carrot contain a protein that stops ice crystals growing. This natural carrot 'anti-freeze' can be extracted and used to preserve body tissues for medical use and improve the shelf-life of frozen food.

DO CARROTS HELP US SEE IN THE DARK?

Not really.

Carrots are a good source of vitamin A, a deficiency of which can lead to night blindness, where the eye adapts very slowly to changes in light.

The retina of the eye is made up of light-sensitive cells called rods and cones. Cones pick up detail and colour, but need plenty of light to function (like a 'slow' film emulsion). The rods can't distinguish colour at all but need less light (like a 'fast' emulsion) so are used for night vision. They contain a light-sensitive chemical called rhodopsin, the key ingredient of which is vitamin A.

The easiest way to treat night blindness is to increase the intake of vitamin A, most commonly found in carotene. Carrots contain carotene, but even better are apricots, dark-leaved vegetables such as spinach, and bilberries.

But improving defective night vision is very

different from making normal night vision better. Eating lots of carrots won't help you see any better in the dark—all it will do, over time, is to turn your skin orange.

During the Second World War, Group Captain John Cunningham (1917–2002) gained the nickname 'Cats Eyes Cunningham'. His 604 squadron operated at night. The British government encouraged rumours that he was able see in the dark because he ate so many carrots.

This was deliberate disinformation designed to cover up the fact that he was testing the newly developed (and top secret) airborne radar system.

It seems highly unlikely the Germans were taken in, but it helped persuade a generation of English children to eat the one vegetable that remained in constant supply through the war.

The Government started to overdo the carrot propaganda. Carrots became 'these bright treasures dug from the good British earth'. A 1941 recipe for Carrot Flan—'reminds you of Apricot Flan—but has a deliciousness all of its own'—fooled no one. And carrot jam and marmalade failed to find their way on to the British breakfast table.

The Portuguese are fond of carrot jam, though. In 2002 this led to the European Union redefining the carrot as a fruit.

WHAT DO BANANAS GROW ON?

There is no such thing as a banana tree.

The banana plant is actually a giant herb and the bananas are its berries.

A herb is defined as 'a plant with a fleshy not a woody stem, which, after the plant has bloomed and set seed, dies down to the ground'. This is not always true: sage, thyme and rosemary have woody stems (though they are not covered with true bark).

As the definition says, after flowering, the part of the herb above the ground dies. With bananas, this gives rises to a strange effect. After the stem dies, another one grows, slightly further along the root. Over a few years, the banana plant will appear to have 'walked' a couple of yards.

Bananas are native to Malaya and have been cultivated for 10,000 years. Wild bananas, which can still be found in South-East Asia, contain large stony seeds and a small amount of flesh. They are pollinated by bats.

The banana in your local supermarket is a cultivated variety, chosen by farmers for its fleshy pulp and lack of seeds. Domestication has produced plants that are sweet and tasty but sterile: they cannot reproduce without human help.

Most banana plants have not had sex for 10,000 years. Almost every banana we eat has been propagated by hand, from a sucker of an existing plant, whose genetic material has not changed in 100 centuries.

258

As a result, bananas are extremely susceptible to disease. Many species have already succumbed to fungal infections like black Sigatoka and Panama disease, which are impervious to fungicides. Unless a genetically modified version can be developed soon, all bananas may become extinct.

This is a serious problem. Bananas are the most profitable export crop in the world. The industry is worth $12 billion dollars a year and supports 400 million people, many of them living well below the poverty line.

Most bananas come from hot countries, but Europe's largest producer is Iceland. The bananas are grown in large greenhouses heated by geothermal water, just two degrees below the Arctic Circle.

Fyffe's, the banana multinational that buys the entire crop of Belize each year, is Irish.

WHICH OF THE FOLLOWING ARE BERRIES?

a) Strawberry
b) Raspberry
c) Peach
d) Watermelon

A berry is defined as 'a fleshy fruit containing several seeds'.

Strictly speaking, strawberries, raspberries and blackberries are not berries but 'aggregated drupes'—a drupe being a fleshy fruit containing a single stone or pit.

Peaches, plums, nectarines and olives are drupes. The world's largest drupe is the coconut, which,

259

because of its hard flesh, is called a 'dry drupe'.

Strawberries, raspberries and blackberries are called 'aggregated' drupes because each individual fruit is actually a cluster of miniature drupes—the characteristic bumpy bits which make up blackberries and raspberries.

Each one of these drupelets contains a single tiny seed—these are the bits that get stuck in your teeth when you eat a blackberry.

Tomatoes, oranges, lemons, grapefruit, watermelons, kiwi fruit, cucumbers, grapes, passion fruit, papaya, peppers and bananas are all berries.

Blueberries are also berries. They are variously known as bleaberries, bilberries, whortleberries, huckleberries, hurtleberries, myrtleberries and trackleberries.

WHICH OF THE FOLLOWING ARE NUTS?

a) Almond
b) Peanut
c) Brazil nut
d) Walnut

Nuts are defined as a simple, dry fruit with one seed (very occasionally two) in which the seed-case wall becomes very hard at maturity.

True nuts include walnuts, butternuts, hickory, pecan, chestnut (but not conkers), beech, oak acorns, tan oak, hazel, filbert, hornbeam, birch and alder.

Peanuts, almonds, pistachios, Brazils, cashews, coconuts, horse chestnuts and pine nuts are not nuts. So the legendary health warning on a packet of peanuts ('may contain nuts') is, strictly speaking, untrue.

Brazil nuts are not nuts but seeds. The wooden pods they come in (up to twenty-four to a pod) grow right at the top of the tree, 45 metres (150 feet) above the ground, and are lethal if they fall on you. In Brazil, the pods are called *ouricos*, 'hedgehogs'.

Almonds are the stone of a once fleshy drupe.

Peanuts, also known as groundnuts, earthnuts, goobers, goober peas, pindas, pinders, Manila nuts and monkey nuts, are actually a type of pea which grows underground.

They are native to South America but now widely cultivated, notably in Georgia, USA. Some people are so severely allergic to peanuts that eating a tiny amount (or even inhaling peanut dust) can be fatal; these people may or may not also be allergic to true nuts.

Pistachios are deadly dangerous. They are classified under Class 4.2. of the International Maritime Dangerous Goods code: Flammable Solids (Substances Liable To Spontaneous Combustion). Fresh pistachios, if stacked under pressure, can burst into flames and cause a cargo fire.

Pistachios continue to absorb oxygen and excrete carbon dioxide even after harvesting. This can be a serious problem when transporting them by sea. If there is inadequate ventilation, seamen entering the hold of a cargo ship can die from carbon dioxide poisoning or from lack of oxygen.

Pistachios have been eaten by humans for at least

If you don't mind smelling like peanut butter for two or three days, peanut butter is darn good shaving cream.
BARRY GOLDWATER

261

9,000 years. According to Muslim legend, the pistachio was one of the foods brought to Earth by Adam when he came down from Heaven.

WHO GOES GATHERING NUTS IN MAY?

No one. There are no nuts to gather in May. The children's song is a corruption of the phrase 'Here we go gathering knots of may'. It refers to the ancient custom of picking bunches (knots) of flowers on May Day to celebrate the end of winter, or 'to go a-maying'.

May, the blossom of the hawthorn, is the only British flower to be named after the month in which it blooms. The may-tree is the origin of both the maypole and the phrase 'Ne'er cast a clout before May is out'—which refers not to the ending of the month, but to the opening of the flowers.

Though the may-tree is closely associated with May Day, it blossoms in the middle of the month not at the beginning of it. This is due to the change to the Gregorian calendar in 1752. Before this, May Day would have occurred eleven days later, exactly the time when the may-tree breaks into flower.

It is considered extremely unlucky to bring hawthorn flowers inside the house, a superstition more widely believed for may than for any other species of plant in the British Isles.

There are many possible reasons for this but the most convincing is to do with its smell. Hawthorn flowers have a heavy, complicated scent, the distinctive element of which is triethylamine, which is also one of the first chemicals produced by a dead human body when it starts to decay.

In some areas it is still referred to as 'the smell of the Great Plague' and people who know say it reminds them of the smell of gangrene. In the old days, bodies were laid out at home for up to a week before burial, and everybody would have been familiar with the smell of death. Hawthorn brought inside the house would have instantly triggered the association.

On the other hand, triethylamine is also the smell of sex: specifically of semen; hence its positive association with wild springtime rogering *outside* in the fields.

As well as 'may', hawthorn is also known as usual by scads of bizarre vernacular names including 'bread-and-cheese', 'arzy-garzies' and 'aglets'. 'Aglet' is also the word for the little metal or plastic tip on the end of a shoelace.

WHAT'S INSIDE A COCONUT?

Not milk, but coconut water. Coconut milk has to be made by boiling the white coconut 'meat' with water and straining it. Boil this down further and you get coconut cream.

Coconut is the only plant to produce such a seed liquid. As the coconut grows, the seed inside changes into a sweet, spongy mass called the 'coconut apple'. From this the young plant shoot emerges out of one of the three holes at the end.

Fresh coconut water is an excellent hangover cure. It is completely sterile, full of vitamins and minerals and has the same balance of salts as human blood (the technical term for this is isotonic).

263

Because of this it can be used in place of a saline drip and is being commercially exploited as a sports drink, particularly in Brazil, where it is now a $75-million industry. Coconut water also ferments quickly and can be made into wine or vinegar.

Coconut oil is used to treat AIDS. Far from being the world's most dangerously fatty oil, it is now being marketed as the healthiest. It is rich in lauric acid, the saturated fat found in mother's milk, and full of anti-viral and anti-bacterial properties. It's also been shown to reduce cholesterol, as it doesn't enter the bloodstream but travels straight to the liver.

Some less well known uses for the coconut palm: DaimlerChrysler now use the husk (or coir) to make biodegradable seats for their trucks (springier than plastic foam); the root is liquefied to make mouthwash and a flour made from the shell is used to clean jet engines. The first car body to be made of coconut is already on the drawing board.

The coconut palm has been heralded as the world's most useful tree for more than 3,000 years. In early Sanskrit texts it was referred to as *kalpa vriksha*—the tree that fulfils all needs.

You could survive on a desert island by eating and drinking only coconut.

WHAT DID CAPTAIN COOK GIVE HIS MEN TO CURE SCURVY?

a) Limes
b) Lemons
c) Sauerkraut
d) Rum and blackcurrant

Cook never carried fresh limes or lemons on board. The closest he got to a remedy was barrels of sauerkraut and a concentrated fruit-juice mixture called 'rob'. Both had been boiled to preserve them on the long voyage and so had lost most of their vitamin C.

Cook had been dead for twenty years before the supply of lemon juice to British sailors became standard practice.

Scurvy was a huge problem on long voyages. Magellan lost most of his crew to it crossing the Pacific. Now we know it is a combination of a lack of vitamins C and B, causing the body's cells to break down, but in the eighteenth century it was treated with more superstition than knowledge. Many sailors believed that the touch of earth would cure it.

The breakthrough came with the publication of Edinburgh physician James Lind's *Treatise on Scurvy* in 1754, which advocated the use of citrus fruit and fresh vegetables.

The legend is that Cook's enlightened approach kept his ships free of the disease. The truth seems to be that Cook simply ignored it. The journals of his fellow officers indicate that it was widespread on all three voyages, although there were few deaths.

Eskimo/Inuit people don't suffer from scurvy because whale blubber is a rich source of vitamin C.

When, in 1795, the Admiralty finally ordered ships to be supplied with citrus fruit (on Lind's recommendation), it was lemon, not lime, juice that was supplied. This had a dramatic effect on the disease.

By the 1850s, lemons were being replaced by limes for economic reasons (limes were grown by

British businessmen in the colonies; lemons were grown by Johnny Foreigner in the Mediterranean). Scurvy returned with a vengeance as, ironically, limes contain very little vitamin C.

The first recorded use of the term lime-juicer (later limey) for a Brit was in 1859. Vitamin C wasn't identified and named until the 1930s. Its chemical name is ascorbic acid. Ascorbic means 'anti-scurvy'.

WHO DISCOVERED AUSTRALIA?

You still hear 'Captain Cook' trotted out at dinner parties (though very rarely at Australian ones).

Let's take it from the top: he wasn't a Captain, for a start, he was Lieutenant Cook on the *Endeavour*'s first voyage (1768–71). And he wasn't the first European to see the continent—the Dutch beat him by 150 years—or even the first Englishman to land there. That was William Dampier who, in 1697, was also the first to record a 'large hopping animal'.

Dampier (1652–1715) was a sea captain, navigator, explorer, cartographer, scientific observer, pirate and buccaneer. Alexander Selkirk—the model for *Robinson Crusoe*—was a member of his crew. He circumnavigated the world three times, invented the first wind map and is cited more than 1,000 times in the *OED*, introducing words like avocado, barbecue, breadfruit, cashew, chopsticks, settlement and tortilla into English.

In recent years, there has been a lot of lobbying in favour of the Chinese as the continent's first foreign visitors. There is some archaeological evidence that the great Ming Dynasty admiral Zheng He (1371–1435) landed near Darwin in 1432.

Without having to swallow the whole 'Zheng He discovered the entire world' theory cooked up by Gavin Menzies in his best-selling *1421: The Year the Chinese Discovered America*, there seems to be a good chance that this extraordinary fifteenth-century voyager (he was a Muslim and a eunuch) did reach the northern coast of Australia.

After all, Indonesian fishermen, crazed for the local sea cucumbers (which they traded with the Chinese), had managed it many years before the earliest recorded Europeans.

Some of the Northern Aboriginal peoples, like the Yolngu, even learnt to sail and fish from these visitors from overseas, picking up words, tools and the usual bad habits (alcohol and tobacco) along the way.

The real 'discoverers' are, of course, the Aboriginal peoples who reached Australia over 50,000 years ago. They have been present on the continent for 20,000 generations, in comparison to just eight generations of Europeans.

That is long enough for them to have witnessed dramatic changes in their environment. The landscape of the Australian interior 30,000 years ago would have been one of green vegetation, brimming lakes and snow-capped mountains.

WHAT DOES 'KANGAROO' MEAN IN ABORIGINAL?

It doesn't mean 'I don't know', despite the endless websites and trivia books that tell you otherwise, citing it as a hilarious early example of cultural misunderstanding.

The real story is much more interesting. In eighteenth-century Australia there were at least 700 Aboriginal tribes speaking as many as 250 different languages.

Kangaroo or *gangaru* comes from the Guugu Ymithirr language of Botany Bay, where it means the large grey or black kangaroo, *Macropus robustus*.

As the English settlers moved into the interior they used this word to refer to any old kangaroo or wallaby.

The Baagandji people lived 2,250 km (1,400 miles) from Botany Bay and didn't speak Guugu Ymithirr. They heard the English settlers using this unfamiliar word and took it to mean 'an animal that no one has ever heard of before'.

Since they had never seen them before, they (quite reasonably) used the word to describe the settlers' horses.

WHAT IS 'POM' SHORT FOR?

   a) Port of Melbourne
   b) Prisoners of Her Majesty
   c) Prisoner of Old Mother England
   d) Permit of Migration
   e) Pomegranates

Most of these are easy to discount because they are acronyms. Folk etymologists seem to be drawn to acronymic explanations, which are almost never right.

Fondness for acronyms is a military habit, dating from the First World War (an early example is AWOL, or 'Absent Without Leave', though even this wasn't consistently pronounced as a word at the time). Acronyms didn't get into general circulation until the Second World War.

There are almost no examples of words of acronymic origin before 1900. Indeed, the very word 'acronym' wasn't coined until 1943.

In the case of 'pom', most reliable authorities agree it is a shortening of 'pomegranate'.

In his 1923 Australian novel, *Kangaroo*, D.H. Lawrence wrote: ' "Pommy" is supposed to be short for pomegranate. Pomegranate, pronounced invariably pommygranate, is a near enough rhyme to immigrant, in a naturally rhyming country. Furthermore, immigrants are known in their first months, before their blood 'thins down', by their round and ruddy cheeks. So we are told.'

The term is first recorded in 1916, suggesting that it dates to the latter stages of the nineteenth century, and not to the original convict ships.

Michael Quinion in *Port Out, Starboard Home* (2000) also accepts 'pomegranate', citing H.J. Rumsey's 1920 introduction to a book called *The Pommie or New Chums in Australia*, in which the word is sourced to children's rhyming slang of the 1870s.

The older term 'Jimmy Grant' used for 'immigrant' became 'Pommy Grant', which was irresistible as the fierce Australian sun turned their 'new chums'' skin 'pomegranate red'.

WHAT'S THE BIGGEST ROCK IN THE WORLD?

It's not Ayers Rock.

Mount Augustus, or *Burringurrah,* in a remote part of Western Australia is the largest single rock in the world, more than two and a half times bigger than *Uluru* or Ayers Rock and one of the natural world's least known but most spectacular sites.

It rises 858 metres (2,815 feet) out of the surrounding outback, and its ridge is more than 8 km (5 miles) long.

Not only is it bigger and higher than Uluru, its rock is much older. The grey sandstone that is visible is the remains of a sea floor laid down 1,000 million years ago. The bedrock beneath the sandstone is granite dated to 1,650 million years ago. The oldest sandstone at Uluru is only 400 million years old.

The rock is sacred to the Wadjari people, and is named after Burringurrah, a young boy who tried to escape his initiation. He was pursued and speared in the leg, and then beaten to death by women wielding clubs. The shape of the rock reflects his prostate body, lying on its stomach with its leg bent upward towards his chest and a stump of the spear protruding from it.

A final sting in the tail for Ayers Rock snobs: Mount Augustus is a monolith—a single piece of rock. Uluru isn't. It's just the tip of a huge underground rock formation that also pokes out at Mount Conner (*Attila*) and Mount Olga (*Kata Tjuta*).

WHAT WERE BOOMERANGS USED FOR?

Knocking down kangaroos? Think about it. Boomerangs are designed to come back. They are lightweight and fast. Even large ones are unlikely to give an 80-kg (180-lb) adult male kangaroo much more than a sore head, and if it did knock them down, you wouldn't need it to return.

In fact, they weren't clubs at all. They were used to imitate hawks in order to drive game birds into nets strung from trees—a kind of wooden, banana-shaped bird dog.

Nor are they exclusive to the Aboriginal peoples. The oldest returning throwing stick was found in the Olazowa Cave in the Polish Carpathians and is more than 18,000 years old. Researchers tried it out, and it still worked.

This suggests there was already a long tradition of using them—the physical properties have to be so exact to make a successful boomerang that it's unlikely to be a one-off.

The oldest Aboriginal boomerangs are 14,000 years old.

Various types of throwing woods were used in Ancient Egypt, from 1,340 BC. In Western Europe a returning throwing stick called a *cateia* was used by the Goths to hunt birds from around AD 100.

In the seventh century, the Bishop of Seville described the *cateia*: 'There is a kind of Gallic missile consisting of very flexible material, which does not fly very long when it is thrown, because of its heavy weight, but arrives there nevertheless. It only can be broken with a lot of power. But if it is thrown by a master, it returns to the one who threw it.'

Australian Aboriginals probably became adept with the boomerang because they never developed the bow and arrow. Most Aboriginal peoples used both boomerangs and non-returning throwing sticks (known as 'kylies').

The first recorded use of the word 'bou-mar-rang' was in 1822. It comes from the language of the Turuwal people of the George's River near Sydney.

The Turuwal had other words for their hunting sticks, but used 'boomerang' to refer to a returning throwing stick. The Turuwal belong to part of the Dharuk language group. Many of the Aboriginal words used in English are from Dharuk languages, including wallaby, dingo, kookaburra and koala.

WHAT'S WRONG WITH THIS PICTURE?

What's wrong with it is the size of the pot.

Producing a watertight metal pot large enough to hold a person requires industrial technology that was new, even to the West, in the nineteenth century. In reality, you were much more likely to be butchered and roasted in small joints, or else smoked and salted for snacking on later.

The word 'cannibal' comes from a misrecording of the name for the Central American Carib tribe by Columbus in 1495. He reported finding a recently abandoned 'Canib' feast of human limbs simmering in small cauldrons and roasting on spits.

Other explorers reported cannibalism in South America, Africa, Australia, New Guinea and throughout the Pacific. Captain Cook was in no doubt that the Maori ate enemies taken in battle. During his second voyage, his lieutenant, Charles Clerke, grilled a portion of head at the behest of a Maori warrior and records that he 'devour'd it most ravenously, and suck'd his fingers ½ a dozen times over in raptures'.

William Arens's influential *The Man-Eating Myth* (1979) argued that these stories were racist lies invented to justify Western colonialism. It resulted in a period of 'cannibal denial' among anthropologists.

However, more recent discoveries have led most historians and anthropologists to accept that cannibalism was practised by many tribal cultures, mostly for ritual purposes, sometimes for food.

The last society to admit to ritual cannibalism, the Fore tribe of New Guinea, stopped in the mid-1950s after an outbreak of *kuru*, a brain disease contracted through eating human brain and spinal tissue.

There is also archaeological evidence. Collections of butchered human remains have even been found in France, Spain and Britain. Some of the British remains date from 30 BC to AD 130, suggesting that the Romans' belief that the ancient Britons ate people was justified.

In October 2003, the inhabitants of a Fijian village announced that they would be making a formal apology to the family of the Rev. Thomas Baker, an English missionary killed and eaten by their ancestors in 1867. They'd even tried to eat his boots, but these proved too tough and were returned to the Methodist Church in 1993.

WHICH RELIGION CURSES PEOPLE BY STICKING PINS INTO DOLLS?

There is no tradition of sticking pins in dolls to harm people in voodoo (known as *vodun* in Benin; *voudou* in Haiti and *vudu* in the Dominican Republic).

The magical practices of voodoo are complex and originated in West Africa before being exported to the Caribbean and America.

Healing is at the heart of most of the rituals. The closest thing to a 'voodoo doll' is a wooden figure called a *bocheo* (literally 'empowered figure') that contains small peg holes. Twigs are inserted into the appropriate hole, and used to channel healing energy.

One is all for religion until one visits a really religious country. Then, one is all for drains, machinery and a minimum wage.
ALDOUS HUXLEY

The voodoo doll of popular myth derives from a *European* figure called a 'poppet' (from the Latin *pupa* for 'doll'), traditionally used in witchcraft. It originated in ancient Greek dolls used as protective effigies called *kolossoi*. The poppet doll, made from clay, wax, cotton, corn or fruit, became a symbol of the life of the subject—whatever was done to the doll would happen to the person.

King James I mentions them in his *Demonology* (1603):

'To some others at these times he [the Devil] teacheth, how to make Pictures of wax or clay: that by the roasting thereof, the persons that they bear the name of, may be continually melted or dried away by continual sicknesse.'

It was the early colonists and slave owners who projected forbidden European 'black magic' practices on to voodoo, adding their suspicions of cannibalism, zombies and human sacrifice to spice up their stories. It was these that captured the popular imagination, and stimulated the appetites of early film-makers and dime-store novelists, fixing the idea of voodoo as dark and fearful.

The idea of sticking pins into people and meditating on suffering is not entirely foreign to Christianity. Some of the more grisly Counter-Reformation images of the Crucifixion leave little to the imagination.

Voodoo has made its peace with Christianity: the two traditions co-exist quite happily. A common Haitian saying is that 'Haitians are 80 per cent Catholic and 100 per cent Voodoo'.

HOW MANY WISE MEN VISITED JESUS?

Somewhere between two and twenty.

It has generally been assumed that there were three of them because they brought three gifts, but it is quite possible that there were four and one forgot to get a present until after the shops were closed and had to come in on the frankincense.

In St Matthew's Gospel the number of wise men is never mentioned. Besides, Jesus seems not to have been a baby but a young child, living in a house not a stable.

Most scholars agree that the Magi were Zoroastrian astrologer-priests but their number varies from two to twenty. It wasn't until the sixth century that three was settled on as the standard.

The Church has now started to backtrack on this. In February 2004, the General Synod of the Church of England agreed a revision to the Book of Common Prayer. Their committee decided that the term 'Magi' was a transliteration of the name used by officials at the Persian court, and that they could well have been women.

'While it seems very unlikely that these Persian court officials were female, the possibility that one or more of the Magi were female cannot be excluded completely,' the report concluded. '"Magi" is a word which discloses nothing about numbers, wisdom, or gender. The visitors were not necessarily wise and not necessarily men.'

WHERE DOES SANTA CLAUS COME FROM?

Depending on your age, the answer is likely to be the North Pole, Lapland or Coca Cola. None of them is right: Santa, like St George, is Turkish.

St Nicholas—the real Santa—lived and performed miracles in what is now the sun-baked town of Demre in south-western Turkey. His most famous miracles usually involved children. In one, he restored to life three children who'd been chopped up by the local tavern owner and kept in a brine tub.

Being kind to children explains his suitability as a Christmas saint, but St Nick is also the patron saint of judges, pawnbrokers, thieves, merchants, bakers, sea travellers and, oddly, murderers.

Italian sailors stole St Nicholas's miraculously

myrrh-exuding bones in 1087. Turkey is still demanding their return.

In the rest of Europe, the benign St Nicholas fused with older darker mythological types—in eastern Germany he is known as Shaggy Goat, Ashman or Rider. In Holland he is Sinterklass, attended by the sinister 'Black Peters'.

The jolly 'Coca Cola' Santa existed well before Haddon Sundblom's famous advertising images of the 1930s. His illustrations, and those of Thomas Nast in the 1860s, were based on New Yorker Clement Clarke Moore's 1823 poem 'A Visit from St Nicholas' (better known as 'The Night before Christmas').

Moore was an unlikely author—his day-job was as a Professor of Hebrew and Oriental Languages—but the poem's importance in fuelling the Santa myth would be hard to exaggerate. It moves the legend to Christmas Eve and, instead of the dour St Nick, describes a rotund, twinkly-eyed, white-bearded elf, with fur-trimmed red clothes, reindeer with cute names, a sledge that landed on rooftops and a sack full of toys. It became one of the most popular children's poems of all time.

It's not clear when the North Pole and the factory of elves became attached to the story, but it was established enough by 1927 for the Finns to claim that Santa Claus lived in Finnish Lapland, as no reindeer could live at the North Pole because there was no lichen.

Santa's official post office is in Rovaniemi, capital of Lapland. He receives 600,000 letters a year.

As if in revenge for his secular success, the Vatican demoted St Nicholas's saint's day (6 December) from obligatory to voluntary observance in 1969.

WHAT DO BUGS BUNNY, BRER RABBIT AND THE EASTER BUNNY HAVE IN COMMON?

They are all hares, not rabbits.

Bugs Bunny and Brer Rabbit are both modelled on North American Jack Rabbits, which are long-eared, large-legged hares.

Bugs Bunny, who won an Oscar in 1958 for *Knighty Knight*, made his screen debut in 1938 in *Porky's Hare Hunt*. Mel Blanc, the voice of Bugs Bunny, loathed carrots: nevertheless he still had to chew them during recordings as no other vegetable produced the desired crunch.

The origins of Brer Rabbit are in the story-telling traditions of African American slaves, who told tales about the hare being more wily than the fox. Robert Roosevelt, uncle of President Theodore and a friend of Oscar Wilde, was the first person to write down the stories but it wasn't until 1879 that the 'Uncle Remus' stories, transcribed by Joel Chandler Harris, became national classics.

The insufferably cute Easter Bunny is also a modern American invention. It's a commercial sanitisation of the hare as fertility-rebirth-moon symbol. In Saxon culture, the hare was sacred to Eostre, the goddess of spring, which is where we get the word 'Easter'.

Few animals have such rich mythological associations. From Ancient Egypt and Mesopotamia through to India, Africa, China and Western Europe, hares have been portrayed as sacred, evil, wise, destructive, clever and, almost always, sexy.

Maybe it's because they are so fast—they can run

at 77 kph (48 mph) and leap 2.5 metres (8 feet) in the air. Or maybe it's their astonishing fertility: a female hare (doe) can produce 42 leverets in a single year. Pliny the Elder believed eating hare would make you sexually attractive for up to nine days.

Hares and rabbits are not rodents but 'lagomorphs' (which derives from the Greek for 'hare-shaped'). Lagomorphs are peculiar in being able to close their nostrils and choosing to eat their own droppings.

They do this for the same reasons cows chew the cud—to extract the maximum amount of nutrients and energy from their food. Unlike cows, hares and rabbits don't get to stand around for hours ruminating.

The familiar spring ritual of ' boxing hares' is not a male dominance contest but a doe fighting off unwanted suitors.

WHAT WERE CINDERELLA'S SLIPPERS MADE FROM?

Squirrel fur.

Charles Perrault, who wrote the familiar version of the story in the seventeenth century, misheard the word *vair* (squirrel fur) in the medieval tale he borrowed and updated for the similar-sounding *verre* (glass).

Cinderella is an ancient and universal story. A Chinese version dates back to the ninth century and there are over 340 other versions before Perrault's. None of the early versions

Did you know that squirrels are the Devil's oven mitts?
MISS PIGGY

mentions glass slippers. In the 'original' Chinese story 'Yeh-Shen' they're made of gold thread with solid gold soles. In the Scottish version 'Rashie-Coat' they're made of rushes. In the medieval French tale, adapted by Perrault, her shoes are described as *pantoufles de vair*—slippers of squirrel's fur.

One source says the *vair–verre* error occurred before Perrault and he merely repeated it. Others think glass slippers were Perrault's own idea and that he intended them all along.

The *OED* states that *vair*, in use in English as well as French since at least 1300, comes from the Latin *varius*, 'parti-coloured', and refers to fur from a species of squirrel that is 'much used for trimming or lining garments'.

Snopes.com states that Perrault could not have misheard *vair* as *verre* because *vair* 'was no longer used in his time'. This seems extremely doubtful— the word was continuously in use in English until at least 1864.

Perrault was an upper-class Parisian author who rose to become Director of the Académie Française. His *Tales of Mother Goose* (1697), originally devised as Court entertainment and published under the name of his 17-year-old son, were immediately popular and opened up a new literary genre: the fairytale. Apart from Cinderella, his famous versions of classic tales include Sleeping Beauty, Little Red Riding Hood, Bluebeard and Puss-in-Boots.

As well as polishing up Cinderella—adding the mice, the pumpkin and the fairy godmother—Perrault reduced their peasant bloodthirstiness. In the medieval original, the ugly sisters cut off their toes and bunions to try on the slipper, and after the Prince marries Cinders, the King takes revenge on them and the wicked stepmother by forcing them to dance themselves to death wearing red-hot iron boots. Much of this bloodthirstiness was later reinstated by the Brothers Grimm.

In *Three Contributions to the Theory of Sex*, Freud claimed slippers were a symbol for the female genitals.

WHERE DO LOOFAHS COME FROM?

Trees.

Not from the sea—that'll be sponges you're thinking of—loofahs grow on trees. They are a kind of gourd and are regarded as a tasty snack throughout Asia.

Smooth loofah (*Luffa aegyptiaca*) is a rampant, fast-growing annual vine that produces pretty yellow flowers and strange-looking fruits that are edible when immature and useful when fully grown. The vine can grow more than 30 feet (9 metres) long and scrambles over anything in its path.

Probably native to tropical Africa and Asia, it is grown throughout most of Asia and is cultivated commercially in the United States for export to Japan.

The immature fruits, 7.5 to 15 cm (3 to 6 inches) in length, can be stir-fried whole or sliced, or they can be grated and used in soups and omelettes. Any fruits longer than 10 cm (4 inches) need to be peeled because the skin becomes bitter.

Allowed to mature on the vine until they start turning brown and their stems go yellow, loofahs are easy to peel for use as back scrubbers, skin exfoliators or general kitchen pot scrubs.

WHAT'S THE STRONGEST WOOD?

Balsa

It's the strongest wood in the world when measured in three categories of stiffness, bendability and compressibility—stronger than oak or pine.

Although it is the softest of woods, it is not, botanically, a softwood, but a hardwood. 'Hardwood' is a botanical term that describes broadleaved, mostly deciduous trees which are angiosperms (flowering plants such as balsa) as opposed to coniferous gymnosperms (non-flowering plants such as pine).

It is also light, of course, though it is not the lightest in the world—the lightest practical wood is a New Zealand native, the small *whau* tree (pronounced 'phow') which is used by Maori fishermen to make floats.

Balsa is Spanish for 'raft'. Balsa wood is mothproof.

WHAT DO YOU GET IF YOU SUCK YOUR PENCIL?

Nothing bad, apart from being told not to.

Pencils don't contain lead and never have done. They contain graphite, one of the six pure forms of carbon, which is no more poisonous than the wood it's wrapped in. Even the paint is now lead-free.

The confusion comes from the fact that sharpened

lead was used for more than 2,000 years to draw on papyrus and paper.

Even what can appear to be the most common, small and simple of objects, can reveal itself to be on its own terms as complex and as grand as a space shuttle or a great suspension bridge.
HENRY PETROSKI

The only deposit of pure, solid, graphite ever found was uncovered by accident in Borrowdale, Cumbria in 1564. It was protected by strict laws and armed guards and mined for just six weeks a year.

The so-called 'black lead' it produced was cut into thin square sticks to make the first pencils. English pencils were adopted quickly across Europe. The first recorded use was by the Swiss naturalist Konrad Gessner in 1565.

Henry David Thoreau, author of *Walden*, was the first American to successfully fire graphite with clay to make a pencil 'lead' but the big commercial breakthrough came in 1827, when Joseph Dixon of Salem, Massachusetts introduced a machine that mass-produced square graphite pencils at the rate of 132 per minute.

By the time he died in 1869, the Joseph Dixon Crucible Company was the world leader, producing 86,000 round cased pencils a day. Today (now called Dixon Ticonderoga) it is still one of the world's leading pencil-makers.

Roald Dahl wrote all his books using a yellow Dixon Ticonderoga medium pencil. The traditional yellow pencil goes back to 1890 when Josef Hardmuth manufactured the first one at his Prague factory and named it after Queen Victoria's famous yellow diamond, Koh-i-Noor (she'd called his luxury line 'the Koh-i-Noor of pencils'). Other manufacturers copied it. In North America, 75 per cent of all pencils sold are yellow.

The average pencil can be sharpened seventeen times and can write 45,000 words or a straight line 56 km (35 miles) long.

The rubber attached to the end of a pencil is held in place by a device known as a *ferrule*. The patent was first granted in 1858, but they were unpopular in schools because teachers believed they encouraged laziness.

The 'rubber' in most pencils is actually made from vegetable oil, with a very small amount of rubber binding it together.

WHERE WAS THE LOG CABIN INVENTED?

Probably in Scandinavia 4,000 years ago.

The development of metal tools during the Bronze Age made them possible. As a quick-to-build, durable, warm form of building they were used widely across northern Europe.

The ancient Greeks may also have a claim, because although the ancient coniferous forests have now receded from the Mediterranean, there is a theory that the Minoan's and Mycenaean's one-roomed house or *megaron* was originally made from horizontal pine logs.

It was through the Swedish and Finnish settlements in Delaware in the 1630s that the log cabin reached America, its spiritual home. British settlers, incidentally, constructed their homes of wooden planks, not logs.

A museum in Hodgenville, Kentucky, proudly

displays the famous log cabin in which Abraham Lincoln was born, though it was, in fact, built thirty years after his death. This is uncomfortably close to the old schoolboy howler: 'Abe Lincoln was born in a log cabin he built with his own hands.'

Despite this ludicrous fakery, the US National Park Service solemnly tells tourists not to use flash photography, in case they damage the historic logs.

WHERE DID STONE AGE PEOPLE LIVE?

Put away that cliché.

'Cavemen' isn't a good description of Stone Age or palaeolithic people. It's part of the 'couldn't-care-less-about-anything-much-before-the-Romans' school of history teaching, much favoured in the late nineteenth century. It's not used by modern historians or archaeologists at all.

Palaeolithic humans were nomadic hunter-gatherers who occasionally used caves. There are 277 sites that have been identified in Europe—among them Altamira in Spain, Lascaux in France and Creswell Crags in Derbyshire. They left paintings and evidence of fires, cooking, rituals and burials, but they were not designed as permanent dwelling-places.

The earliest European cave art has been dated to 40,000 years ago, although the precise age is notoriously difficult to establish. Paint isn't organic, so can't be carbon-dated.

The most persuasive explanation of its function relates it to more recent cave painting among hunter-gatherer people in southern Africa and Australia. Here the paintings were the work of shamans, who entered the dark and often remote caves in order to connect with the spirit world. Another theory suggests they were simply palaeolithic teenage graffiti.

In northern China, an estimated 40 million people currently live in cave homes known as *yaodong*. As the human population of the entire planet in 8,000 BC was probably only five million, there are eight times as many cavemen now than there were people of any kind then.

People who live in caves are called troglodytes, from the Greek for 'those who get into a hole'.

Other places where there have been troglodyte dwellings in modern times include Cappadocia in Turkey, Andalucia in southern Spain, New Mexico in the USA and the Canary Islands.

This may be the beginning rather than the end of a trend. Research from the University of Bath has demonstrated that an underground home uses 25 per cent less energy than a normal house.

WHAT WAS THE FIRST ANIMAL TO BE DOMESTICATED?

a) Sheep
b) Pig
c) Reindeer
d) Horse
e) Dog

Around 14,000 years ago, palaeolithic hunter-gatherers on what is now the Russian/Mongolian border learned to lure reindeer away from their huge migratory groups and breed them to create their own small herd.

Reindeer were like walking corner-shops, offering meat, milk, and fur for clothing. It is possible that they trained dogs at the same time to help them domesticate the reindeer.

Today, there are about three million domesticated reindeer, most of them in the wastes of Lapland, which stretches across Sweden, Norway, Finland and Russia.

The Lapps, who herd them, prefer to call themselves the Sami. Perhaps they don't know that Sami is ancient Swedish for 'chavs'.

'Caribou' is the North American name for reindeer. It comes from *xalibu,* 'one who digs' in the Mi'Maq (or Micmac) language of eastern Canada. Reindeer/caribou use their large feet to dig through to the lichen beneath the snow. Lichens provide two-thirds of a reindeer's food.

Reindeer are nomadic and travel up to 4,800 km (3,000 miles) a year, the mammal travel record. They're fast, too, reaching speeds of 77 kph (48 mph) on land and 9.6 kph (6 mph) in water. Because of a clicking tendon in their feet, a herd of migrating reindeer sounds like a castanet convention.

Here are the estimated dates for domestication of the major animals:

Reindeer	*c.* 12,000 BC
Dogs (Eurasia, North America)	*c.* 12,000 BC
Sheep (SW Asia)	8,000 BC
Pig (SW Asia, China)	8,000 BC
Cattle (SW Asia, India, N Africa)	6,000 BC

Domestication is different from taming. It implies selective breeding. Elephants can be tamed, but are not domesticated.

WHAT WAS ODD ABOUT RUDOLF THE RED-NOSED REINDEER?

He was a girl.

Despite being called Rudolph and referred to as 'him', like all Santa's reindeer 'he' must in fact have been female. Male reindeer lose their antlers at the beginning of the winter. Females keep their antlers until they give birth in the spring.

Reindeer/caribou are the only female deer to have antlers. They are shed and regrow every year. They are shorter and simpler than those of the males but still grow at a rate of more than 2.5 cm (1 inch) a day, making them the fastest-growing tissue of any mammal.

The other possibility is that Rudolph was a eunuch. The Sami sometimes castrate male reindeer, thus enabling them to keep their antlers, and to carry especially heavy loads.

WHERE DO TURKEYS COME FROM?

Despite being native to North America, the domesticated turkeys that graced the tables of the Pilgrim Fathers had travelled out with them from England.

Turkeys first reached Europe in the 1520s, brought

back from their native Mexico first to Spain and then sold throughout the continent by Turkish merchants. They quickly became a favourite food for the richer classes.

By 1585, turkey had become a Christmas tradition in England. Norfolk farmers set to work to produce a heavier-breasted, more docile version of the wild bird. The Norfolk Black and the White Holland were both English breeds reintroduced to America, and most domestic turkey now consumed in the USA derives from them.

From the late sixteenth century, English turkeys walked the 160 km (100 miles) from Norfolk to Leadenhall Market in London each year. The journey would take three months and the birds wore special leather boots to protect their feet.

A flock of 1,000 turkeys could be managed by two drovers carrying long wands of willow or hazel with red cloth tied on the ends. Traffic jams were caused by the vast flocks entering London from Norfolk and Suffolk in the weeks before Christmas.

Turkeys have nothing to do with Turkey. They were called 'Turkie cocks' in England because of the traders who supplied them. Maize, also originally from Mexico, was once called 'turkie corn' for the same reason.

In most other countries—including Turkey—they were named after India, perhaps because the Spanish returned with it from the 'Indies' (as America was called).

Only the Portuguese got close to the truth, calling the turkey a *peru*. The Native American word for turkey was *furkee*, according to the Pilgrim Fathers, although no one seems to know which Algonquin language it comes from. In Choctaw they are called *fakit,* based on the sound the bird makes.

Even science seemed unsure what to call the turkey. The Latin name *Meleagris gallopavo* translates literally as the 'guinea-fowl chicken-peacock', which looks like linguistic spread-betting.

A male turkey is called a stag, gobbler or tom. The female is always a hen. Turkeys are the largest creatures able to give birth without sex: the offspring of such virgin births are male, and invariably sterile.

Most languages write the turkey's gobble as *glu glu* or *kruk, kruk.* In Hebrew, however, they go *mekarkerim.*

WHO WAS BORN BY IMMACULATE CONCEPTION?

Mary.

This catches out a lot of non-Catholics. The Immaculate Conception refers to birth of the Virgin Mary, not the virgin birth of Jesus.

It is commonly confused with the doctrine of the Virgin Birth, by which Mary became pregnant with Jesus through the Holy Spirit.

Under the doctrine of the Immaculate Conception, Mary was granted immunity from all suspicion of sin at the moment she was conceived.

Unfortunately, the Bible doesn't make any reference to this happening. It only became an official Catholic dogma in 1854.

Many theologians believe the doctrine to be unnecessary because Jesus redeemed everyone anyway.

The Virgin Birth is a core doctrine of the Church

but that doesn't mean it is beyond controversy. It is explicitly mentioned in Luke and Matthew's Gospels but not by the earlier Gospel of St Mark, or the even earlier letters of St Paul.

St Paul, in his letter to the Romans, states clearly that Jesus 'was made of the seed of David, according to the flesh'. We also know that the earliest Jewish Christians, called Nazarenes, didn't believe in the virgin birth either.

The 'supernatural' elements of Jesus's life story became exaggerated as the new religion gradually absorbed pagan ideas to broaden its appeal.

The virgin birth wasn't a part of Jewish tradition. But Perseus and Dionysus in Greek mythology, Horus in Egyptian and Mithra, a Persian deity whose cult rivalled Christianity in popularity, were all 'born of virgins'.

WAS JESUS BORN IN A STABLE?

No.

Not according to the New Testament. The idea that Jesus was born in a stable is an assumption made only because St Luke's Gospel says he was 'laid in a manger'.

Nor is there any biblical authority for the presence of animals at the Nativity. Of course, we're all familiar with the scene from the crib we see in churches and schools, but it was 1,000 years before it was invented.

St Francis of Assisi is credited with making the first crib, in 1223 in a cave in the hills above Greccio. He placed some hay on a flat rock (which can still be seen), put a baby on top and added carvings of an ox and an ass (though no Joseph, Mary, Wise Men, Shepherds, angels or lobsters).

HOW MANY SHEEP WERE THERE ON NOAH'S ARK?

Seven. Or fourteen.

The relevant passage in the King James Bible appears in Genesis 7: 2, where God tells Noah: 'Of every clean beast thou shalt take to thee by sevens, the male and his female: and of the beasts that are not clean by two, the male and his female.'

Every scientific truth goes through three stages. First, people say it conflicts with the Bible. Next they say it had been discovered before. Lastly they say they always believed in it.
LOUIS AGASSIZ

'Unclean' beasts are the extensive range of creatures that Jews were (and are) forbidden to eat, including pigs, camels, rock-badgers, chameleons, eels, snails, ferrets, lizards, moles, vultures, swans, owls, pelicans, storks, herons, lapwings, bats, ravens, cuckoos and eagles.

'Clean' (edible) animals include sheep, cattle, goats, antelopes and locusts.

So there were at least seven sheep on the Ark, not two as taught in Sunday school. But the passage is slightly ambiguous: does it mean seven males and seven females, or seven altogether? Those who know say that seven of each would be a disaster: fights would break out between the rams. A more practical solution would be one ram and six ewes.

However, the Douay-Rheims Bible, the

authoritative Catholic translation of the Latin Vulgate published in 1609, is quite clear on the matter: 'Of all clean beasts, take seven and seven, the male and the female.' So it looks like there were fourteen sheep on the Ark.

Medieval rabbis spent a good deal of time debating whether fish were left to fend for themselves in the Flood, or whether Noah dutifully brought them on board the ark in an aquarium. In the mid-sixteenth century, Johannes Buteo calculated that Noah's Ark would have had a usable space of 350,000 cubits, of which 140,000 must have been taken up by hay.

But the flood really happened. More than 500 different flood-myths exist in cultures all over the world.

Human beings evolved during the last Ice Age. Towards the end of it, as the temperature rose, there were vast catastrophic rises in sea level caused by the melting ice-caps. The story of Noah is thought to describe the disappearance of the Tigris–Euphrates Delta under the Persian Gulf.

The sudden shortage of land could no longer support hunter-gathering, and, for the first time, human beings were forced to turn to farming.

Aborigines, whose culture and oral tradition reaches back to the last Ice Age, can name and locate mountains that have been under the sea since the ice-caps melted 8,000 years ago.

WHERE WERE THE FIRST MODERN OLYMPICS HELD?

At Much Wenlock, Shropshire, in 1850. The games were held there annually and inspired Baron Coubertin to organise the Athens Olympiad of 1896:

'Much Wenlock is a town in Shropshire, a county on the borders of Wales, and if the Olympic Games that modern Greece has not yet been able to revive still survive today, it is due not to a Greek, but to Dr W. P. Brookes.'

Brookes believed a rigorous programme of physical training would help make people better Christians by keeping them out of the pubs. His knowledge of the ancient Olympics inspired him to found the Much Wenlock Society for the Promulgation of Physical Culture in 1841.

The first of the annual 'Brookes' Olympian Games' was held in 1850 with small cash prizes for running, long jump, football, quoits and cricket. Other events were gradually added, such as a blindfold wheelbarrow race, a pig race and a medieval tilting contest. Winners were crowned with laurel wreaths and medallions inscribed with Nike, the Greek goddess of victory.

The fame of the Wenlock Olympics quickly spread, attracting entries from all parts of Britain. They were even noticed in Athens and King George I of the Hellenes sent a silver medal to be awarded as a prize.

With visions of reviving the ancient games on an international scale, Brookes founded the National (British) Olympic Association in 1865 and staged its

294

first games at the Crystal Palace in London. Without sponsors, it was snubbed by the leading sportsmen of the day.

In 1888 Brookes began a correspondence with Baron Coubertin. In 1890, the Baron came to see the Wenlock Games for himself, planting an oak that still stands in the village. He returned home determined to re-establish the ancient games, founding the International Olympic Committee in 1894.

Through his wealth, prestige and political connections, Coubertin succeeded where Brookes had failed. He staged the first international revival of the games in Athens in the summer of 1896.

Dr Brookes had died the previous year, aged 86. The Wenlock Games are still held annually in his honour.

WHY IS A MARATHON 26 MILES AND 385 YARDS LONG?

For the convenience of the British royal family.

At the first three modern Olympics, the marathon was run over a distance of roughly 42 km (26 miles), varying from games to games. In 1908 the Olympic Games were held in London and the starting line was put outside a window at Windsor Castle from which one half of the royal family could watch, with the finish in front of the royal box in the White City stadium where the other half of the family was waiting. This distance was 26 miles and 385 yards: the standard length of a marathon ever since.

The origin of the 26-mile run dates to a Greek messenger called Pheidippides, who ran this distance from Marathon to Athens to relate the victory of the Athenians over the Persians in 490 BC. According to popular legend he delivered the message and then dropped dead.

It's a heroic tale but it doesn't hold water. Very few marathon runners die after the event, and professional ancient Greek couriers were regularly required to run twice as far.

This version of the story first appears in the work of the Roman historian Plutarch (c. AD 45–125) more than 500 years later. He calls the runner Eucles. It seems to have become confused with the much older story of Pheidippides recorded by Herodotus, who was born six years after the battle, and whose account is the nearest we have to a contemporary one.

According to him, Pheidippides ran from Marathon to Sparta (246 km or 153 miles) to ask for help in beating off the Persian attack. The Spartans were busy with a religious festival, so he ran all the way back and the Athenians had to fight the Persians on their own. They won a resounding victory, losing 192 men to the Persians' 6,400. Pheidippides didn't die.

Ultra-running is the discipline that covers any running event that's longer than a marathon. In 1982, the American Ultra-running Association ran the authentic Pheidippides route (as agreed by a consortium of Greek scholars) and established it as the International Spartathlon in 1983. The first winner was a modern legend: the Greek long-distance runner, Yannis Kouros.

Kouros currently holds every world record from 200 to 1,600 km (125 to 1,000 miles). In 2005, he retraced Pheidippides' complete route, running from Athens to Sparta and back.

WHAT DOES THE QUEEN SAY TO SOMEONE SHE'S KNIGHTED?

Not a lot.

According to the official website of the British monarchy, www.royal.gov.uk:

'. . . after his name is announced, the knight-elect kneels on a knighting-stool in front of The Queen who then lays the sword blade on the knight's right and then left shoulder. After he has been dubbed, the new knight stands up (contrary to popular belief, the words 'Arise, Sir —' are not used), and The Queen then invests the knight with the insignia of the Order to which he has been appointed (a star or badge, depending on the Order). By tradition, clergy receiving a knighthood are not dubbed, as the use of a sword is thought inappropriate for their calling.'

The actual meaning of the English word *accolade* is 'the salutation on the bestowal of knighthood'. It comes from Latin *ad,* 'to', and *collum,* 'neck'—hence, 'an embrace round the neck'.

There also used to be a ceremony associated with the removal of a knighthood: degradation. The last public degradation was in 1621, when Sir Francis Mitchell was found guilty of 'grievous exactions' and had his spurs broken and thrown away, his belt cut and his sword broken over his head. Finally, he was pronounced to be 'no longer a Knight but Knave'.

Unlike Lord Kagan (jailed for theft in 1980), Baron Archer of Weston-super-Mare was never knighted and so hasn't faced degradation following his own 'grievous exactions'. He keeps his peerage but has inspired reforms—so far not carried out—that will make it impossible for a convicted criminal to serve in the House of Lords.

WHO WAS THE FIRST KING OF ENGLAND?

Alfred the Great's grandson.

King Aethelstan (924–39) was the first true King of all England. His grandfather, Alfred the Great, was only King of Wessex, even though he did refer to himself rather optimistically as 'King of the English'.

When Alfred came to the throne, England was still made up of five separate kingdoms. During Alfred's life, Cornwall came under his control but Mercia, Northumbria and East Anglia fell to Viking invaders.

After a period hiding in the Somerset levels (where he *didn't* burn any cakes), Alfred fought back against the Danes, eventually restoring his old kingdom. But in the treaty he made following his defeat of the Viking warlord Guthrum at Edington in 878, he chose to give half the country (everything east of a line from London to Chester) to the enemy. This was known as the Danelaw. In return, Guthrum agreed to convert to Christianity.

Alfred was keen to ensure that any future Scandinavian raiders wouldn't find it quite so easy and set about creating a network of defended towns to protect his territory.

It worked. By his grandson's reign, Wessex's control of England was complete. At the battle of Brunanburh in 937, Aethelstan defeated the Kings of Scotland, Strathclyde and Dublin to establish the Anglo-Saxon kingdom of England.

No one is sure where 'Brunanburh' is: Tinsley

Wood near Sheffield seems the best guess.

The last King of 'England'—that is, the last King to rule England and nothing else—was Harold Godwinson or Harold II. William, his successor, was already Duke of Normandy, and the English crown controlled substantial portions of France until Calais was finally surrendered in 1558.

WHO FOUGHT AT THE BATTLE OF CULLODEN?

Essentially, it was Scotland v. Scotland.

There were more Scots in the army that defeated Bonnie Prince Charlie in 1746 than there were in his own army.

As well as three battalions of Lowland Scots, the Hanoverian army under General Cumberland included a well-trained battalion of Highland Scots from Clan Munro, a big contingent of the Highland Clan Campbell's militia, and a large number of Highland foot soldiers from Clans MacKay, Ross, Gunn and Grant, fighting under English officers.

Three-quarters of the Jacobite army were Highlanders, the rest were Lowland Scots, with a small contingent of troops from France and Ireland. Jacobite mythology has re-interpreted the battle as a Scotland versus England affair, but it was, for the most part, Scotland versus Scotland.

The Jacobite Rebellion of 1745 started with some early success for the Highlanders at the battle of Prestonpans, near Edinburgh, followed by an invasion of England which took them as far as Derby. With the bulk of the British army fighting the French in Flanders, this caused a panic in London, and contingency plans to evacuate the King to Hanover were drawn up.

But the Jacobites failed to recruit supporters in England, and the planned French invasion was postponed. Despite a brilliantly executed retreat by Lord George Murray, the army that entered the field of battle at Culloden were starving, exhausted by weeks of marching, and poorly armed. Only a quarter of them had swords.

They fought bravely, but in just over an hour 1,250 of them lay dead. The Hanoverian army lost just fifty-two men. The Duke of Cumberland—known to Scots as 'the Butcher' ever since—executed all the prisoners and wounded on the battlefield, and rode into Inverness waving his bloody sword.

More than 3,000 Jacobite sympathisers were arrested in the aftermath, most of them being imprisoned or transported to the colonies. One in twenty were selected at random for 'show' executions. The Highland way of life never recovered. The Clan system was destroyed and the wearing of Highland dress made illegal.

Modern Jacobites still maintain that the true line of succession to the British throne runs through the Stuarts and their descendants. They acclaim Duke Franz of Bavaria as Francis II, King of England, Scotland, France and Ireland. He keeps a dignified silence on the issue.

WHICH WAS THE LAST COUNTRY INVADED BY SCOTLAND?

Panama.

One of the last acts of Scotland, before the 1707 Act of Union joined it to England and Wales to form Great Britain, was an ill-fated attempt to colonise the isthmus of Darién.

The scheme was dreamt up by William Paterson, the founder of the Bank of England. He saw an opportunity to establish a trading post in Central America which could act as link between the riches of the Pacific and the trading nations of Western Europe.

The English are not happy unless they are miserable, the Irish are not at peace unless they are at war, and the Scots are not at home unless they are abroad.
GEORGE ORWELL

The English quickly ruled themselves out as partners. They were at war with France at the time, and did not want to risk angering the Spanish (who had claims on Panama). When the government heard of the scheme, it barred Englishmen from investing. Paterson decided to gather all his funding north of the border. Such was the Scot's enthusiasm that he raised £400,000 in six months, a vast sum equal to a third of the total collective assets of the nation. Almost every Scotsman who could put his name to £5 invested.

In 1698, the first fleet of five ships set sail from Leith, arriving in November. They were woefully underprepared and ill-informed. The land they had hoped to turn into New Caledonia was an unfarmable, mosquito-infested swamp. The Indians had no use for the crates of wigs, mirrors and combs they had hoped to trade. The English colonies in the region were barred from trading with them and the Spanish were implacably hostile.

Within six months, 200 of the 1,200 settlers had died of malaria and other tropical diseases and the death rate had reached ten a day. As well as the backbreaking work of trying to drain a swamp, all their supplies had spoiled and by the beginning of the summer they were each trying to live on a pound of maggot-infested flour a week. The news of an imminent Spanish attack was the final straw. Only 300 people made it back to Scotland.

The Darién Venture was an unmitigated disaster for Scotland. It shattered morale and left the economy almost £250,000 in debt. Seven years later, the country was forced to sign the Act of Union with England. The popular consensus was that the English had refused to help in order to humiliate Scotland and make union inevitable. Much of the support for the Jacobite cause over the next forty years can be traced back to the horrors and shattered aspirations of Scotland's lost colony.

As for Darién, it remains a pretty inhospitable place covered with dense jungle. Even the Pan-American highway, which will eventually connect Alaska in the north to Argentina in the south, is forced to break for the Darién Gap.

WHERE DO PANAMA HATS COME FROM?

Ecuador.

They first appeared in Europe and North America in the early nineteenth century where they were called 'panama' hats because they were exported through shippers based in Panama.

In England, they were chosen as perfect summer headgear by the royal family, and quickly became indispensable accessories for sporting and outdoor social occasions. When Queen Victoria died in 1901, the black band was added in her honour.

In the Americas, the hats were standard issue for the men digging the Panama Canal. President Theodore Roosevelt visited the site in 1906 and was photographed wearing one. The panama's fame was assured.

The hat's origins are ancient: ceramic figures wearing curious headpieces have been discovered on the Ecuadorian coast and date back to 4000 BC. Some archaeologists believe that the weaving skills needed to make a panama were acquired through contact with the Polynesian people of the Pacific, famous for their woven flax. The first Spaniards were so unnerved by the material's translucent quality that they believed it was vampire skin.

The modern hats date back to the sixteenth century and are made from the woven fibres of the ten-foot-tall panama-hat palm, the *jipijapa* or *toquilla* (its scientific name is *Carludovica palmata*). They are mostly produced in the town of Cuenca, although the finest examples come from the towns of Montecristi and Biblian.

The time it takes to make a panama hat varies enormously. The *toquilla* can be harvested only five days a month, during the moon's final quarter, when the palm fibre holds less water, making it lighter and easier to weave. A skilled weaver can extract a fibre that is as fine as silk. A low-grade hat can be knocked out in a matter of hours, whereas a top quality, or *superfino*, hat can take five months to finish and sell for £1,000.

In 1985 the Conran Foundation nominated the panama hat as one of the '100 best designs ever' for an exhibition at the V&A.

Ecuador is named after the Spanish word for 'equator'. As well as hats, it is the world's largest exporter of bananas and balsa wood for model aircraft.

CAN YOU NAME AN IRISH SAINT?

St Patrick (*c.*385–461) is the patron saint of Ireland but he wasn't born there, nor was he of Irish stock.

He was a Briton, from the north or west of the country. His birthplace is traditionally given as *Bannavem* or *Bannaventa Taberniae*. This has long been thought to be a lost settlement near the Severn or in Pembrokeshire, but a recent and convincing suggestion is the village of Banwell in Somerset.

While still a teenager Patrick was abducted and taken to Ireland as a slave. After six years he escaped to the Continent, where he became a monk. Eventually, following a vision, he returned to Ireland to Christianise it.

Ireland isn't short of home-grown saintly talent, however.

St Brendan (?486–?578) was from County Kerry. Born near Tralee, he was ordained a priest in 512. A famous traveller, he is believed by many to have reached America centuries before Columbus, who didn't.

St Columba (521–97) was born into the Irish nobility. After many years wandering round Ireland, preaching and founding monasteries, at the age of forty-two he settled on Iona from where he and his monks converted the Picts to Christianity.

The history of saints is mainly the history of insane people.
BENITO MUSSOLINI

St Kevin (?498–618) was also born of noble Irish parents and destined for the priesthood. Instead he became a hermit. A blackbird famously laid an egg in his outstretched hand and he kept perfectly still until the baby bird hatched.

St Malachy (?1094–1148) was appointed abbot of Bangor, County Down and bishop of Connor by the age of 30, and became archbishop of Armagh. According to legend, he had a vision of all the popes. If his prophecy is correct, the present pope, Benedict XVI, will be the last but one.

St Oliver Plunket (1629–81) was born in County Meath, educated by the Jesuits in Rome and appointed archbishop of Armagh and primate of all Ireland in 1669. In 1678 an English conspirator, Titus

Oates, implicated him in a plot to kill Charles II. Plunket was found guilty of treason and hanged at Tyburn, mercifully dying before he could be drawn (disembowelled) and quartered.

St Bridget (?453–?523), the abbess of the first Irish women's community which she founded at Kildare, was noted for the miracle of transforming her used bathwater into beer for visiting clerics.

WHAT NATIONALITY WAS THE DUKE OF WELLINGTON?

Irish.

Despite his reputation as one of England's greatest generals, Arthur Wellesley, the 1st Duke of Wellington, was unarguably an Irishman.

He was born in Dublin in 1769 into the Wesley family, whose seat was Dangan Castle, near Trim in County Meath. He later married into one of Ireland's most notable families, the Longfords, and served in the Irish parliament in 1790.

If further proof were needed of his nationality, there is also his decision to play for the All Ireland team in the first recorded game of cricket played in Ireland in August 1792. Their opponents were a team from the local British garrison in Dublin. The Duke notched up a distinctively unimpressive total of six runs from his two innings.

The Duke's grandfather, the 1st Baron Mornington, was called Richard Colley, but assumed the surname of Wesley after inheriting the estates of a distant relative. While the Colleys had been in

Ireland for several centuries, the Wesleys were wealthier and could claim that their ancestor had arrived in Ireland as Henry II's standard-bearer. In 1798, the Duke and his family changed their names to Wellesley, just because it sounded grander.

Debate about the Duke's Irishness was widespread during his lifetime. It is often claimed that he repudiated his link to Ireland by saying that 'A man can be born in a stable, and yet not be an animal.' However, there is no evidence he ever said this: it probably originated as scurrilous court gossip.

Wellington remained as proud of his connections with Ireland as the Irish were of him; a monument 62.5 metres high (205 feet) stands in Phoenix Park in memory of his achievements.

The other quote that he famously didn't say was: 'The Battle of Waterloo was won on the playing fields of Eton.' It was first attributed to the Duke four years after he died in a work of Catholic propaganda by the French historian, Count de Montalembert.

It's worth pointing out that when Wellington briefly—and unsuccessfully—attended Eton, the school had no playing fields and he was a pupil noted for his lack of enthusiasm for, or talent at, games.

WHO WAS BRITAIN'S FIRST PRIME MINISTER?

a) Sir Robert Walpole
b) William Pitt the Elder
c) The Duke of Wellington
d) Sir Henry Campbell-Bannerman

Sir Henry Campbell-Bannerman. The expression 'Prime Minister' was first officially used in 1905 just five days after he became one. Before then the term had been one of abuse.

Sir Robert Walpole, generally recognised as the first *de facto* Prime Minister, never used the word: he and his successors were 'First Lords of the Treasury'. This included Campbell-Bannerman until 10 December 1905, when—in the first official use—a Royal Warrant placed the 'Prime Minister' in order of precedence after the Archbishop of York.

Sir Henry Campbell-Bannerman (1836–1908) was born Henry Campbell. The name Bannerman was added in 1871, as a condition to his inheriting his uncle's estate. After succeeding Arthur James Balfour, who resigned in 1905, Campbell-Bannerman became Britain's first official Prime Minister. His unusually strong cabinet included two future Prime Ministers (Asquith and Lloyd George) and he led the Liberals to a landslide victory in the 1906 General Election.

More radical than liberal, he supported women's suffrage and Irish devolution; introduced the Old Age Pension; improved the lot of the poor; denounced British 'barbarism' in the conduct of the Boer War; arranged self-government for much of South Africa; and pushed through the Trade Disputes Act in 1906 which gave unions considerable freedom to strike.

In 1907, the year after the election, he had a heart attack, followed by a second one in 1908, after which he resigned in favour of Asquith. Just over two weeks later, he died at No. 10 Downing Street.

His last words were: 'This is not the end of me.'

WHO INVENTED THE PENNY POST?

Once upon a time every schoolboy's hand would have shot up and the class would have shouted 'Roland Hill in 1840, Sir!' in unison. Not these days.

This isn't such a disaster, because those clever-clogs were wrong. William Dockwra had already established the London Penny Post 240 years earlier. It handled packets up to one pound in weight, there were several deliveries a day, and items were also delivered to addresses within ten miles of London for an extra charge of one penny. In 1683, Dockwra was forced to surrender his business to the government-operated General Post Office, a monopoly controlled by the Duke of York, later King James II.

In 1764, Parliament authorised the creation of Penny Posts in any town or city of the UK. By the beginning of the nineteenth century several were in existence. In 1840, Rowland Hill's Uniform Penny Post was established throughout the UK, and soon afterwards postage could be prepaid with the adhesive stamp known as the Penny Black. In 1898, the Imperial Penny Post extended the rate throughout the British Empire.

There are several candidates for the first true postal service. Egyptian pharaohs had an organised courier system as early as 2400 BC. The envelope was invented in Assyria around 2000 BC: both letters and envelopes were made of pottery. Cyrus the Great (568–528 BC), the founder of the Persian Empire, had a swift courier service that greatly impressed Herodotus. Confucius (551–479 BC) wrote: 'News travels faster than the mail,' so presumably the

Chinese had one around that time too.

The word 'post' comes from the Latin *posita*, 'placed', from the verb *ponere*, 'to place'. The Roman postal service was two-tier: first class went by horse and second class by ox-cart. The word 'mail' comes from Old French *male*, a wallet or bag

The Postmaster General in 1840, Lord Lichfield, criticised Hill's scheme as 'wild and visionary' but it was an immediate success, especially with Queen Victoria. She liked the profile portrait of her on the Penny Black so much that she ordered that the same image be used on all subsequent issues of the stamp for the next sixty years.

The first philatelist surfaced within a year of the first stamp being issued: a young woman who advertised in *The Times* for sufficient stamps to cover her bedroom walls. Because the UK was the first to issue them, British stamps have the unique distinction of not carrying the name of the issuing country.

WHAT DO YOU GET WHEN YOU'RE 100 YEARS OLD?

A telemessage.

It's no longer a telegram from Her Majesty and it isn't automatic—you have to apply for it.

UK inland telegrams were abolished in 1982 and replaced by telemessages which are delivered the next day, along with the normal post. BT describes the new service as: 'an efficient means of contacting customers with vital information, integrating into their whole customer communication strategy to produce real added value results.' Sounds enticing, doesn't it?

In the United Kingdom, the Queen (if asked) sends telemessage greetings on the 100th birthday and on every birthday after the 105th. In the United States, centenarians receive a letter from the President. Today, centenarians are the fastest-growing demographic group in the UK—increasing by 7 per cent each year. In 2000, there were 7,000 people in the UK aged 100 or more. Worldwide, there were an estimated 100,000. By 2050, there could be more than two million.

According to Genesis 5: 27, Methuselah lived to be 969 years old. It has been suggested that this was a translation error in which lunar cycles were mistaken for the solar ones, and the actual ages are 13.5 times less. This makes Methusaleh a rather ordinary seventy-two. However, other patriarchs such as Mahalalel (Genesis 5:15) and Enoch (Genesis 5:21) were said to have become fathers after sixty-five 'years'. If the lunar cycle theory is accepted this would translate to an age of about four years and ten months.

Jeanne Calment of Arles is the oldest person whose age has definitely been verified by modern documentation. Born in 1875, she lived to the age of 122.

At 116 years, Christian Mortensen (1882–1998), a Danish-born American, is the oldest documented male. His closest rival, Shigechiyo Izumi (?1865–1986) from Japan, is supposed to have reached 120, but there are rumours that his birth certificate was actually his brother's. His

Time is a great teacher. Unfortunately, it kills all its pupils.
HECTOR BERLIOZ

311

claim is recognised by the *Guinness Book of World Records*.

On her 121st birthday, Jeanne Calment was asked for the secret of her longevity. She attributed it to olive oil, which she ate nearly every meal as well as rubbing it into her skin. 'I only have one wrinkle,' she gurgled coquettishly, 'and I'm sitting on it.'

WHAT IS QUITE INTERESTING?

Ignorance is like a delicate, exotic fruit; touch it and the bloom has gone.
OSCAR WILDE

QI stands for Quite Interesting. We do not claim to be Quite Right.

If you have better answers to any of these questions, or if you have new questions of your own, we'd love to hear from you.

Join us online at www.qi.com/books or come and visit us at our bar/bookshop in The QI Building, 16 Turl St, Oxford.

The book is the distillation of many people's attempts to understand the world around them, but owes most of all to the QI research team, a collection of people with high curiosity levels, low boredom thresholds and a knack for asking difficult questions. Special thanks are due to Piers Fletcher, Justin Gayner, Chris Gray, James Harkin, Mat Coward, Justin Pollard, Garrick Alder, Molly Oldfield and Dan Schreiber. They'd make the world's best pub quiz team.

We also doff our caps to the professionalism and

taste of our publishers Julian Loose, Stephen Page and their colleagues at Faber & Faber; to our production partners, Sarah Chaloner, Beatrice Gay and the team at TalkbackThames; and to Mark Freeland and Peter Fincham at the BBC, for having the courage of their convictions.

John le Carré once complained that having a book made into a movie was 'like seeing your oxen turned into bouillon cubes'. With that in mind, we should acknowledge the hundreds of scientists, philosophers, historians, inventors, saints and visionaries whose original work we have diced, skimmed, boiled and puréed to make the book you now hold in your hands.